Jeremiah
The Fate of a Prophet

מגיד

MAGGID

Binyamin Lau

JEREMIAH
THE FATE OF A PROPHET

TRANSLATED BY
Sara Daniel

Maggid Books

Jeremiah
The Fate of a Prophet

First English Edition, 2013
Second Printing, 2020

Maggid Books
An imprint of Koren Publishers Jerusalem Ltd.

POB 8531, New Milford, CT 06776-8531, USA
& POB 4044, Jerusalem 91040, Israel
www.korenpub.com

Original Hebrew Edition © Binyamin Lau 2010

Cover image © Sistine Chapel Ceiling:
"The Prophet Jeremiah," Michelangelo /
Vatican Museums and Galleries / The Bridgeman Art Library

The publication of this book was made possible through
the generous support of *Torah Education in Israel*.

ISBN 978 159 264 194 9, *hardcover*

A CIP catalogue record for this title is
available from the British Library.

Printed and bound in the United States

This work is dedicated with love to my parents

Joan (née Lunzer)
&
Naphtali Lau-Lavie

*"I will rejoice in doing good for them
and will assuredly plant them in this land
with all My heart and soul."*
(Jer. 32:41)

Thus said the Lord: There will yet be heard in this place, about which you say, "It is a desolate wasteland".... The sound of joy and the sound of gladness, the sound of the bridegroom and the sound of the bride, and the voices of those who cry, "Give thanks to the Lord of Hosts, for the Lord is good; His kindness endures forever!"

(Jer. 33:10–11)

I screamed out in song and thrust it
Like a divine chariot wheel of fire along those sedated streets
Of yours, silent and like shallow waters ...

And before the debauchery had abated, before another festival
Of dance and chattering greetings at parties,
With my spirit I breathed of the coming woes
And I heard the ravens calling in the nights,
White ... unusual for ravens –

And my fate shall be the fate of a prophet:
Gravely I am amongst you and you are my grave:
Like a fleshy kind of earth, your bodies
And through this grave I walk and I scream
The scream of a vision buried alive amongst its people
And the depth of the grave amplifies the sound
Of the beguiling song of the heretics and the weaklings
Who are the rulers of the ground above.

(Uri Zvi Greenberg,
from "A Song That I Screamed Out," *Streets of the River*)

Contents

Preface

> *My Creator, endow me with the insight to inherit*
> *Your legacy.*
>
> (from *Shaḥarit* of Rosh HaShana)

With God's blessing, I have merited to present my readers with my interpretation of the Book of Jeremiah. In my previous works, I have delved into the world of Torah scholars, seeking to sketch their characters for a modern audience. This is my first attempt to represent the Bible itself. Both those volumes and the book that you now hold are part of an overall attempt to build a bridge within Israeli society in particular, and the Jewish community in general, between modern culture – our world today – and the multilayered Jewish tradition over the generations. I will endeavor to explain why I have begun with Jeremiah in the introduction. Here, I would like to simply thank everyone who has been a partner in my Torah study and my attempts to apply this study to everyday life.

First and foremost, my wife Noa, my partner in all I do.

Second only to her, the members of the Ramban community in Jerusalem, whose Shabbat afternoon lectures formed the initial outline of this work.

My friend Shlomo Greenberg, the director of the circulation department in the National Library, who offered ready and willing help to find every scrap of research that related to the Book of Jeremiah and its period.

My dear friend Dr. Micha Goodman and the people of the Ein Prat Academy for Leadership, who provided wonderful accommodation and the right environment for the creation of this book.

The dedicated team of Maggid Books, who worked diligently to bring this volume to an English-speaking audience. Translation is not just the technical conversion of words from one language to another; it is an act of alchemy, capturing the mood, the music, the deeper meaning of the text. The English edition of this book, I am delighted to say, achieves this alchemy. I am grateful to Sara Daniel for the translation, to Elli Fischer and Deena Glickman for the editing, to Judy Lee, Tali Simon, and Leo Mercer for the proofreading, and to Tomi Mager for coordinating all the work. A special thanks to Gila Fine, editor in chief of Maggid Books, who expertly led this project from manuscript to print.

Binyamin Lau
Jerusalem
Summer 5773/2013

Introduction

On May 11, 2009, at the president's residence in Jerusalem, President Shimon Peres presented Pope Benedict XVI with a gift: the smallest Bible in the world. In its entirety, the Bible was half a millimeter square. Developed by the Technion, Israel's Institure of Technology, to showcase its progress in the field of nanotechnology, the cutting edge of high tech, the nano-Bible declared: "Look how tiny the Bible can be!" I seem to be stuck in the old world; this book was written to show how *great* the Bible can be. How great and how relevant.

The present volume was born from the desire to spark a deep and meaningful dialogue about the Bible within the Jewish world in general, and the Jewish state in particular. It is a sad truth of our time that the Bible – the foundational text and traditional cornerstone of Jewish existence – no longer occupies the space it once did in our lives. From a vital, pertinent guide to all matters spiritual and ethical, social and political, it's become a relic of days past – monumental and obscure and utterly distant. There are many who do not study it at all; there are many who study it, though scarcely; and there are many who study it extensively, but even they fail to infuse the word of God with any contemporary relevance.

This state of affairs is unfortunately no better in the Jewish state, where the unique and often challenging circumstances of daily life, coupled with a growing alienation toward religion among large segments of Israeli society, preclude any serious discussion of the question of Israel's

Jewish identity, and of the Bible's place in it. While other discourses have successfully penetrated the country's public debate, the Bible, and certainly the words of the prophets, are studied disjointedly, in a socio-political vacuum: "a bit here and a bit there" (Is. 28:10).

This work aims to render the Book of Jeremiah accessible to the contemporary reader, reinstating the words of the prophets into the heart of our political, social, and cultural discourse. Before delving into the book itself, I will attempt to establish Jeremiah's status in modern society and explain why I have chosen to focus on him, of all prophets.

THE STATUS OF THE PROPHET WITHIN SOCIETY: "FOOL IS THE PROPHET, MAD IS THE MAN OF LETTERS"

In terms of today's social milieu, the prophet might be regarded as something of a public intellectual, a man of letters.[1] An eternal critic, an outsider to the system, a gadfly who must summon all his literary or oratory powers to persuade his audience of the truth of his words – and of the mortal danger of ignoring them. A prophecy does not depend upon its being heard. On the contrary, more often than not it is disregarded, though the speaker's own belief in it does not allow him to remain silent.[2] How does society relate to one who determinedly, doggedly repeats his unheeded words? Practical men, when faced with adversity, will often state, unfazed, "The dogs may bark, but the caravan moves on." But while this might encourage the caravan on its way, what will be of the dogs? How does one shake the people of their complacency and alert them to the danger that is looming?

---

1. This section was inspired by A. Kasher's article "Fool is the Prophet, Mad is the Man of Letters," in Tamar Brosh, ed., *A Speech for Every Occasion* (Tel Aviv, 1993) [Hebrew]. The article is based on a speech given during the awarding of an honorary doctorate to Prof. Yeshayahu Leibowitz by Tel Aviv University in 1993. The title of the article, and of this section, is taken from Hosea 9:7.
2. The suggestion that the journalist fulfills the role of the prophet appears in Rabbi A. Steinsaltz, "King and Prophet," in A. Tzurieli, ed., *Prophesy, Son of Man* (Jerusalem, 5767), 174–75 [Hebrew]. Steinsaltz claims that the media has become a form of entertainment and has consequently lost its status as the heir of the prophets due to the entertainer's dependency on public opinion.

Throughout biblical history, prophets have repeatedly failed to penetrate the collective consciousness. Moses, the greatest of the prophets; Elijah and Elisha, the oratory prophets; Isaiah, Jeremiah, Ezekiel, and the other twelve literary prophets – none were successful in getting their message across and inspiring the people to repentance. Jonah is perhaps the only prophet who may be said to have fulfilled his mission, making the people of Nineveh see the error of their ways.

The words of the prophets have been preserved for us, their distant descendants, so that we may learn what is right in the eyes of God and man. But in their own days, in real time, there is hardly a prophet who has redressed the social, religious, or political wrongs of Israel; the prophets barked, but the caravan kept moving. Moreover, when a prophet dared to deviate from his usual message of morality and challenged the existing order, he was declared an enemy of the people. Thus, the prophet Amos was banished by the priest of Bethel, Amaziah, in the name of King Jeroboam: "Get thee out, seer!" (Amos 7:12).

The comparison of the prophet to a public intellectual is intended not to diminish the importance of the former, but to emphasize the responsibility of the latter. While the significance of the prophetic overture "Thus said the Lord" may be disputed, and it is difficult to distinguish a true prophet from a false one, certain hallmarks of true prophecy may be found. First among these is the prophet's readiness to pay a personal price for his vision; thus, the "prophet" who is eager to reinforce the dominant zeitgeist and the prevailing mores – who tells the people exactly what they want to hear – is immediately suspect. One of the most striking examples of this phenomenon is the story of King Ahab of Israel and King Jehoshaphat of Judah, who joined forces to free their territories from the Arameans. Before making the final decision to wage war, Jehoshaphat asked Ahab to seek the word of God. Ahab acceded to his ally's request:

> Then the King of Israel gathered the prophets together, about four hundred men, and said to them, "Shall I go to Ramoth-Gilead to battle, or shall I withhold?" And they said, "Go up; for the Lord shall deliver into the king's hand." (1 Kings 22:6)

When the press all sing the same tune, something rings false; the King
of Judah indeed suspected that the four hundred "prophets" were merely
pandering to the King of Israel. He could see that their unanimous declaration had more to do with choreography than with actual prophecy.
When Jehoshaphat asked if any others claimed to be a "prophet of the
Lord" (22:7), Ahab admitted that there was indeed another prophet
who had not been summoned, "for I hate him, for he foretells for me not
good but evil" (22:8). Ahab preferred the cheerleading of false prophets
to the foreboding word of God, and hated the bearers of such warnings.

The story goes on to describe how the hated prophet, Micaiah
son of Imla, is summoned to prophesy before the king. The four hundred reiterate their prophecy, calling, "Go up to Ramoth-Gilead and
be victorious, for the Lord shall deliver into the king's hand!" (22:12),
and one of their number, Zedekiah son of Kenaana, triumphantly bran-
dishes a pair of iron horns, declaring, "With these shall you gore Aram!"
(22:11). When the king asks for Micaiah's prophecy, he weakly repeats
the words of his false peers: "Go up and be victorious, for the Lord shall
deliver into the king's hand" (22:16). Sensing that Micaiah's words are
disingenuous, the king urges him to deliver the true message of God.
Micaiah then pours forth a terrible vision of Israel scattered over the
hills like sheep without a shepherd.

Upon hearing Micaiah's words, the King of Israel irritably turns
to the King of Judah: "Didn't I tell you that he wouldn't prophesy any
good about me, only evil?" (22:18). Micaiah, undeterred, ominously
describes God sitting on His throne, asking the heavenly hosts,

> "Who will entice Ahab to ascend and fall in Ramoth-Gilead?" One
> said this and one said that. Then a spirit came … and said, "I will
> entice him … I will go out and be a false spirit in the mouths of
> all his prophets." And [God] said, "You will succeed in enticing
> him. Go out and do so." (22:20–22)

The strength of the prophet as public intellectual derives from his faith
and his deference to the word of God. His intent is never to mollify the
masses. Four hundred prophets forecasting in perfect unison do not a
true prophecy make. Does society want to hear that other still, small

voice? Generally not. Wherever the government, press, and tycoons form a controlling triad, any dissenting opinions will be quickly snuffed out. Worse, prophets are sometimes bought off by interested parties and, through the combined forces of money and media, forcibly mold public opinion. The voice of God should therefore be sought in those discordant voices that do not toe the party line. Of course, prophetic opposition is not necessarily right. Sometimes the ruling power finds itself torn between two opposing prophets, unable to declare a winner. Jeremiah himself faces such opposition, clashing with serious prophets who present their own systematic worldview, and it is wholly unclear which of them is the true messenger of God.

However, there is another criterion for a true prophet. He must love his people. Even when the harshest reproach is called for, the prophet must consider himself a divine emissary whose role is to help redeem the people, not to stand aloof and condemn. Indeed, journalists today take on the role of moral and social critics, though more often than not their criticism is laced with the venom of loathing. Criticism based on love, of the kind that distinguished Jeremiah, is not often found.

WHY JEREMIAH?

Some prophets were defrocked or harmed because of their prophecies. First and foremost among these few was Jeremiah. As a prophet, his life was endangered more than once. The inner truth that burned within him took him to such extremes that he eventually betrayed the Kingdom of Judah. Under siege, during an attempt to expel the enemy from the walls of Jerusalem, he called for his people to cross the battle lines and surrender. He thus became despised and disparaged in the streets of Jerusalem, a menace to the public good. All rejected him – kings, priests, noblemen, and the masses.

Three kings were subject to the prophecies of Jeremiah: Josiah, Jehoiakim, and Zedekiah. The first barely acknowledged him, possibly due to his tender age; the second sought to eliminate him in order to ensure the stability of his reign; the third actually believed him, but could not overcome his own weakness and fears. The priests of the Temple regarded Jeremiah as one regards a gadfly – a pest and troublemaker. The Temple wardens restricted his every step. Among the noblemen there were different leanings; some pandered to the king, while most took a belligerent stance against the rising Babylonian Empire. For the latter, Jeremiah was a menace. And the masses? They behaved as masses do. At times they sought to kill the prophet; other times they needed him desperately, their loyalties changing with the wind. Among the people, Jeremiah's most formidable opponents were the false prophets. They aroused the men of Zedekiah's time to rebel against the Babylonians and encouraged the king to form a pro-Egyptian alliance with the surrounding nations. For Jeremiah, these false prophets were the true enemy.

JEREMIAH IN ZIONIST EYES

There is no doubt that the greatest prophet who arose in the days of the kings before the destruction of Jerusalem, as well as the most despised, downtrodden, and daring, was Jeremiah. He was not afraid of imprisonment, of torture, even of death itself – and always chose to speak the bitter truth, until the bitter end.... He knew that invincibility would not last forever, and was sure that soon enough – certainly within seventy years – Babylonia would tumble and fall.... Jeremiah loved his people and had faith in its posterity – and his faith has proven true until this very day.[3]

In today's world, Jeremiah is perceived as the prophet of the Temple's destruction, the composer of our Tisha B'Av lamentations. The modern word "jeremiad," meaning a work that mourns society and its imminent downfall, reinforces this perception. The Zionist ethos and the national Israeli spirit (secular and religious alike) have ignored Jeremiah and embraced Isaiah as the prophet who comforts Israel and announces its rebirth, and Amos as the prophet entrusted with the moral rehabilitation of society.[4] Enlightenment-era Jewish society and the founders of

3. David Ben-Gurion, on his eighty-fourth birthday, Sde Boker, October 1970. See D. Ben-Gurion, "Kingship and Prophecy," in B. Luria, ed., *Studies in the Book of Jeremiah – Remarks of the Bible-Study Circle in the President's Residence*, 1 (Tel Aviv, 1971), 20 [Hebrew].
4. In a celebratory Knesset session marking one hundred years of Zionism, Shimon Peres (then the head of the opposition) praised Bible study as a basis for

Zionism scorned Jeremiah. This scorn was reinforced in the late nineteenth century by Judah Leib Gordon, whose poem "Zedekiah in the Prison House" depicts a blinded Zedekiah, shackled in Babylonia, asking himself why he deserved such punishment:

> But what crime have I committed? What was my sin?
> That to Jeremiah I would not give in?
> To the softhearted man of defeatist disposition
> Who prescribed for us slavery, shame, and submission?
> Yea, I refused to follow his word,
> Preferring instead to meet sword with sword.

Ben-Gurion, in the speech excerpted above, recounted that as a child he was greatly affected by Gordon, opposing Jeremiah in with all his heart. He was certainly not the only one. Jeremiah was an exilic Jew, hero of the assimilated and religious. Stefan Zweig, a thoroughly assimilated Austrian Jew, recast him as the antiwar protagonist of his World War I play.[5] Just prior to World War II, Franz Werfel, the Czech Jewish human-rights activist, wrote a novel entitled *Jeremiah*. This monumental work is based on a vigorous reading of the Bible, but sheds no light on the tension and conflicts in the Kingdom of Judah in the prophet's time.[6]

Anyone perusing the Bible curriculum in Jewish high schools will immediately notice what short shrift Jeremiah is given. In Israel, the only chapters studied are those of the assassination of Gedaliah – presumably

---

developing a renewed Jewish identity. Peres asserted that "the Labor party views [Amos and Isaiah] as the two great ideological harbingers." MK Yossi Sarid interjected that "In light of the national situation, it could be that Jeremiah is the most relevant." This was said during Prime Minister Benjamin Netanyahu's first term of office, a month after the opening of the Western Wall tunnels, the resurgence of Saddam Hussein's regime, and the Taliban's victory in Kabul. Protocol of the fourteenth Knesset, October 28, 1996 [Hebrew].

5. S. Zweig, *Jeremiah: A Drama in Nine Scenes*, trans. P. Cedar (New York, 1922). See also A. Hameiri, "The Prophet: On *Jeremiah* by Stefan Zweig," in S. Zweig, *Jeremiah* (Jerusalem, 1950), 215–22 [Hebrew].

6. F. Werfel, *Hearken Unto the Voice* (or *Jeremiah*), trans. William Rose (New York, 1938).

because of their parallels to the assassination of Prime Minister Yitzchak Rabin.[7] Jeremiah's own story is known to so few that it has practically become esoteric. This is the void I seek to fill.

JEREMIAH: A PRELIMINARY SKETCH

Jeremiah began prophesying at a young age, and learned to bear this prophetic burden during one of the most turbulent periods in Israel's history. His career commenced during the reign of Josiah, when there was a general sense that the nation was returning to the glory days of King Solomon. Josiah was seen as not only a religious reformer, but a national leader who strove toward the reunification of the kingdoms of Judah and Israel. His vision was not unrealistic; Josiah exploited a political window of opportunity, when the great powers – Assyria, Egypt, and Babylonia – were too busy fighting among themselves to notice what was taking place in the lands of the Israelites. Jeremiah was torn between his desire to participate in this glorious vision of redemption and the ingathering of Israel, and his perception of the hypocrisy of Judean religious reform. His prophecies during Josiah's reign largely reflect this inner conflict: They appealed to the northern tribes to reconnect with Jerusalem and harshly condemned the corrupt lifestyle of those living in Judah and Jerusalem. The fall of Josiah during the unnecessary battle of Megiddo broke Jeremiah's heart.

The second phase of Jeremiah's prophecy began with the reign of Jehoiakim, a faithful follower of Egypt and its culture. During this period, the prophet focused on condemnation of the alienated and violent ruling class. Halfway through Jehoiakim's reign, Nebuchadnezzar rose to power, and Jeremiah started calling for surrender and subjugation to the Babylonian Empire. For the rest of his life, his refrain was "Serve the King of Babylon, and live." Jeremiah believed that there was no point in dying on the altar of imaginary independence. Subjection to Babylonia

---

7. The story of Gedaliah son of Ahikam changed dramatically in Israel after the Rabin assassination. The Fast of Gedaliah, on 3 Tishrei, has become associated with Rabin's murder and is marked by dialogue panels around the country. See "The Murder of Gedaliah," below.

would allow religious and cultural autonomy in Judah and Jerusalem, whereas resistance would lead to destruction. The people around him docilely followed their Egypt-infatuated king. Jeremiah desperately tried to breach this wall of indifference and was eventually persecuted by the king for undermining the kingdom's stability.

Jeremiah's final prophecies took place under Babylonian rule in the Land of Israel. King Zedekiah, a puppet of Nebuchadnezzar, ruled a kingdom split between the pacifist followers of Jeremiah and the nationalist faction spurred on by the other prophet, Jeremiah's rival, Hananiah son of Azzur. Even those exiled to Babylonia during the reign of Jeconiah, Zedekiah's immediate predecessor and the last independent King of Judah, were divided along these lines. The prophecies that span this final period are frightening, unsettling; no one could say for certain which side would prevail, including Jeremiah himself. The king finally sided with Hananiah, bringing destruction upon himself and his people.

This three-act drama has not yet been adequately presented to a modern Jewish audience. While all the elements of conflict in Jeremiah's world can be found in today's newspapers, the lessons of his story have never been applied to contemporary debates about questions of nationalism, autonomy, and identity.

THE STRUCTURE OF THIS BOOK

The Book of Jeremiah is hard to follow. Some chapters seem coherent and complete, while others appear to be disjointed, as if the pages of the original manuscript had been scattered and haphazardly rearranged. Perhaps it's time they should be.

> The difficult question that faces anyone who opens the Book of Jeremiah is: What is the connection, the bridge, between the historical personality and the book that lies before us? .... It contains all manner and type of prophecies, all mixed up.[8]

---

8. M. Haran, "The Composition of the Book of Jeremiah," *Studies in the Book of Jeremiah* III, 105 [Hebrew]. A. Rofei dealt extensively with the issue of the book's structure. See his article "Questions about the Composition of the Book of Jeremiah," *Tarbiz* 40

I have therefore disassembled the Book of Jeremiah and reconstructed it according to the chronology of Jeremiah's life and the development of his prophecy. I have not inserted any ideas not found in the text. I have not embellished the narrative by indulging my imagination, or even that of the sages (with a few clearly indicated exceptions). This is essentially the original Book of Jeremiah, rearranged and reedited. The talmudic rabbis determined that "Jeremiah wrote his own book" (Bava Batra 15a), claiming that the prophet recorded his own visions but not ruling out the possibilty that they were later edited.[9] I have recompiled Jeremiah's prophecies chronologically in an attempt to explore the prophet's personal development. In writing this book, I have attempted to read, and absorb the explanations, interpretations, and research of my predecessors, whom I have cited in footnotes.[10] I emphasize, however, that this work is not a complete running commentary on the Book of Jeremiah, nor is it meant to replace any other commentaries, old or new.

It is my hope that my rearrangement of the Jeremiah narrative will remove the barrier to plumbing its depths, and serve as a foundation for the in-depth study and systematic interpretation of every chapter and verse. In the course of my work, I found that I needed to interpret individual chapters and passages, and I did not refrain from doing so where necessary. I developed many new insights, and entire chapters suddenly took on new meaning. In restructuring the book in a correct, consistent, and chronological order, I was forced to take

---

(5735): 1–29 [Hebrew]. Y. Hoffman also dedicated many articles to Jeremiah's compilation and structure, and I will refer to them in the relevant chapters. On the difficulties of editing Jeremiah and the dead ends in research in the field, see H.M.I. Gevaryahu, "Baruch Son of Neriah: Outlines and Currents in the History of the Study of the Literary Composition of the Book of Jeremiah," in B. Luria, ed., *Wreath of Might* (*In Honor of Zalman Shazar*) (Jerusalem, 5733), 191–243 [Hebrew].

9. Accordingly, the Septuagint's version of Jeremiah contains several chapters out of order. See Y. Kaufmann's theory in *History of the Religion of Israel* III (Jerusalem, 5720), 404 [Hebrew].

10. I owe special gratitude to one man in particular. The late Prof. Yehuda Elitzur never taught me personally, but over the years I have come to consider myself his student. A collection of his articles, *Israel and Scripture* (Ramat Gan, 5760) [Hebrew], attempts to read the Bible and recover its depth for the contemporary reader. His historical articles have greatly influenced my method of reading the Bible.

issue with several classic interpretations. It is unfair to criticize early commentators, such as Rashi, for their ignorance of local geography or the histories of the great empires. I have thus mentioned the opinions of commentators and academics only when needed for proof or refutation. My greatest wish is that this book will inspire further exploration of the deeper recesses of the Bible, and equip the reader with the tools to master its challenges.

Part 1

The Reign of Josiah (640–609 BCE)

Background

Josiah's Predecessors

After a century of Assyrian domination of the Trans-Euphrates region, King Rezin of Aram and King Pekah son of Remaliah of Israel launched an attack on the Kingdom of Judah, which had refused to join them in a coalition against Assyria. King Ahaz of Judah (mid-eighth century BCE) turned to King Tiglath-Pileser III of Assyria for protection: "I am your slave and dependent; come up and save me" (II Kings 16:7). In return, Ahaz paid a massive tribute to the King of Assyria from the royal treasury and the Temple coffers. Tiglath-Pileser indeed subdued the region and dispossessed Aram as well as significant territories of the Kingdom of Israel. The Judeans did not mourn the destruction of Samaria – the savage wars between the two kingdoms overshadowed the blood ties that had once united them.

The Davidic monarchy's last memory of the Kingdom of Israel was thus a degrading and vexatious one. Tens of thousands of Jerusalemites were crushed and murdered in the Israel-Aram assault. "And the Israelites took their brothers captive, two hundred thousand women, boys, and girls. They also plundered great spoils from them and brought the spoils to Samaria" (II Chr. 28:8). During that same event, "Zichri, hero of Ephraim, killed Maaseiah, the king's son; Azrikam, chancellor of the king; and Elkanah, viceroy to the king" (28:7). These were the last deeds of the Kingdom of Ephraim before its exile, and every child growing up in the Kingdom of Judah knew these stories and vowed to avenge the pride of the House of David.

In the meantime, Samaria was exiled, and King Ahaz of Judah became a vassal to Assyria. To prove his loyalty, he recreated an Assyrian altar he had seen in Damascus and erected it in the Temple. This first instance of Assyria's spiritual penetration of Judah was quickly followed by one of Assyrian culture's cruelest rituals – the worship of the god Molech by sacrificing children on its pyres (II Kings 16:3). Until then, this practice had been completely foreign in Judah. Henceforth, Assyria dominated the Land of Israel with virtually no contest.

When Hezekiah, Ahaz's son, ascended the throne, he attempted to restore Judah's glory. He struggled to return Jewish culture to center stage, and – as part of his state-building endeavor – boldly defied the Assyrian Empire and its king, Sennacherib. The latter retaliated with harsh collective punishment and destroyed dozens of cities in the Judean plain and along the coastain: "The daughter of Zion is left like a booth in a vineyard, like a hut in a cucumber field, like a city under siege" (Is. 1:8). Descriptions of these massacres (which took place in 701 BCE) have been found in Assyrian inscriptions. The prophet Isaiah and King Hezekiah joined forces for the first time and appealed to divine mercy. Jerusalem was miraculously saved. The Assyrian king turned on his heels and fled to his kingdom in the north. The war was over, and Hezekiah had become a national hero.

BABYLONIA'S DEBUT IN JUDAH:
MERODACH-BALADAN'S DELEGATION TO HEZEKIAH

As Hezekiah lay on his deathbed, he received a delegation from the Babylonian monarch Merodach-Baladan (II Kings 20:12–13).[1] It was the first time a leader from the Persian Gulf area had arrived in the Land of Israel. Obviously, this was not merely a visit of the bedridden. The king's aims were clear: He wished to forge a coalition against the Assyrian Empire.

Judah was only one piece in the political puzzle that the King of Babylonia was assembling. He forged alliances with Arabian tribes, visited Syria, and made contact with Elam. For years, he painstakingly

---

1. My description of the meeting between Hezekiah and Merodach-Baladan is drawn from Y. Elitzur's article "Isaiah Versus Hezekiah and Merodach-Baladan," *Beit Mikra* 10 (5725): 81–96 (reprinted in Elitzur, *Israel and Scripture*, 201–9) [Hebrew].

built his coalition, until he was assassinated by Sennacherib. Merodach-Baladan's visit to Judah was one of his last political moves before his death. It is almost certain that Hezekiah's rebellion against Sennacherib was inspired by the Babylonian king's increasing power in the east. A diplomatic visit from such an important leader no doubt increased Hezekiah's self-worth. He clearly had weight on an international political scale.

However, the prophet Isaiah criticized him for forming an alliance with Babylonia – a generation after criticizing Hezekiah's father, Ahaz, for allying with Assyria. Isaiah was no politician and was not inclined to one foreign policy over another; he simply opposed any treaty with another nation, encouraging reliance on the God of Israel alone. The prophet warned both father and son, "Be calm and quiet" (Is. 7:4), that is, he advising them not to get involved. The best course of action during a fight between two powerful kings was to lie low and let them wage their wars among themselves. The small Kingdom of Judah was never a great power. Even if the monarchic ambitions are to restore the glory of the Davidic dynasty, the king should not position himself against the dominant power.

Alas, Isaiah's advice fell upon deaf ears. In II Chronicles 32:25, Hezekiah's sin is attributed to his haughtiness. This pride was closely tied to his political consciousness: The alliance Hezekiah forged with Babylonia was more than the Kingdom of Judah had bargained for. Isaiah warned that the generous gifts Hezekiah bestowed upon Babylonia would come to be perceived as mere appetizers for the ravenous Babylonian Empire destined to rise within a century.[2]

THE REIGN OF MANASSEH: BLUE SKIES OVER ASSYRIA

An ancient Jewish adage advises: "Do not rely on miracles." This adage was familiar to Hezekiah's son and heir, Manasseh. He ascended the throne at the turn of the seventh century (697) BCE and at some point

---

2. This section is based on a lecture given by Y. Elitzur in Sde Boker for Ben-Gurion's Panel of Bible Studies (5725) [Hebrew]. In response, Ben-Gurion commented: "Does faith forbid the forming of treaties?" to which the lecturer replied, "Heaven forbid…. You are not currently worthy of being a power." This snippet of dialogue gives a sense of the drama reverberating around the panel.

decided to deviate from his father's foreign policy. These were the days of Esarhaddon of Assyria, who in 677 BCE vanquished the few who still opposed him and transformed Assyria into the most powerful empire of the time. Manasseh decided it was an auspicious time to re-ally Judah with Assyria, and as a result, the Kingdom of Judah enjoyed an unprecedented half-century of peace and security. Manasseh reigned for fifty-five years without as much as the rattling of a saber. The economy stabilized, and people lived in security and prosperity, with nothing to tend to but their fortunes. Manasseh's religious demands on his people were hardly taxing. The prophet Zephaniah described Judean society at the end of Manasseh's reign as devoid of passion, longing, vision, and ambition: "the nation does not yearn" (Zeph. 2:1). One characteristic of this period was the almost complete lack of prophets and visionaries. The glorious present reigned supreme.

Manasseh inundated Jerusalem with Assyrian idols and other symbols of the imperial culture. The zeitgeist penetrated all corners of Manasseh's kingdom. Assyrian became the official language, the latest fashions were imported from Assyria, and etiquette was dictated by the accepted codes of behavior in the great city of Nineveh. Assyrian rites were instituted in the Temple, and altars were erected in honor of all the hosts of heaven – the Assyrian sun god Ashur foremost among them. An idol of the goddess Ishtar, queen of heaven, was erected in the Temple along with houses for the sacred prostitutes who played an indispensable part in Assyrian ritual. Jerusalem took on the guise of an Assyrian province.

Many, particularly those faithful to God and His commandments, opposed Manasseh's policies. II Kings 21:16 describes the copious blood that he shed – presumably the blood of those who rose up against this deviation from Hezekiah's path, this desertion of Israel's God. It is likely that Manasseh's opponents were forced to the margins – far away from the defiled Temple – where they worked to encourage the worship of God. Traces of this campaign have been discovered in neighborhoods west of biblical Jerusalem (in the area of Kiryat HaYovel and Givat Massua) in the form of tumuli – mounds of earth and stones covering ritual altars. Bible scholar Yehuda Elitzur hypothesized that these tumuli attest to the dramatic struggle against Manasseh. These altars served as spiritual alternatives for the Jews who still served God, "monuments that bear witness to the holy rebellion and self-sacrifice of those who feared God, who opposed Manasseh and his deities, and remained faithful to the God of Israel."[3] The altars of West Jerusalem were not removed until the days of Josiah, when, because they had been used for the worship of God, they were not destroyed, but merely covered in earth.

MANASSEH IN THE JEWISH COLLECTIVE MEMORY

The Book of Kings cuts Manasseh no slack, portraying his reign as a time of the utmost evil, during which Jerusalem's fate was sealed in payment for its sins. Jeremiah, too, attributes Jerusalem's harsh sentence to the sins of Manasseh: "I will make them a horror to all the kingdoms of the earth, on account of King Manasseh, son of Hezekiah of Judah, [and] of what he did in Jerusalem" (Jer. 15:4).

Whereas Manasseh is vilified in the books of Kings and Jeremiah, the author of Chronicles describes the end of his days in a different light. In the Chronicles account, Manasseh was captured by the King of Assyria (who apparently suspected him of treason) and led in chains to Babylonia, where he returned to God:

> In his distress, he entreated the Lord, his God, and humbled himself greatly before the God of his fathers. He prayed to Him, and He granted his prayer, heard his plea, and returned him to Jerusalem, to his kingdom; then Manasseh knew that the Lord was God. (II Chr. 33:12–13)

The debate regarding Manasseh's end continued until the era of the *Tanna'im*, the rabbis of the Mishna. The Mishna (Sanhedrin 10:2) determinedly lists him as one of three kings (the others being Ahab and Jeroboam) who have no share in the World to Come. However, Rabbi Yehuda expunges Manasseh from this blacklist, citing the redeeming description in Chronicles. The controversy surrounding him is also described in a talmudic narrative about the Babylonian Rav Ashi (late

---

3. Y. Elitzur, "On the Essence of the Tumuli in Western Jerusalem," in Elitzur, *Israel and Scripture*, 164–71 [Hebrew].

fourth century CE), who taught Sanhedrin to his students. As prepara-
tion for the next class, he told his students, "Tomorrow, we will begin
discussing our friends," sarcastically referring to these three kings:

> [That night,] Manasseh appeared to him in a dream. He said: "Did
> you call us your friend and the friend of your father?" Manasseh
> began to teach him Torah laws that R. Ashi did not know.
>
> R. Ashi said to him: "If you are so sagacious, why did you
> worship foreign gods?"
>
> Manasseh answered him: "Had you been there, you would
> have tripped over your skirt running after idol worship."
>
> The next day, during the lesson, R. Ashi began by saying:
> "Today we will begin dealing with Israel's greatest." (Sanhedrin
> 102b)

This story seems to mitigate the criticism heaped on a king who, after
all, was trying to put his tiny kingdom back on its feet and, in doing so,
could not resist the attraction of Assyria's culture. In awe and fear of the
ascendant Assyrian Empire, Manasseh forfeited the cultural and religious heritage of the Kingdom of Judah to make it Assyrian in every way.

640 BCE: THE BEGINNING OF JOSIAH'S REIGN AND THE BIRTH OF JEREMIAH

After Manasseh's death, his son Amon ascended the throne for a brief
and historically insignificant period (642–640 BCE). Leaving no lasting
mark upon the Kingdom of Judah, he continued his father's unwavering
support for Assyria. He was assassinated after only two years in power,
and the "people of the land" (*am ha'aretz*) enthroned his son Josiah, then
only eight years old, in his stead. The designation "people of the land"
refers to Judah's upper classes, which included the landed aristocracy
and those with the power to appoint kings. It is possible that these aristocrats killed Amon's assassins and appointed his son in order to prevent
Assyrian retaliation against the assassination of this pro-Assyrian king.

Nothing is known about Josiah's early years. On the international political scene, Assyria continued its unrivaled dominance.
The emperor Ashurbanipal enjoyed a long reign, during which he

continually reinforced his empire. We can only assume that the Judean aristocrats instructed their young king to be faithful to the Assyrian overlord.

Around the same time Josiah was enthroned in Judah, a son was born to Hilkiah in the priestly village of Anathoth, in the territory of Benjamin. Hilkiah was from the line of Abiathar, a descendant of High Priest Eli, whose roots can be traced – according to rabbinic tradition – to Ithamar son of Aaron. Abiathar was banished from Temple service by King Solomon and replaced by High Priest Zadok and his successors, descendants of Phinehas son of Eleazar, Ithamar's brother. The priests of Anathoth had nothing to do with service in the Temple, instead tilling the soil and shepherding in the desert frontier region of Wadi Qelt.[4] Hilkiah's son, Jeremiah, was born in a time of political and cultural stability.

627 BCE: THE FALL OF ASSYRIA, THE BEGINNING OF JOSIAH'S REFORMATION, AND JEREMIAH'S PROPHECY

A turning point came in 627 BCE. The death of Ashurbanipal sparked a power struggle and a war of succession. In addition to Assyria's internal problems, the Babylonian coalition strengthened and reared its head. Babylonia's King Nebopolassar began to attack cities in northeast Assyria. The great metropolis Nineveh fell into Babylonian hands in 612 BCE. For years, Assyria focused on its own problems and failed to notice what was happening to its outer provinces. With this background, we can begin our journey through the Book of Jeremiah.

In the eighth year of Josiah's reign, when he was but sixteen years old, something changed within him. According to Chronicles, Josiah began to oppose the Assyrian culture that had dominated Jerusalem for over half a century:

> In the eighth year of his reign, while he was still young, he began to seek the God of his father David. (II Chr. 34:3)

The first phase of his reformation was his search for a connection to "the God of his father David." For four years, Josiah fortified his bond with

---

4. N. Hareuveni, *A New Light on the Book of Jeremiah* (Jerusalem, 5715), 27–61 [Hebrew].

his ancestral culture and religion, so it was not until the twelfth year of his reign – when he was twenty years old – that he felt strong enough to commence his life's work: the purging of Assyrian worship. As described in Chronicles, he began by cleansing and purifying Jerusalem and Judah, and only then proceeded to the second phase of his revolution – reuniting the kingdoms of Judah and Israel. Josiah began sending envoys to the region of Samaria, where there remained individual families that had not been exiled along with the ten northern tribes.

These steps can be understood only against the backdrop of the crumbling Assyrian Empire and the war of attrition it was waging along its northeastern border. The young king's vision filled the vacuum that had gradually permeated Judah and Israel. He surveyed the political map, returned to his ancestor David's vision of ruling over all the tribes of Israel, and fused his fantasies with reality. He decided that the time was ripe to reunite the tribes, to return those that Assyria had exiled from Samaria and the Galilee a century earlier, and to restore the Davidic dynasty to its glory days under King Solomon.

Of course, this vision met with hostility from without and within. The notion of returning the Israelite tribes and reuniting the kingdoms of Israel and Judah is obvious to anyone who has studied the prophets of Israel, who were unequivocal on this issue. The Jewish redemptive vision seeks to unify all of Jacob's children as one people in one land. However, what is obvious to a Jew in the twenty-first century was not self-evident in 627 BCE.

There were good reasons to oppose the vision of the romantic young king. The elders of his generation still recalled those who had survived Israel's final bloody attack on Judah during the reign of Ahaz (discussed above). They had made their children swear never to forget what Ephraim had done to Judah. Moreover, in the century since the exile of the ten tribes, the Assyrian kings had resettled the desolate cities of Samaria with natives of the northeastern lands. These transplants had accepted the local Jewish God, adopted local customs, and become full-fledged citizens through intermarriage with the remaining native Ephraimites. The Judeans, who saw Israel as "a people that dwells alone" (Num. 23:9), valued cultural and religious isolation, and so took a dim view of such ties.

Josiah was not the first to try reconnecting the split kingdoms. When Hezekiah revived the Paschal sacrifice, he had invited the tribes of Ephraim and Manasseh up to the Temple in Jerusalem. The text describes the scorn heaped on Hezekiah's delegates traveling through the cities of Ephraim:

> As the couriers passed from town to town in the land of Ephraim and Manasseh till they reached Zebulun, they were laughed at and mocked. (II Chr. 30:10)

The enmity between the two kingdoms ran deep. Even when their own kingdom had been destroyed, the inhabitants of Mount Ephraim boycotted Judah's religious rites. Only Israelites from the northern and western Galilee, the tribes of Manasseh and Zebulun, gave in and came to Jerusalem. Hezekiah's attempts to ingather the tribes indicate his approach, but the time was not yet ripe for the reunification of the kingdoms. His son Manasseh was not concerned with renewing the united monarchy; he worshipped the Assyrian gods while trying to strengthen Judah. Josiah broke the ice and attempted to change the climate of hostility that prevailed between the sister states. It is at this point that Jeremiah enlists in the cause of promoting a renewed monarchy and a reunited kingdom.

Jeremiah's Prophetic Initiation

Jeremiah becomes aware of his prophetic message during the thirteenth year of Josiah's reign, or 626 BCE. Josiah's reformation is already under way, and the king is busy purging Assyrian culture from Israel and Judah. Jeremiah, a young man of about thirteen, is fully aware of the spiritual implications of the events unfolding in the vicinity. News of the demise of the Assyrian king and the rise of the Babylonian kingdom has already reached Anathoth. The balance of power remains unclear, the roles of heroes and villains have not yet been assigned, and the implications of the fall of one empire and the rise of another have yet to be discerned.

Jeremiah, presumably, receives his first prophecy in Anathoth. God tells him: "Before I formed you in the womb, I knew you; before you were born, I consecrated you; I appointed you a prophet to the nations" (Jer. 1:5). The expression "to the nations" does not mean, specifically, non-Israelites, but rather indicates that Jeremiah will be speaking to a much wider target audience. He will not be confined to the role of local prophet, concerning himself solely with the moral edification of his coreligionists. The map of the world will be forever before him, and he will prophesy the acts of God toward the nations.[1]

---

1. For different interpretations of Jeremiah as a prophet of Israel and the nations, see S. Zalevski, "I Appointed You a Prophet Concerning the Nations," in *A Volume in Honor of H.M.I. Gevaryahu* (Jerusalem, 5750), 185–210 [Hebrew].

Already here, in Jeremiah's prophetic initiation, we see that prophecy has been branded upon his being, irrespective of his free will. In response to his evasion of God's word – "I do not know how to speak, for I am still a boy" (1:6) – God touches his mouth, saying: "Herewith I put My words into your mouth" (1:9). This is the defining moment of Jeremiah's life. The insertion of God's word into Jeremiah's mouth makes prophecy an inextricable part of his being, whether he likes it or not. God then expounds upon Jeremiah's role as "a prophet concerning the nations":

> I appoint you this day over nations and kingdoms: to uproot and tear down, to obliterate and destroy, to build and plant. (1:10)

The boy is appointed prophet at a fateful moment, as massive upheavals shake the known world. He does not yet know the names of these empires to be obliterated and built, uprooted and planted. He knows only that his hour has come, and that God controls the playing field.

Jeremiah then receives his first prophetic visions – the rapidly budding almond branch and the thorny tumbleweed[2] facing down from the north. These two visions render him fully alert, his ears cocked and his eyes straining, every muscle in his body tensed. When asked, "What do you see?" he immediately answers, "An almond branch I see" (1:11). Having just been initiated and given his prophetic mission of heralding the uprooting and rebuilding of nations, Jeremiah is presented with two symbols that, in a chiastic structure, reflect this dichotomy. The blossoming almond branch symbolizes life and renewal. Therefore, when he answers, "An almond branch I see," God responds, "You have seen well" (1:12). These are words of praise not for his sight, but for his interpretation of the vision – you have envisioned the rise of a nation, corresponding to your future role as one who will "build and plant."[3]

---

2. Translator's Note: Though most translations render this vision as a "seething pot" or the like, "thorny tumbleweed" is more consistent with the interpretation that follows.
3. As suggested by H. Mack, "An Almond Branch I See," *Beit Mikra* 39 (5754): 269–76.

The vision of the almond branch is closely followed by the image of the tumbleweed – "wind-blown brushwood I see, facing down from the north" (1:13). Jeremiah sees a pile of thorny burnet shrubs (*Sarcopoterium spinosum*, or *sira kotzanit* in modern Hebrew), a native Mediterranean shrub burned for cooking and heating purposes.[4] Fierce northern winds threaten to blow the pile of thorns southward. While the almond branch indicates *when* the prophecy will come to fruition (the buds are *about to* burst open), the tumbleweed signifies *where* – "*From the north* will disaster break loose upon all the inhabitants of the land" (1:14). Despite these clues, it remains unclear exactly which northern empire will rise up next.

Jeremiah's prophetic initiation concludes with God's urging him to gird his loins:

> Rise and speak to them all that I command you. Do not cower before them, or I shall make you cower before them. Today I have rendered you a fortified city, a pillar of steel, and bronze walls against all the land – Judah's kings, officers, priests, and aristocrats. They will fight against you, but they will not overcome you, for I am with you – says the Lord – to save you. (1:17–19)

---

4. See Y. Felix's explanation, "Parables of Nature and Agriculture in the Book of Jeremiah," in Luria, *Studies in Jeremiah I*, 119 [Hebrew]. Felix debates whether Jeremiah's vision, a *sir nafuaḥ*, is indeed a nature image or the more common explanation, "a seething." For a summary of possible explanations, see Y. Hoffman, ed., *Jeremiah* (*World of the Bible*) (Tel Aviv, 1999), 25–26 [Hebrew].

627–622 BCE

Prophesying Reunification

The prophecy of Jeremiah emerges during Josiah's reformation. Jeremiah's early prophecy envisions the reunification of Israel and Judah, which suits the spirit of Josiah. As a young boy from a family of priests in Anathoth, Jeremiah is not truly part of either kingdom. Anathoth is a priestly city within the lands of the tribe of Benjamin, on the border between Judah and Israel. It pledges allegiance to neither kingdom.[1] As noted, the priests of Anathoth are not active in the Jerusalem Temple; rather, they live quiet lives, tilling their fields.

CHAPTER 3: "MARKETING" THE VISION OF REDEMPTION TO THE EPHRAIMITES

Jeremiah's first prophecy leads him straight to the territories of the former northern kingdom, Samaria and the Galilee:

> Go out, proclaim these words toward the north, and say: Return, O unruly Israel – says the Lord; I will frown upon you no longer, for I am kind – says the Lord – I will not be angry forever. (3:12)

---

1. See Y. Bin-Nun, "Territory of Benjamin, Territory of the *Shekhina*," http://www.ybn. co.il/mamrim/m47.htm [Hebrew], and a partial English synopsis, http://vbm-torah. org/archive/yeru/18yeru.htm.

Those who have remained in the land after the exile of the ten tribes do not see moving to Judah as an option, nor do they have neighborly relations with it. They live a relatively autonomous life under Assyrian rule. Jeremiah voices a new promise to the Israelites of Samaria. Whereas Isaiah prophesied, during the final war between Judah and Israel, that "within sixty-five years, Ephraim will be too shattered to be a people" (Is. 7:8), there now arises a fresh young prophet, calling, "Return, O unruly Israel." Israel's sins are but the unruly rebellions of youth. Considering Isaiah's harsh prophecies and Hosea's comparison of Israel to a prostitute constantly betraying her husband (Hos. 2), we can understand how differently the soft words of a young prophet from Benjamin ring in the ears of Ephraim:

> Return, O mischievous children – says the Lord – for I am your caretaker, and I will take you, one per city, two per family, and I will bring you to Zion. (Jer. 3:14)

In these lines, Jeremiah offers insight into the process of return that he set out to spearhead together with King Josiah.[2] First, Jeremiah announces in God's name that "I will not be angry forever." God bears no grudge against His wayward children; repentance and atonement are possible in His world. Though Samaria has been inundated with idolatry for centuries, and even Judah has been worshipping idols for three generations since Hezekiah's death, their fate has not been sealed for destruction.

Second, Jeremiah wishes to outline the process of return to Jerusalem for the remnants of the Israelite kingdom. The inhabitants of Jerusalem must merely purge their hearts of idolatry, whereas the northerners must resolve to return to this city, which they have forsaken since the days of Jeroboam 1. The profound, centuries-old gap between the kingdoms can be bridged only by an intense process of repentance and return. What can make the people of Ephraim accept the tidings that they are to come back to Jerusalem, having mocked Hezekiah's invitation eighty years before?

---

2. Y. Ben Shem, "The Prophet Jeremiah and the Exiled of the Ten Tribes," *Beit Mikra* 18 (5733): 221–26 [Hebrew].

Young, inexperienced Jeremiah must repackage and market an old, unwanted product. He expects the Ephraimites to reject his invitation for three reasons: As descendants of Rachel, who believe that Joseph was Jacob's chosen son, they are unwilling to embrace the Davidic dynasty; they do not view Jerusalem as the ultimate capital – Mount Ephraim, and within it, Bethel, is nearer and dearer to them; and the Temple is no holier to them than the places of worship that have served their ancestors for over three hundred years. Jeremiah must overcome these prejudices, so he emphasizes new "selling points."

Jeremiah announces to the children of Ephraim that the Jerusalem to which they will return is not the same one abandoned by Jeroboam centuries before. Jeremiah is careful to strike the House of David from his vocabulary, for the Ephraimites are obviously uninterested in that product. He promises that their return to Zion will be guided by faithful shepherds who will lead the people wisely: "I will give you shepherds according to My heart, who shall feed you with knowledge and under-standing" (3:15). In his heart, Jeremiah certainly means Josiah, whom he considers the perfect leader to ingather the exiles of Israel. But to his audience, he remains deliberately vague.

Yet this careful diplomacy is just the first step. He saves the real surprise for last:

> And when you multiply and bear fruit in the land in the days to come – says the Lord – people will no longer mention the Ark of the Lord's covenant or yearn for it; it will be neither remem-bered nor recalled, and another shall not be made. In those days, Jerusalem will be called "Throne of the Lord," and all the nations will be gathered to her, in the Lord's name, to Jerusalem. They will no longer follow the impulses of their evil hearts. In those days, the House of Judah will go to the House of Israel, and they will come together from the north to the land that I allotted to your fathers. (3:16–18)

Jeremiah tells the people remaining in the north that when they return to Zion, to a reunited Kingdom of Israel, the Ark of the Covenant will no longer be so important. It is worth recalling that the Ark was the centerpiece of the Temple. The Kingdom of Judah had reveled in its glorious position as keeper of the Ark since David's time. Ever since Solomon had built the Temple, the Ark had resided in the Holy of Holies, the inner sanctum of the Temple.

The people of Samaria know this well. They have not forgotten one of the formative stories of their kingdom, which took place before David came to rule in Jerusalem, when the Ark of the Covenant was in Shiloh. In that distant past, the Philistines captured the Ark during a war in which two sons of High Priest Eli were killed. The Ark never returned to the territory of the northern tribes (see 1 Sam. 5–6). It became a symbol of the power and glory of the House of David – and of the weakness and inadequacy of the early Israelite kingdom. Jeremiah, himself a descendant of Eli, acts on his awareness of the Israelites' sensitivity about the Ark, freeing it of its symbolic role.

The northerners are loath to trust a Judean prophet promising that the Ark of the Covenant will no longer dominate their worship, so Jeremiah makes considerable efforts to convince his audience. To reinforce his message, he uses five different phrases negating the centrality of the Ark: "people will *no longer* mention the Ark of the Lord's covenant *or* yearn for it; it will be *neither* remembered *nor* recalled, and another *shall not* be made."

In truth, the Ark of the Covenant was already being concealed during the reign of Manasseh, as recorded in Chronicles' description of Josiah's celebration of Passover:

> And [Josiah] said to the Levites, who instructed all Israel, who were holy to the Lord, "Put the Holy Ark in the Temple that Solomon son of David, King of Israel, built – do not carry it on your shoulders; now serve the Lord, your God, and His people, Israel." (11 Chr. 35:3)

Obviously, if Josiah demanded that the Ark be returned to the Temple, it was not there to begin with. Yehuda Elitzur offered an interesting theory regarding the Ark's removal from its proper place: Manasseh, who commissioned secret and labyrinthine royal catacombs, had reinterred those buried in the older royal burial grounds in the new catacombs at the garden of Uzzah:

> Manasseh certainly remembered the events that had occurred in his father Hezekiah's time, when Jerusalem had been about to fall into Assyrian hands and was miraculously saved from destruction at the last minute. Manasseh understood that miracles of this nature do not happen every day, and that Jerusalem was no longer invincible. He therefore transferred the treasures of his forefathers and concealed them deep beneath Jerusalem's rocky terrain. It is almost certain that within those same labyrinthine catacombs, he commissioned a special section for particularly important artifacts, the most important of which was the Ark. He did not do so out of awe of its holiness; rather, the pragmatic leader deemed it vital to hide this most valued and glorious piece, which held such an honored place in the Israelite consciousness.[3]

It emerges that at the beginning of Josiah's reform, the Ark was removed from its hiding place, but Josiah commanded the Levites to conceal it again: "do not carry it on your shoulders." They would no longer have to carry it about, for it was to be concealed permanently. This is also the meaning of the rabbinic tradition: "Who concealed the Ark? Josiah concealed it" (Yoma 52b).

Jeremiah, enticing the northerners back to Jerusalem, "liberates" them from any Temple-object fetishism and inspires them to rise from idolatry to the worship of God. Jerusalem, in his vision, becomes God's throne. Josiah, in his eyes the greatest of kings, will lead Israel to the Kingdom of Heaven, which will reinforce the earthly kingdom of David.

---

3. Y. Elitzur, "The Controversy Surrounding the Ark of the Covenant in the Days of Josiah," in Elitzur, *Israel and Scripture*, 230–34 [Hebrew].

CHAPTER 31: CHILDREN SHALL
RETURN TO THEIR BORDERS

For Jeremiah, voicing a prophecy of the return of the northern tribes is a simple matter. His task is to sell the idea that the time has come for the children of Rachel and Leah to reunite. Ephraim's infrastructure is in shambles, desperately in need of adoption by a more stable government. Since its destruction at the hands of Assyria, Samaria has become an Assyrian backwater. Until this point, native and immigrant Samaritans have lived together while enjoying the patronage of the occupying empire. Now, with war ravaging Assyria, their future is less secure.

Josiah's invitation to Samaria to return to Judah, reinforced by Jeremiah's prophecy, strikes a chord. The third chapter of Jeremiah is directed entirely to Samaria, as is chapter 31, in which the prophet gently entices Ephraim as a loved one who has grown distant and needs to be appeased and cajoled into coming home again:

> Thus says the Lord: The people who have survived the sword have found favor in the wilderness, for I will give rest to Israel. From afar, the Lord appeared to me, saying: And with a great love I have loved you, so I have drawn you close to Me tenderly. I will rebuild you, My maiden Israel, and you will be built; you will again play your tambourine and go out and dance with joy. You will again plant your vineyards on the Samarian hills; the planters will plant and enjoy the fruit. For the day will come when watchmen will shout from the hills of Ephraim, "Come, let us go up to Zion, to the Lord, our God!" (31:1–5)

The chapter opens with the promise that the hills of Samaria will once again be cultivated and their fruits enjoyed.[4] But it goes on to describe that the vineyard watchmen will call out from the Ephraimite hills to arise and go up to Zion. This festive announcement symbolizes the

---

4. The prophet uses the word *hillelu* (lit., "be redeemed"), referring to the Jewish law of *neta revai*, by which fruits may not be enjoyed until the fourth year after planting. The implication is that the people will remain on their own soil long enough to eventually enjoy the fruit of their labor.

renewed fraternal love between Judah and Samaria, as well as the latter's recognition of Jerusalem as the locus of God's presence.

Though the chapter is devoted to the people of Samaria, it seems that this last verse addresses the people of Jerusalem. Like a professional mediator conducting political negotiations, flitting back and forth between the parties, Jeremiah tries to present each one with what it wants to hear, what it stands to gain. He promises a stable economy and security to the people of Samaria ("you will again plant vineyards") while offering geopolitical superiority to the people of Jerusalem ("Come, let us go up to Zion").

Jeremiah must also consider that it is more difficult to convince the Judeans of the revolutionary idea of ending the conflict between the two states, which means forgetting past injuries and forging a shared identity that will bind them under one kingdom. Having nodded in Judah's direction, Jeremiah quickly returns to the vision of a new Samaria: "For thus says the Lord: Sing with joy for Jacob; shout out on the hilltops of the nations; make your praises heard, and say, 'Lord, save Your people, the remnant of Israel'" (31:6).

In chapters 3 and 31, Jeremiah makes frequent use of the name "Jacob." The name resonates with the Samaritans, recalling their forefather Jacob and the city of Bethel, where he encountered God, as well as stressing the origins they share with the people of Judah (who identify with David and his city, Jerusalem). Jeremiah prophesies optimistically, already hearing the sound of the salvation of the remnant of Israel:

> I will bring them from the north country and gather them from the ends of the earth, and with them the blind, the lame, the expectant mother together with those in childbirth: a great throng will return here. They will come in weeping, and I will lead them as they pray; I will guide them to running water along a straight path, on which they will not stumble; for I am a father to Israel, and Ephraim is My firstborn. (31:7–8)

"Ephraim is My firstborn" – such an expression could never escape Jeremiah's lips in the Judean hills or the courtyards of Jerusalem. This prophecy declares that in the struggle for succession between Judah and Joseph and their descendants, Ephraim, of Joseph's line, is the rightful firstborn.[5]

The rest of the prophecy is directed to the entire world, so all should know what is to come:

> Hear the word of the Lord, O nations, and proclaim it on distant islands, and say: "He who scattered Israel will gather it and guard it as a shepherd over his flock." For the Lord will deliver Jacob and redeem him from the hand of one stronger than he. They will come and shout for joy on the heights of Zion; they will stream to the Lord's bounty, for grain, for wine, and for oil, and for the young of the flocks and herds; their soul will be like a well-watered garden, and they will languish in sorrow no more. (31:9–11)

To conclude this prophecy of comfort and redemption, Jeremiah invokes the memory of Rachel, mother of the tribes of Joseph and the Kingdom of Ephraim:

> Thus says the Lord: A voice is heard in Ramah, of mourning and great weeping – Rachel weeping for her children; she has refused to be comforted for her children, for they are no more. Thus says the Lord: Restrain your voice from weeping and your eyes from tears, for your work will be rewarded – declares the Lord; they will return from the enemy's land. And there is hope for your descendants – declares the Lord; [your] children will return to their border. (31:14–16)

---

5. This passage is a reaction to the interpretation of Rabbi David Kimḥi (Radak) regarding the words "Go out, proclaim these words toward the north" (Jer. 3:12):

    > [God] does not tell the prophet to go north to the place where the ten tribes were exiled. Rather, "go out" signifies haste. "Proclaim" means that he should proclaim these words in Jerusalem, before the elders of Judah.

    Radak explains thus because he understands the order to refer to the distant north. However, I submit that Jeremiah went on a diplomatic mission to Samaria, within walking distance of his home in Anathoth.

Jeremiah, serving at this early stage as a tailwind for the vision of national healing, sounds like a prophet deeply rooted in Samaria. His prophecy tells of the children of Rachel, the tribes of Ephraim and Manasseh, who were exiled from their lands by Assyria. He has already promised her children that they will again plant vineyards on the Samarian hills, for that is their home, and none will remove them from it again. Now he illuminates his words with a precious, evocative light: Those who passed by Ramah (the village of a-Ram, adjacent to Ramallah) as they were exiled to the northern Assyrian territories will return. The procession of exiles passed Rachel's Tomb on the "road to Ephrath." There is much disagreement about the location of this tomb. However, in the context of this chapter, the opinion of Noga Hareuveni seems most plausible. He identifies Ephrat with Naḥal Perat (Wadi Qelt) and its spring, known as Ein Perat.[6]

Rachel, weeping for her children, is called upon to hold back her tears, for her children will return from hostile lands to their own borders – to Samaria. By turning directly to the tribes of Israel and mentioning Rachel, the mother of Joseph, the beloved wife of Jacob who watches over her children, Jeremiah reaches the climax of his prophecies of consolation. The conflict between Rachel and Leah, between Joseph and Judah, between the House of David and the House of Saul, is about to end. Ephraim is the firstborn, and Rachel is the true mother.

Jeremiah does not stop at his mention of Rachel weeping for her children. He recasts his gaze upon the children of Ephraim themselves:

> I have heard Ephraim bemoaning himself: "Chastise me, and I will be chastised, like an untrained calf; turn me back, and I will return, for You, Lord, are my God. For after I had turned away, I regretted it, and after I was made aware, I struck my thigh; I was ashamed and humiliated, because I bore the disgrace of my youth." Ephraim is My dear son, My playful child; for whenever I speak

---

6. N. Hareuveni, "Rachel's Tomb," in Hareuveni, *New Light*, 143–51. For a range of opinions regarding the tomb's location (between Benjamin and Judah), see Y. Elitzur, "'A Voice is Heard in Ramah' and the Location of Rachel's Tomb," *Shmaatin* 59 (5740): 16–22 [Hebrew].

of him, I miss him even more; therefore My innards ache for him; I will surely show him love – declares the Lord. (31:17–19)

"Ephraim bemoans … like an untrained calf" – this is one of the greatest defenses of Israel ever proclaimed by a prophet. Look at Ephraim, urges Jeremiah; he is like a newborn calf, whose legs tremble unsteadily. Israel, the inhabitants of Samaria, heard the opposite prophecy from Hosea: "Ephraim is a well-trained calf that loves to thresh" (Hos. 10:11) – a calf habituated in sin. Now Jeremiah compares them to a baby calf that cannot even stand yet. This calf requests of its mother, "Chastise me, and I will be chastised" – I can be trained, if you will only guide me. Jeremiah then concludes, "Turn me back, and I will return, for You, Lord, are my God." His innovation here lies in envisioning Ephraim's asking God to take the first step: "Turn me back."

In Jeremiah's prophecy, Ephraim confesses his sins: "I bore the disgrace of my youth." Faced with the pathetic lowing of his unruly offspring, the loving parent, without a trace of anger or bad memories, responds: "Ephraim is my dear son," even if he is occasionally mischievous and "playful." "Whenever I speak of him, I miss him even more." Just as a parent's heart fills with love the more he thinks of his child, so too, God pines for the son who stormed out in his youthful passion. The parent concludes with an oath: "I will surely show him love." Thus, Jeremiah completes his promise to the tribe of Ephraim. He arrives at a climax of love and promises that the days of estrangement and alienation have ended at the dawn of a new age.

Jeremiah then says, perhaps to himself, perhaps to us,

With that, I awoke and saw how sweet my sleep had been. For days are coming – declares the Lord – when I will plant the House of Israel and the House of Judah with the seed of man and the seed of beast. And just as I watched over (*shakadeti*) them to uproot and tear down, to obliterate, destroy, and afflict, so I will watch over (*eshkod*) them to build and plant – declares the Lord. (31:25–27)

Upon awakening from his vision, Jeremiah sees all that he has seen in his prophecy. In his prophetic initiation, he beheld an almond branch (*shakeid*) accompanying the echo of God's voice, promising that He would uproot and tear down, obliterate and destroy, and eventually build and plant. And indeed God quickly draws His children close, ready to build and plant. The comfort comes swiftly, and the days of dreading the evil from the north are over.

A NOTE ON CHAPTER 31: "A VOICE IS HEARD IN RAMAH" IN THE POST-BIBLICAL COLLECTIVE JEWISH MEMORY

Our interpretation of Jeremiah's famous words "A voice is heard in Ramah … Rachel weeping for her children" undermines two basic, highly charged premises within Jewish tradition. First, tradition places Rachel's Tomb in Bethlehem, south of Jerusalem in Judah, at a site that has been sanctified by thousands of years of Jewish tears. Second, Rachel is one of the most beloved figures in all of Jewish tradition: in Midrash, liturgy, poetry, literature, and art. Her children's great love for her stems from the midrashic image of her weeping figure, watching over the procession of exiles making its way to Babylon. The explanation offered here – that Rachel is buried in the portion of Benjamin and weeps only over her direct descendants, Ephraim and Manasseh – detracts from the raw emotion and power of these midrashim.

When discussing these famous lines, it is impossible not to mention the midrashic tradition – and all subsequent Jewish traditions – of Rachel comforting Leah's descendants as they go into exile, forty years after Jeremiah spoke these words. Rashi cites this midrash in his commentary on the verse in which Jacob explains Rachel's death and burial to Joseph:

> When I was coming from Padan, Rachel died in the land of Canaan, on the road, with a way to go before Ephrath; and I buried her there, on the road to Ephrath, that is, Bethlehem. [Gen. 48:7]
>
> "I buried her there" – Know that I buried her there at God's command, so that she would aid her children. When Nebuzaradan exiled them, they passed by there, and Rachel left her grave and wept and begged for mercy on their behalf, as it says: "A voice is heard in Ramah, of mourning and great weeping – Rachel

weeping for her children" [Jer. 31:14]. And God responds: "your work will be rewarded – declares the Lord…your children will return to their borders" [31:15]. (Rashi, ad loc.)

This midrash, and Rashi in its wake, has an awesome power. It has elicited Jewish tears throughout the generations, irrevocably sanctifying the site. And Rachel has become the mother of all Jews, including those descended from her sister, Leah.[7]

CHAPTER 23, VERSES 1–8: REBUKE OF THE LEADERSHIP AND FAITH IN JOSIAH

As the months pass, Jeremiah begins to sense the profound failure of his people's return. Josiah means well and has great aspirations, but does not realize that his campaign to return to God is not penetrating the people's hearts. Defective local leadership has caused the people of Judah to remain unaware that this period of imperial downfall and radical reform carries great potential for the redemption of Judah and Israel. These regional rulers are the shepherds Jeremiah condemns in his prophecy:

> Woe to the shepherds who destroy and scatter the sheep of My pasture – declares the Lord. Therefore, thus says the Lord, God of Israel, to the shepherds who tend My people: You have scattered My flock and driven them away and have not taken care of them; I will punish you for the evil you have done – declares the Lord. I Myself will gather the remnant of My flock out of all the countries where I have driven them, and I will bring them back

---

7. In marking the joint anniversary of Rachel's death and Yitzchak Rabin's murder, Hanan Porat, a former Knesset Member, stated:

    The agreement with Arafat had already been initialed, stating that Rachel's Tomb would be designated as Palestinian territory, as part of Bethlehem, when suddenly Menahem Porush [an Ultra-Orthodox Israeli MK] grabbed Rabin and shook him, shouting, "Reb Yitzhak, we're talking about Mama Rochel!" Tears streamed down his face and drenched Rabin's suit. I saw Rabin flush, then pale. He didn't know what to do with himself. He said, "Give me a moment to consider." Then, right in front of us, he called Shimon Peres – then foreign minister – and said to him, "Regarding Rachel's Tomb, I wish to reconsider."

to their pasture, where they will be fruitful and increase. I will place shepherds over them who will tend them, and they will no longer be afraid or terrified, nor will any be missing – declares the Lord. (23:1–4)

Jeremiah could have expressed such sentiments only early in his career, when he was still optimistic about the redemption and reunification of Judah and Israel, when he could still draw from the vision of the blossoming almond branch, and when he still had high hopes for the scion of the House of David. The problem he addresses here is local: The shepherds are unfit and must be replaced.

Jeremiah views this discrepancy between the king and the local leadership as a generation gap. Whereas Josiah is young and revolutionary, the local leaders continue to represent the sinful generation of Manasseh. Therefore, God will rid the kingdom of these shepherds, gather the scattered flock from Samaria, and establish a new, worthy leadership. Despite Jeremiah's withering criticism of the old guard, this chapter remains full of hope and joy regarding the impending fulfillment of Josiah's messianic vision. Just as Isaiah prophesied hopefully about Hezekiah and the flourishing (*tzemaḥ*) of the Davidic dynasty (Is. 4:2), Jeremiah says of Josiah:

Days are coming – declares the Lord – when I will raise up a righteous branch (*tzemaḥ*) of David's line: He shall reign as king and prosper, and do what is just and right in the land. In his days, Judah will be saved, and Israel will live in safety; and this is the name by which he will be called: The Lord is our righteous Savior. (Jer. 23:5–6)

Here, a messianic vision bursts forth from Jeremiah.[8] He beholds Josiah, selects him as the one in whose days "Judah will be saved, and Israel will

8. Throughout the books of the prophets, from Isaiah through Zechariah, the term *tzemaḥ* – branch, sprout, growth, flourishing – is associated with the house of David. See B. Oppenheimer, "The Historical Testimony of the Books of Haggai and Zechariah," in Oppenheimer, *The Visions of Zechariah: From Prophecy to Apocalypse* (Jerusalem, 5721), 5–7 [Hebrew].

live in safety," and assigns him the epithet: "The Lord is our righteous Savior."[9] Jeremiah does not shrink from his tidings at this stage, for Josiah is restoring Israel's fallen glory. He declares that the period of disgrace that began with Assyria exiling the ten tribes, and extended through Manasseh's defilement of Judah, has come to an end:

> For days are coming – declares the Lord – when they will no longer say, "By the Lord who brought up the Israelites from Egypt," but "By the Lord who brought up the seed of Israel from the northern land and from all the countries where He had banished them." Then they will live in their own land. (23:7–8)

Israel's recent enslavement to Assyria and the return of those lost in its empire will eclipse the Israelites' enslavement in Egypt and their entrance into their land, led by Moses. Whoever witnesses this miracle will no longer refer to the Exodus from Egypt as the definitive example of God's glory. The return of the lost tribes from the north will surpass all the miracles Israel has ever known.

Jeremiah is convinced that God's promise to rebuild after the destruction will soon be realized. He feels that the people have already experienced destruction with the exile to Assyria. Now, with the ascent of a Davidic king, the days of resettling and replanting are imminent.

CHAPTER 30: MOCKING THOSE WITH LITTLE FAITH IN REDEMPTION

> The word that came to Jeremiah from the Lord, saying: Thus said the Lord, God of Israel: Write all the words I have spoken to you in a book. For days are coming – declares the Lord – when I will bring back the captivity of My people, Israel and Judah – says the

---

9. It has been claimed that Jeremiah is referring to Zedekiah, whose name may be interpreted as "the Lord is our righteous Savior (*tzidkenu*)." See J. Klausner, *The Messianic Idea in Israel* (Jerusalem, 1926), 64–66 [Hebrew]. But at this stage it seems that Jeremiah still believed in Josiah as a hope for the renewal of the Davidic reign; we may thus assume that the king is alluded to in the phrase "in his days he will save (*beyamav tivasha*)," thereby referring to both Judah and Israel.

Lord – and I will return them to the land I gave their ancestors, and they will inherit it. (30:1–3)

God's order to inscribe all of Jeremiah's prophecies in a scroll is no doubt intended "to preserve them for a long time" (32:14), and ultimately to demonstrate their authenticity to the faithless of a later era. This may have been the first of the scrolls that Jeremiah inscribed, and its main message is one of great consolation. In the days of Jehoiakim (ch. 36), Jeremiah will write a second scroll, filled with lamentations. But for now, he wishes to inform Israel and Judah of God's promise:

And these are the words that the Lord spoke to Israel and Judah: For thus says the Lord: We have heard a voice of trembling, of fear and no peace. Ask now, and see: Does a male bear children? Then why do I see every man with his hands on his loins like a woman in labor, every face turned pale? O how great that day will be, like no other; and it will be a time of strife for Jacob, but he will be saved from it. On that day – declares the Lord of Hosts – I will break his yoke off your neck and rip off your bonds; no more will strangers enslave him. Instead, they will serve the Lord, their God, and David their king, whom I will raise up for them. So fear not, My servant Jacob – declares the Lord – and do not be dismayed, O Israel, for I will rescue you from afar and your descendants from the land of their captivity, and Jacob will again have peace and tranquility, with none to strike fear in him. For I am with you – declares the Lord – to rescue you; for I will put an end to all the nations among which I have scattered you, but I will not put an end to you; I will chastise you in due measure; I will not let you go entirely unpunished. (30:4–11)

Jeremiah is describing society in Judah and Israel at a time of great unrest in the northern empires. For him, a young prophet in Anathoth, the impending tremors that will announce the collapse of Assyria signify the "day of the Lord." He playfully mocks the men cowering in the face of world events, their faces pale. The image of a man grabbing his loins like a woman in labor is borrowed from Isaiah, who compares the future redemption to birth pangs: "Like a pregnant woman nearing delivery, trembling and screaming in her pangs, so are we before You, O Lord" (Is. 26:17).[10]

Jeremiah is bursting with joy and yearning when he declares: "O how great that day will be, like no other!" His predecessors also foresaw the turbulence that would precede redemption: Amos (ch. 5) and Isaiah (ch. 2) described the "day of the Lord," as did others.[11] "It will be a time of strife for Jacob, but he will be saved from it," has become the motto of the Jews during times of national crisis, as it promises that redemption will follow the bleak periods. Jeremiah continues to soothe the people's defeated spirits, promising that the heavy yoke imposed by oppressive nations will soon be broken. In his mind's eye, he again sees the House of David rising up:

> Instead, they will serve the Lord, their God, and David their king, whom I will raise up for them. So fear not, My servant Jacob – declares the Lord – and do not be dismayed, O Israel, for I will rescue you from afar and your descendants from the land of their captivity, and Jacob will again have peace and tranquility, with none to strike fear in him. (Jer. 30:9–10)

Once again, Jeremiah addresses not Judah, but the united "sons of Jacob," the unified Kingdom of Ephraim and Judah. He promises the destruction of Assyria – "I will put an end to all the nations among which I have scattered you" – but foretells that Israel will endure forever. The prophet continues to meditate on this vision of redemption, culminating with a coda that relates to the end of days:

> At that time – declares the Lord – I will be a God for all the families of Israel, and they will be My people. (30:25)

---

10. This verse is the source of the literary tradition of the "birth pangs of the Messiah," referring to the calamities preceding the redemption. See Sanhedrin 98b.
11. See Hoffman, *Jeremiah*, 147–48.

Judah's Decay

J eremiah's prophetic outburst of optimism is directed at the cities of Ephraim in Samaria. Perhaps because they have been scarred by exile and lacked independent leadership he deems it important to console them and urge them to reunite with the tribes of Judah. No trace of such optimism is found in his words to Benjamin and Judah. There, the prophet focuses on the powerful pagan culture introduced by King Manasseh and watches bleakly as the eager new king tries to reconnect God and His people. Jeremiah has already borne his prophetic consciousness, which gives him no rest, for several years. He witnesses the people of Benjamin, engrossed in their land and wealth, wrapped up in everyday life, and awash in paganism. His prophecies warn of a volcano about to erupt, but no one has noticed and no one is listening.

For decades, there have been no prophecies of reproach in Israel. Moreover, prophets have attempted to lull the people to sleep and approve the abuses of King Manasseh. In the words of the prophet Zephaniah: "Her prophets are arrogant men of treachery; her priests defile the holy and violate the Torah" (Zeph. 3:4). From the days of Isaiah at the end of the eighth century BCE, until the deaths of Manasseh and Amon and Josiah's ascent in the last quarter of the seventh century BCE, no prophetic voice has been heard. With the demise of Manasseh and his son, prophecy reemerges: Zephaniah, the prophet of doom who envisions the day of God's wrath, and young Jeremiah, who describes Israel's lechery, inspire Israel's religious renewal. At precisely the same time, Josiah awakens and seeks to restore the glory of the Davidic crown.[1] It is unnecessary to ask what comes first, who influences whom – for it is the zeitgeist that inspires all.

CHAPTER 2: JUDAH HAS ABANDONED GOD

Jeremiah's prophecy describes a society that, even if it has begun to exhibit the effects of Josiah's religious reformation, is still up to its ears in Assyrian idolatry. This prophecy hardly differs from others depicting a society that has forgotten God, worships foreign deities, and loses its autonomy.

By following young Jeremiah's words in this chapter, we get a sense of the social and spiritual state of Judean society at the end of Manasseh's reign and the beginning of Josiah's. This portrait is unique in the Book of Jeremiah, as it describes a pagan society whose chain of command has completely lost its way:

> The priests have not asked, "Where is the Lord?" The handlers of the Torah know Me not, the shepherds have sinned against Me, and the prophets prophesy by Baal and follow what is worthless. (2:8)

This verse explains the division of responsibility at the beginning of Josiah's reign, explaining why each group of potential leaders deserves Jeremiah's criticism. First, we should note that the king is not explicitly mentioned here. The term "shepherds" signifies leadership, but not necessarily that of a monarch. On the contrary, Jeremiah greatly esteems Josiah and his efforts to cure Judean society's spiritual ills.

THE PRIESTS HAVE NOT ASKED, "WHERE IS THE LORD?"

The priests are the first in Jeremiah's line of fire. He does not address the Temple. That is not his focus. He seeks out those responsible for the spiritual deterioration of the people. He is concerned with the question of education in Israel, which is first and foremost a priestly duty.

---

1. For a similar description, see Kaufmann, *Religion of Israel* III, 451.

According to Jewish tradition, the role of the priests is not limited to service in the Temple, but extends out to the streets of Judah and Israel:

> They shall teach Your laws to Jacob and Your doctrines to Israel; they shall offer incense in Your nostrils and whole offerings on Your altar. (Deut. 33:10)

Teaching the people Torah requires the priests to wander among the cities of Israel. Yet it emerges that Jeremiah's priestly contemporaries have been cloistered in the Temple and singularly focused on its service, living off public funds and neglecting their primary role – teaching Torah.[2] Jeremiah, a priest himself, can rebuke the priests of the Temple without hypocrisy, because his family has long been banned from the Temple services and forced to earn an honest living as farmers in Anathoth. This is just the beginning of the prophet's settling of accounts with the Temple priests; his criticism of them will increase with time.

THE HANDLERS OF THE TORAH KNOW ME NOT

Next, Jeremiah attacks the "handlers of the Torah," who "know Me not." Rashi explains that this censure is aimed at the judges. They are the Torah's handlers, running the Torah-based judicial system, but without really knowing God. What does this mean? How can one run a system of Torah law without knowing God?

In several places, Jeremiah elucidates what it means to "know God." Referring to Josiah, the prophet states that "he upheld justice for the poor and destitute – all was well; this is what it means to know Me – declares the Lord" (Jer. 22:16). Knowing God does not mean simply grasping the Torah intellectually. Knowledge of God emerges through action. As God says of Abraham: "For I know him, that he will instruct his children and household after him to keep the way of the Lord, to do

---

2. At the beginning of the Second Temple period, the prophet Malachi says so explicitly: "You have strayed from the path, you have led many away from the Torah" (Malachi 2:8). The priests' rejection of this role and its transfer to the sages is discussed in my book *The Sages I: The Second Temple Period*, trans. Michael Prawer (Jerusalem: Maggid Books, 2010), 8–9.

what is right and just" (Gen. 18:19). Here too, it appears that the "way of the Lord" is doing what is right and just. This radical idea removes the religious act from the realms of meditation and seclusion and places it squarely within the sphere of social action and concern for others. A person's religiosity is measured by his attention to those around him. Jeremiah stresses this again in chapter 9, when he confronts people who take pride in their abilities rather than their actions:

> A wise person should not revel in his wisdom, nor the strong in his strength, nor the wealthy in his riches. For only in this should the reveler revel: understand and know Me, that I am the Lord, who exercises kindness, justice, and righteousness on earth, for in these I delight – declares the Lord. (9:22–23)

THE SHEPHERDS HAVE SINNED AGAINST ME

By "shepherds," Jeremiah generally means the leaders who direct the people and their behavior. Relating to such leaders as shepherds is a favorite metaphor of his; after all, he grew up on the edge of the desert. Throughout his childhood, he watched the shepherds and determined that the behavior of the flock depends on the shepherd. More than thirty images in the Book of Jeremiah are drawn from the realm of raising livestock, in all its variations.[3]

THE PROPHETS PROPHESY BY BAAL AND
FOLLOW WHAT IS WORTHLESS

In the eighty years since the death of Isaiah, there has been no prophecy in Israel. But there can be no monarchy without institutional prophecy serving as the nation's moral compass. As noted, the prophets of Manasseh's era served the king instead, endorsing his cultural and religious projects, reinforcing paganism, and lulling the people into a contented stupor.

Young Jeremiah's prophecy deals with the spiritual state of Judah. At this point, he still has no interest in politics. Even as Assyria struggles for survival against the rising Babylonian Empire, he speaks of the coun-

---

3. N. Hareuveni, "Shepherds and Their Flocks," in Hareuveni, *New Light*, 66–88.

try as the only northern superpower, whose only rival is the southern superpower of Egypt. From Jeremiah's point of view, it makes no difference whether Judah is entrenched in the culture of Egypt or Assyria – north and south are both sources of evil: "Why do you go to Egypt to drink the water of the Nile, and why do you go to Assyria to drink the water of the Euphrates?" (2:18). This chapter reinforces the impression that the young prophet has not yet been impacted by Josiah's revolution.

The second half of chapter 2 likens Israel's abandonment of God to a wife's infidelity:

> How can you say, "I am not defiled, I have not run after Baal"? See how you behaved in the valley! Consider what you have done! You are a restive she-camel running about. A wild donkey accustomed to the desert, sniffing the wind in her desire – in her heat, who can turn her away? All who seek her need not weary themselves; at mating time they will find her. (2:23–24)

The prophet wanders among his people, shouting at all sectors of society about their rejection of God. He is met with total indifference: "I am not defiled." His reaction is indignant – "How can you say, 'I am not defiled, I have not run after the Baal'?" Your whoring is blatant, obvious to all! As a native of Anathoth, used to seeing desert animals, Jeremiah recalls she-camels and she-donkeys in heat, feverishly seeking a mate. The males need make no effort, for the females are all too ready and willing.

This graphic depiction of Israel's lust for idol worship concludes with a despondent description of the people's behavior:

> In addition, your garments are stained with the lifeblood of the innocent destitute – you did not catch them breaking in. (2:34)

For the first time, the young prophet adds social criticism to his religious reproach. (This criticism will be reinforced after Josiah's attempted reformation.) "In addition, your garments are stained with the lifeblood of the innocent destitute" – this refers to overt, shameless social violence. After this great prophetic reprimand regarding the spiritual prostitution spreading across Israel, its painful conclusion is presented at the opening of chapter 3. Jeremiah describes the exile of Samaria as "a bill of divorce" that God has given the ten northern tribes as a result of their betrayal. The prophet is amazed that Judah could witness the messy divorce of its neighbor yet "not be afraid; she too has gone and played the harlot" (3:8). This section concludes by condemning the entire Kingdom of Judah: "And despite all this, her faithless sister Judah has not returned to Me wholeheartedly, only pretentiously – declares the Lord" (3:10).

CHAPTER 10: A CONFRONTATION WITH IDOLATORS AND A PRAYER

Jeremiah's descriptions of idol worship in the streets of Jerusalem leave no room for doubt regarding its ubiquity within the city. Josiah's reformation is still in its infancy, and great efforts must be made to convince people to cast away the idols of their fathers. In chapter 10, Jeremiah uses three rhetorical strategies to help purge the land of idolatry: public relations, parody, and prayer:[4]

> Hear the word that the Lord has spoken to you, O House of Israel. Thus said the Lord: Learn not the way of the nations, and fear not signs in the heavens, though the nations fear them. For the laws of the peoples are empty: a tree from the forest is cut down, the work of a craftsman's hands, with his chisel. They adorn it with silver and gold; with nails and hammers they reinforce it, that it not teeter. They are like a rigid post and cannot speak; they must be carried, for they cannot walk. Do not fear them, for they can do no evil, nor can they do good. (10:1–5)

Jeremiah turns to the "House of Israel," a collective name for the kingdoms of Judah and Ephraim, and appeals to them to abandon the ways of foreign nations. He contends with those who plan their every move based on the constellations. Astrology was well-developed in Babylo-

---

4. This topic is covered in depth in M. Margaliyot, "Jeremiah's Diatribe Against Idolatry," in Luria, *Studies in Jeremiah* III, 73–89 [Hebrew].

nian religion, and his plea not to fear the heavens may be the first indication that the people are beginning to absorb a new and increasingly prevalent pagan culture. Jeremiah's call to Israel not to fear heavenly signs is echoed in a later, well-known rabbinic saying: "Israel is not subject to constellations."[5] A midrash based on our chapter depicts the human experience of divination based on the stars:

> R. Eliezer says: A solar eclipse is an ominous sign for the nations of the world, and a lunar eclipse is an ominous sign for the enemies of Israel [a euphemism for Israel itself], for Israel is likened to the moon, and the nations of the world to the sun.... If [the eclipse] is in the west, it bodes ill for those in the west; if it occurs at the zenith, it bodes ill for the whole world. If its face looks like blood, the sword is coming to the world; if it looks like sackcloth, famine is coming to the world.... When Israel carries out the will of God, [it] shall not fear, as it says, "Thus said the Lord: Learn not the way of the nations, and fear not signs in the heavens, though the nations fear them" – the nations will fear, but [Israel] will not. (*Tanna DeVei Eliyahu Zuta* 16)

After addressing those who place their faith in horoscopes, Jeremiah turns to those who worship idols of wood and stone. A similar style of mockery can be found in Isaiah 44 as well as other prophetic works. Jeremiah describes the absurdity of idol worship: The worshippers themselves cut down trees, carve statues out of the wood, decorate them with gold and silver, hammer them full of nails, and finally, worship their own creations. Israel's faith in the God of heaven and earth contrasts with prostration before replaceable, man-made statues:

> But the Lord, God, is true, the living God and King of the world; at His wrath the earth shakes, and the nations cannot withstand His fury. (Jer. 10:10)

---

5. B. Benedict, "Sustenance Depends on the Stars," in Benedict, *The Torah Center in Provence* (Jerusalem, 1985), 243–67 [Hebrew].

At this point in the chapter, a verse appears in Aramaic, beckoning to the idolaters in the *lingua franca* of the era, confronting them with the futility of their service:

> Tell them this: these gods, which did not create the heavens or the earth, will perish from the earth and from under the heavens. (10:11)

Later, Jeremiah prays for Israel to be released from the all-absorbing grip of pagan ritual:

> The portion of Jacob is not like these, for He is the Maker of all, and Israel is the tribe of His inheritance – the Lord of Hosts is His name. (10:16)

Jeremiah concludes his prayer with the famous words that made their way into the Haggada:

> Pour out Your wrath upon the nations that do not know You, and upon the families who do not call Your name. For they have devoured Jacob, devoured him and consumed him, and have made his homeland desolate. (10:25)

This verse calls on God to avenge the tribes of Jacob, who were devoured by the nations. With this call for revenge, Jeremiah concludes his prophecy against idol worship.

CHAPTER 17: A CALL TO OBSERVE THE SABBATH

In the early days of Josiah's reform, the culture promoted by his grandfather Manasseh is still palpable within Jerusalem. Ignorance and abandonment of the Torah are rampant. One of the most prominent signs of this neglect is the desecration of the Sabbath. The commercial culture of that era utilizes all seven days of the week for the rat race, regarding Sabbath observance as a symptom of laziness. When prophets and leaders draw attention to the Sabbath – particularly in the public sphere – their words express the very real crisis underlying the state of affairs in

Israel. The chapter in Jeremiah imploring the people to resume their observance of the Sabbath is one such example:[6]

> Hear the word of the Lord, kings of Judah, and all people of Judah, and everyone living in Jerusalem, who come through these gates. Thus says the Lord: Heed yourselves, and do not carry a burden on the Sabbath day or bring it through the gates of Jerusalem. Do not carry a burden out of your houses on the Sabbath, or do any work – rather, sanctify the Sabbath day, as I commanded your forefathers. (17:20–22)

It seems that the residents of Jerusalem are not yet meticulous about the prohibition of commercial dealings on the Sabbath, despite Josiah's initial religious enactments. The revolution is still in its early stages. In his early prophecies, Jeremiah still believes he has a receptive audience. His prophecy is not yet pessimistic, and he contrasts the blessings inherent in Sabbath observance with the curses stemming from its desecration:

> And it shall come to pass if you diligently hearken to me – declares the Lord – and bring no burden through the gates of this city on the Sabbath day, but sanctify the Sabbath day by not doing any work on it, then kings and princes who sit on David's throne will come through the gates of this city, riding on chariots and horses,

---

6. Gordon's "Zedekiah in the Prison House," cited earlier in the text, describes Jeremiah as a preacher detached from the existential political concerns of the king:

   And what is this priest of Anathoth's petition?
   Not to carry burdens on the Sabbath day?
   Was then a time for Sabbatical celebration?
   The enemy had besieged the land; the cities had gone to fray
   The battering rams had reached the castle gates

   [...]

   And he stands among the people, day after day
   Calling out in the ear of all comers
   Not to carry burdens on the Sabbath day

   This poem is but one example of the stereotype that Israel's prophets were out of touch with reality and fixated on archaic rituals.

accompanied by the men of Judah and those living in Jerusalem, and this city will be inhabited forever. People will come from the towns of Judah and the vicinity of Jerusalem, from the land of Benjamin and the Shephelah, from the hill country and the Negev, bringing burnt offerings and sacrifices, grain offerings and frankincense, and bringing thanksgiving offerings to the House of the Lord. But if you do not listen to me to sanctify the Sabbath day by not carrying any burden as you come through the gates of Jerusalem on the Sabbath day, then I will kindle a fire in her gates, and it will consume the fortresses of Jerusalem and not be extinguished. (17:24–27)

Here Jeremiah clearly invokes the language of Deuteronomy (*vehaya im shamoa tishme'u* – "and it shall come to pass if you diligently hearken").[7] He makes the novel claim that the consecration or desecration of the Sabbath is the key to the peace and glory of Jerusalem, or, God forbid, to its destruction. This insight is derived from the extent of Jerusalem's syncretism prior to Josiah's reformation, as described by the prophet Zephaniah in the first chapter of his book. Among other things, Zephaniah emphasizes the bustling trade that filled the streets of Jerusalem on the Sabbath day, in which all the neighboring peoples participated. Sabbath observance will reunite Judah and Israel against the surrounding nations and symbolize a renewal of the covenant between God and His people.[8]

---

7. Based on this language, many scholars have declared the prophecy a later addition, probably from the era of Nehemiah. Y. Kaufmann counters that their position stems from a blatantly Christian outlook. See Kaufmann, *Religion of Israel* VII, 436.
8. Based on a lecture by Moshe Greenberg, "The Passage Regarding the Sabbath in Jeremiah," in Luria, *Studies in Jeremiah* II, 23–37 [Hebrew].

622 BCE

Renewing the Covenant

While chapter 2 is orated prior to the religious reawakening inspired by Josiah, Jeremiah utters his next prophecies to reinforce the people's gradual return. The people, so steeped in their betrayal of God, so immersed in their forgetting of Him, so utterly estranged from their roots, begin to repent. This process comes in the wake of King Josiah's reforms, which commenced in the eighteenth year of his reign (five years after Jeremiah's prophetic initiation). Josiah orders a complete renovation of the Temple and, to his amazement, discovers the Book of God's Covenant there. The discovery is described at length in II Kings 22–23 as well as in II Chronicles 34–35:[1]

> Then Shaphan the scribe told the king, "Hilkiah the priest has given me a book," and Shaphan read it before the king. When the king heard the words of the book of the Torah, he tore his clothes. The king ordered Hilkiah the priest, Ahikam son of

---

1. Traditional exegetes and modern Bible critics debate the nature of the book found in the Temple. The former maintain that the book was the actual Torah written by Moses himself, which had been preserved in the Temple and hidden by the priests in the days of Ahaz or Manasseh. Others believe it was the Book of Deuteronomy alone (see Seforno on Deut. 31:26). The critics deal extensively with the book's identity vis-à-vis the authorship of Deuteronomy. See Y.M. Grintz's summary in B. Luria, ed., *Studies in the Book of Kings* (Jerusalem: Kiryat Sefer Publishing, 1985) [Hebrew].

Shaphan, Akhbor son of Mikhaya, Shaphan the scribe, and Asa-
iah the king's attendant, saying: "Go and inquire of the Lord on
my behalf and on behalf of the people and on behalf of all Judah
concerning the words of this book that has been found, for great
is the Lord's anger that burns against us, because our fathers have
not listened to the words of this book to act in accordance with
all that is written concerning us." (11 Kings 22:10–13)

The discovery of this book triggers a spiritual crisis for the king and
his entourage. A midrash describes the moment the book was read to
Josiah:

When Hilkiah the priest found the book in the Temple courtyard, it was scrolled to this verse: "Cursed is he who does not
uphold the words of this Torah." At these words, Josiah tore his
garments and said, "We must uphold them!" (*Midrash HaGadol*,
Deut. 27:26)

The last verse of the scroll levels a curse at one who does not uphold
the Torah. According to the midrash, Josiah reacts instinctively, declaring, "We must uphold them!" At this moment, he launches a vigorous
campaign of repentance. He immediately sends a delegation to the most
veteran prophetess in Jerusalem – Huldah, unmentioned until now – in
order to hear God's words through her. Although it may seem obvious
to us that young, inexperienced Jeremiah does not yet serve as a prophetic address for Josiah, the rabbis of the Talmud overlook his age (only
eighteen) and discuss why he is not consulted:

The students of R. Shilo's academy said: It is because women are
compassionate. R. Yoḥanan said: Jeremiah was not there, for he
had gone to return the ten tribes. (Megilla 14b)

The first answer is that the king decided to turn to a prophetess because
of the greater potential for compassion on her part. The second, more
technical answer is that Jeremiah was simply not available. He was in the
middle of his campaign to return the lost tribes. R. Yoḥanan's explana-

tion fits what we have seen regarding Jeremiah's prophecies about the return of the northern tribes.

Huldah's answer is short and sharp:

> Thus said the Lord: Behold, I am bringing evil upon this place and its inhabitants – all the words of the book that the King of Judah read. Because they have forsaken Me, and burned incense to other gods in order to anger Me with all their handiwork, My wrath has been ignited against this place and will not be extinguished. (II Kings 22:16–17)

Like Jeremiah in chapter 2, Huldah despairs at the extent to which idolatry has contaminated Israel, and she confirms that the fire that will one day consume Jerusalem has been ignited and will not be extinguished.

Now Josiah is trapped. The prophetess has condemned Jerusalem to destruction, leaving no possibility for the repairs and reforms he advocates. Yet Josiah "rebels" against Huldah's prophecy, resuming his plan with renewed vigor. He understands that decades of spiritual disconnection cannot be overcome with a single ceremony. He therefore plans an assembly to renew the covenant with God in the presence of the entire nation, thereby declaring to all of Judah the magnitude of the process he has undertaken. The king is about to shatter and purge every last trace of idolatry from the kingdom, summoning the full power of his throne in order to do so. Josiah razes the centers of idol worship across the land, annihilates the priests of the pagan high places, and concentrates the entire spiritual workforce of Judah in Jerusalem. This is the first and fullest implementation of the vision of Deuteronomy, which repeatedly emphasizes the importance of centralized worship.

Obviously, such a course of action generates formidable opposition: All the pagan priests are liable to lose their positions and status and to become enemies of the state. Jeremiah undertakes to help Josiah accomplish this mission impossible, but unlike the king, who has chosen to ignore Huldah's prophecy and attempt to repeal her terrible decree, Jeremiah is torn.

CHAPTER 11: THE PROPHET'S PERCEPTION
OF JOSIAH'S COVENANT

Josiah's public assembly to renew the covenant stirs up great excitement. By virtue of his faith and leadership, the king instigates a movement to purge Israel of idolatry. The beginning of this process awakens much hope in the hearts of the people, but Jeremiah's own heart is troubled. He hears the words of the covenant and cannot help but recall his own prophetic initiation. He knows deep down that destruction is inevitable. Nevertheless, the renewal of the covenant between God and His people must offer an opening, a final opportunity. He resolves to encourage the people to repent even as he secretly weeps over the irreparable depth of their corruption. Elsewhere in the Book of Jeremiah, the prophet explicitly describes Josiah's covenantal assembly, as heard by his prophetic ears:

> The word that came to Jeremiah from the Lord: Hear the words of this covenant, and tell them to the people of Judah and the inhabitants of Jerusalem. Tell them: Thus says the Lord, God of Israel: Cursed is the one who does not obey the terms of this covenant, which I commanded your forefathers when I brought them out of the land of Egypt, the iron furnace, saying: "Obey Me and do everything I command you, and you will be My people, and I will be your God," in order to fulfill the oath I swore to your forefathers, to give them a land flowing with milk and honey – as you possess today. And I responded: Amen, O Lord. The Lord said to me: Call out all these words in the towns of Judah and in the streets of Jerusalem, saying: Listen to the terms of this covenant, and follow them. For I have repeatedly warned your forefathers, from the day I brought them out of the land of Egypt until today, saying: "Listen to Me." But they did not listen or pay attention; instead, they followed the stubbornness of their evil heart; so I brought upon them all the curses of this covenant, for they did not do what I commanded them to do. (11:1–8)

Jeremiah's description echoes the assembly on Mount Gerizim and Mount Ebal soon after entering the Promised Land, during which the tribes of Israel entered into a covenant with God (Deut. 27:11–28:69). The final curse on the list is "'Cursed is he who does not uphold the words of this Torah, and do them,' and all the people shall say: Amen." During Josiah's covenantal assembly, Jeremiah returns to that primal and festive ceremony of centuries before, but instead of hearing the priests administering the oaths of "cursed is he," he hears God Himself doing so. The oath-taking that Jeremiah prophetically hears is a clear expansion of the passages in Deuteronomy. He even responds, "Amen, O Lord" at the conclusion. The word of God beats within him, calling him to embark on a journey to awaken the people in the cities of Judah and the courtyards of Jerusalem. There is a spark of hope.

CHAPTER 18: GOD ANSWERS JEREMIAH – THE DESTRUCTION MAY YET BE AVERTED

Jeremiah is vacillating between the king's message of hope and his own knowledge that even reform will not save Jerusalem. He waits for God to guide him through this maze of uncertainty, and ultimately he receives a prophetic vision. Chapter 18 describes Jeremiah's visit to a potter's workshop. The opening verses of the chapter suggest that God has bidden him to go to the workshop after his pleas to hear the word of the Lord:

> The word that came to Jeremiah from the Lord: Arise and go down to the potter's workshop, and there I will make My words heard to you. (18:1–2)

The prophet has been seeking God's word in an effort to resolve the conflict burning within him. How can he live with the knowledge that God will uproot and tear down, obliterate and destroy, alongside the hope of spiritual renewal, the ingathering of exiles, and the promise of security in the land? In the workshop, Jeremiah meets the potter sitting at his wheel and creating vessels, constantly destroying his handiwork in order to form a vessel he considers superior. As Jeremiah watches the potter at work, a prophecy bursts forth from within him:

> Then the word of the Lord came to me, saying: Can I not do with you, O House of Israel, as this potter does? – declares the Lord –

like clay in the hand of the potter, so are you in My hand, O House of Israel. At any moment I may speak of a nation or kingdom to be uprooted, torn down, and destroyed. But if that nation, against which I have pronounced, turns from its evil, then I will change My mind about the evil I have planned for it. And at any moment I may announce that a nation or kingdom is to be built up and planted. But if it does evil in My sight and does not obey Me, then I will reconsider the good I had intended to do for it. (18:5–10)

God guides Jeremiah through an understanding of his first vision, which indeed foretold destruction and eventual flourishing. However, despite Huldah's fatalistic diagnosis, in Jeremiah's world there is room for correction and healing.

Hopelessness and despair have seized the people in view of the enormity of their sin. Even those who hear the king reading from the newly discovered Torah scroll do not believe in the power of repentance:

Now, say to the people of Judah and the inhabitants of Jerusalem: Thus said the Lord: I am preparing a disaster for you and devising a plan against you, so let each man turn from his evil way, and reform your ways and actions. But they will say: "It is hopeless; we will follow our own notions," and each man will act on the wickedness of his stubborn heart. (18:11–12)

The people are convinced that the king's campaign will not alter the harsh decrees, and that there is no way to survive the wrath of God. As a result, a familiar attitude coalesces: "Eat and drink, for tomorrow we die." Let us at least enjoy life while it lasts.

Jeremiah's prophetic encounter at the pottery workshop inspires him to support the king's program.

CHAPTER 5: THE PROPHET'S FRUSTRATIONS – SUPERFICIALLY PENITENT BUT CORRUPT TO THE CORE

The next period of Jeremiah's life brings him from the heights of hope to the depths of despair. After experiencing the renewal of the covenant and receiving a prophetic promise at the potter's workshop, he returns to wandering the streets of Benjamin and Judah. These thoroughfares are filled with spiritual and cultural revolution. The king's emissaries patrol every corner, stamping out any traces of idol worship still to be found. Pagan priests are arrested, and inspectors go from house to house enforcing the king's orders. Jerusalem no longer tolerates idolatry, for it has returned to its religious roots – the Lord is God of the land, and He alone shall be worshipped by all.

But Jeremiah views the scene differently. He immediately recognizes this great Jewish awakening as superficial. Nothing has stirred inside the people's hearts. Over the course of several chapters, the prophet expresses his disappointment and frustration at the great national deception. He is torn between embracing the king's optimism – delighting in the vision of the ingathering of the exiles, the reunification of Judah and Israel, and the renewal of the covenant – and despairing over the people's religious ambivalence.

At first glance, Josiah's reform has achieved the impossible. The idols have been smashed, the Temple purified, and worship centralized. Topheth, the site of child sacrifice, has been declared impure and condemned, and Torah study has expanded. People are proudly declaring, "We are wise, and we have the Lord's Torah!" The sounds of redemption seem to echo in the distance – but all this is only an illusion. Jeremiah sees behind this façade and recognizes the falsity and hypocrisy, the thin veneer of piety serving as a fig leaf for corruption and warped social values. He enters Jerusalem to examine the process of alleged repentance:

> Wander the streets of Jerusalem, look around and inquire, and seek in her squares, whether there is but one man who does justice, who seeks truthfulness, and I will forgive her. Though they say, "As surely as the Lord lives," they are surely swearing falsely. O Lord, do Your eyes not look for truthfulness? You struck them, but they felt no pain; You crushed them, but they refused correction; they set their faces harder than stone and refused to repent. I thought: these are only the poor; they are foolish, for they do not know the way of the Lord, the law of their God. I will make my way to the great men and speak to them; surely they know

the way of the Lord, the law of their God; but all of them as one had broken the yoke and burst the bonds. (5:1–5)

In these verses, Jeremiah describes how he hopes to find the key to true repentance. As in several of his other prophecies, he asserts that executing justice is constitutive of reform and of the "way of the Lord." Though there is much talk about faith, it is no indication of who truly serves God. If there is but one man who executes justice, on his account alone God will forgive the entire city. In this verse, Jeremiah is ready to fight for Jerusalem more fiercely than Abraham argued for Sodom to be spared. In Abraham's famous haggling with God, he contended: "Perhaps there are fifty righteous people in the city; will You still destroy and not spare the place for those fifty righteous people within it?" (Gen. 18:24). Abraham eventually bargained God down to ten righteous people in whose merit the city would be saved. Jeremiah goes further: "Whether there is but *one* man … and I will forgive her!" This wording alludes to a chilling realization on Jeremiah's part: that Jerusalem is like Sodom.

Jeremiah hears many oaths "as surely as the Lord lives," but he knows that "they are surely swearing falsely." He tries to give these oath-takers the benefit of the doubt, explaining that they "are only the poor; they are foolish, for they do not know the way of the Lord." The educational system is malfunctioning; the spiritually weak people do not know any better and cannot by themselves break out of the vicious cycle of ignorance. Until now, there has been no systematic teaching of the ways of God. So Jeremiah redirects his appeal to the leaders of the people, for "surely they know the way of the Lord, the law of their God." However, there too, Jeremiah meets with great disappointment: "But all of them as one had broken the yoke and burst the bonds." Sadly, they are no better than their students.

THE SECOND HALF OF CHAPTER 7: THE PROPHET'S TURBULENT SOUL – BETWEEN LOVE AND ACCUSATION

Just as Jeremiah's first prophecy heralded the coming of both destruction and rebuilding, just as his first visions were of a flowering almond branch as well as a wind-blown tumbleweed, the prophet constantly oscillates between hope and despair. There are many indications that these chapters relate his early forays into prophecy, while he is yet discovering the nation's impatience and the Godless leadership that is lulling the people to sleep. Jeremiah perceives Josiah as a genuinely righteous leader, but he alone is not strong enough to extricate the people from the mire of idolatry. On the one hand, Jeremiah wishes to emulate Moses, who implored God even after the sin of the Golden Calf, begging Him to rescind His anger. On the other hand, he feels that Israel's fate has been sealed and that the gates of prayer have been locked before him. Despite the constant updates on the purging of all idolatry from the land, Jeremiah portrays Jerusalem's backyards, where almost every family still participates in the worship of heavenly bodies:

> As for you, do not pray for this people; do not utter a cry or prayer for them, and do not beg Me, for I will not listen to you. Do you not see what they are doing throughout the towns of Judah and in the streets of Jerusalem? The children gather wood, and the fathers build fires, and the women knead dough in order to make cakes to offer to the queen of heaven, and they pour libations to foreign gods in order to provoke Me.... Tell them: This is the nation that has not obeyed the Lord, their God, and has not accepted correction; truthfulness has perished, cut from their mouths. (7:16–18, 28)

CHAPTER 8: "NO ONE REGRETS HIS WRONGDOING"

The flimsiness of the people's repentance shatters Jeremiah's hope. It dawns on him that nothing will change. The reformation is not being accompanied by an inner process. The king, absorbed in his efforts, does not yet see what Jeremiah sees.

> And you shall say to them: Thus said the Lord: When they fall, shall they not rise again? If they turn away, shall they not turn back? Why then have these people of Jerusalem strayed perpetually, clinging to deceit and refusing to return? I have listened and heard; they do not speak truthfully; no one regrets his wrongdoing, saying: "What have I done?" Each pursues his course like a horse charging into battle. Even the stork in the sky knows her

> seasons, and the dove, the swift, and the thrush observe the time
> of their migration, yet My people do not know the Lord's law.
> How can you say, "We are wise, and we have the Lord's Torah,"
> when in fact the pen has wrought in vain, in vain the scribes?
> The wise have been shamed, they are dismayed and trapped, for
> they have rejected the word of the Lord; what wisdom do they
> have? Therefore I will give their wives to others and their fields
> to dispossessors, for from the least to the greatest, all are greedy
> for gain; from prophet to priest, all practice deceit. (8:4–10)

The prophet articulates a question that echoes ceaselessly in his heart
throughout the great reformation: "If they fall, shall they not rise again?
If they turn away, shall they not turn back?" Is there no rehabilitation
after punishment? If they repent of their evil ways, will God not retract
His anger and have mercy on His people? If, in the potter's workshop,
Jeremiah found cause for hope, now he is given to understand that all
is lost. He wanders the streets of Jerusalem and Anathoth, listening to
people's conversation and knowing that in truth "no one regrets his
wrongdoing." People live their lives like "horses charging into battle," a
simile explained beautifully by Rabbi Moses Ḥayyim Luzzatto:

> Jeremiah laments the evil of his contemporaries, for whom
> this defect is like a plague. They turn a blind eye to their own
> actions, without taking heed to determine whether they should
> be engaged in or abandoned. He says about these men (8:6),
> "No one regrets his wrongdoing…. Each pursues his course
> like a horse charging into battle." He means that they act out of
> impulse and habit, without leaving themselves time to evalu-
> ate their actions and ways, and, as a result, fall into evil without
> noticing. (*Path of the Just* 2)

Jeremiah draws upon both human and natural phenomena to express
his feelings. He lifts his eyes toward the birds soaring above and notes
that every migration follows a specific direction and pattern. In contrast
to nature's robust health, Israel follows a sick and tortuous path. Again
Jeremiah finds himself bearing a prophecy of hopeless destruction: "from

the least to the greatest, all are greedy for gain; from prophet to priest, all practice deceit."

Despair floods Jeremiah, and he is overcome with a prophecy that in time will become a hymn of destruction, read on the most tragic day of the Jewish calendar, Tisha B'Av: "I will surely consume them – declares the Lord" (8:13). This vision spills out of him with terrible pain. He begs to escape the role that has been forced upon him, that of the prophet of doom. In his mind's eye, he sees the fruit trees of the Land of Israel – the emblematic grapevine and the fig tree – fruitless. There is nothing to hope for; the enemy will arrive and devour all who inhabit this land.

This chapter expresses the anguish of complete failure. Despite his great love for his people, Jeremiah is powerless to prevent the impending evil: "If only my head were water and my eyes wells of tears, that I could weep day and night for the slain of the daughter of my people" (8:23). This wounded love song bursts forth from his throat, painfully entwined with a prophecy of reproach: "If only I had a place of lodging in the desert, that I could leave my people and abandon them, for they are all lecherous, a treacherous band" (9:1). These two tormented wishes express the paradox of Jeremiah's feelings for his people – he is torn between wounded love and rising anger.

CHAPTER 11: THE CONFLICT WITH
THE PEOPLE OF ANATHOTH

Jeremiah roams the streets of Jerusalem, inundated by frustrating prophecies. In his early days as a prophet, as a young man in his twenties, he would accost people on the street and curse them and the end they would come to, and they would perhaps write him off and go on their way. As the years pass, however, and Josiah's national project of repentance takes hold, Jeremiah's audience comes to despise him. He claims that the sages do not teach Torah, that the priests do not seek God's presence, that the prophets prophesy falsely, and that all shall perish by a vengeful sword – even as the king is purifying the land and serving the God of Israel faithfully and fearfully. Jeremiah's words are therefore most outrageous. Chapter 18 (after the vision in the potter's workshop) describes the fierce opposition forming against him:

> They said, "Let us devise a plan against Jeremiah, for there is no lack of Torah from the priest, or counsel from the wise, or word from the prophet; let us go and slander him, and we will not have to listen to his words anymore." (18:18)

Jeremiah's adversaries are not wrong. If the whole chain of leadership is filling us with optimism and confidence, why is this madman spouting poisonous prophecies? The people of Judah mock Jeremiah as Jacob's sons mocked Joseph. This is the golden age of Josiah's reign, secure and prosperous, and Jeremiah has the nerve to threaten them with ominous warnings of destruction! In their eyes, he is only stirring up trouble: "They keep saying to me, 'Where is God's word?' So let it come" (17:15).

Throughout Scripture, prophets are known as social hazards. Army officers refer to Elisha's apprentice as "that crazy person" (11 Kings 9:11); Hosea states, "fool is the prophet; mad is the man of letters" (Hos. 9:7). Yet the prophet does not usually risk his life. In the Book of Amos, we read the well-known warning of the King of Israel: "Get thee out, seer; flee to the land of Judah … and prophesy there" (Amos 7:12). Jeremiah, though, is threatened by the residents of his hometown. The people of Anathoth dislike the commotion he is causing. They are solid, salt-of-the-earth men, far from politics and the Temple. Suddenly, they find themselves in the spotlight, for a young prophet from their village is wandering the corridors of the capital, taunting and riling up its inhabitants. The people of Anathoth conspire to put an end to Jeremiah's prophecies and, if necessary, his life: "Let us devise a plan." The deadliness of this scheme emerges explicitly from another plot against him:

> But the Lord has given me knowledge of it, so I knew it; You showed me their scheme. I had been like a tame lamb led to the slaughter; I did not realize they had plotted against me: "Let us destroy the tree and its fruit; let us cut him off from the land of the living, that his name be remembered no more." But You, Lord of Hosts, righteous Judge, who scrutinizes innards and heart, let me see Your vengeance on them, for to You I have committed my cause. (Jer. 11:18–20)

Listen to me, O Lord; hear what my adversaries are saying. Should good be repaid with evil? For they have dug a pit for me. Remember that I stood before You and spoke on their behalf to turn Your wrath away from them. (18:19–20)

Jeremiah's prophecies render him a loner, an outcast, hated, scorned, and scoffed at by all. He begins to curse those who mock him, assuming a posture of violent self-defense. It is painful to read these curses when recalling the great love he expressed for God's people just a few chapters earlier. The closing verses of chapter 18 describe the angry curses that Jeremiah heaps upon those who scorn him:

So give their children over to famine; hand them over to the sword; let their wives be bereft and widowed; let their men be put to death, their young men slain by the sword in battle. Let a cry be heard from their houses when You suddenly bring invaders against them, for they have dug a pit to capture me and have hidden snares for my feet. And You, Lord, know all their plots to kill me. Do not forgive their crimes or blot out their sins from Your sight; let them be overthrown before You; deal with them in the time of Your anger. (18:21–23)

Jeremiah begins to reveal himself as a prophet who explodes with rage whenever he catches sight of falsehood. He acquires a reputation as a disturber of the peace, one who threatens to dissipate the joy that envelops the king and his people as they embark upon their reformation – notorious both in the broad courtyards of Jerusalem and on the dirt roads of Anathoth.

The prophet receives word from God about the retribution awaiting his brethren and the people of Anathoth:

Therefore, thus says the Lord regarding the people of Anathoth, who threaten to kill you, saying: "Do not prophesy in the name of the Lord, or you will die by our hands." Therefore thus said the Lord of Hosts: I will punish them – their young men will die by

the sword, their sons and daughters by famine. Not even a remnant will be left to them, for I will bring disaster to the people of
Anathoth in the year of their punishment. (11:21–23)

This is Jeremiah's first mention of the grief that will wrack Judah. Blood-
shed and famine will afflict all, and "not even a remnant will be left
to them." At this stage, only the people of Anathoth who wish to kill
Jeremiah are cursed, but soon his words of doom will encompass the
entire land.

CHAPTER 16: "DO NOT TAKE A WIFE"

As a symbolic reflection of the terrible prophecies of rebuke against the
people of his hometown, Jeremiah is commanded to remain unmarried
and childless: "Do not take a wife or have sons and daughters in this
place" (16:1). The language of this opening indicates that Jeremiah shares
this particular prophecy with a small, intimate group that has gathered
around him, rather than broadcasting it in public. God then offers an
explanation for this harsh instruction:

> For thus said the Lord regarding the sons and daughters born
> in this place and regarding the women who bear them and their
> fathers who sire them in this land: They will die of deadly dis-
> eases; they will not be elegized or buried, but will be like dung
> lying on the ground; they will perish by sword and famine, and
> their dead bodies will become food for the birds of the heavens
> and the animals of the earth. (16:3–4)

Usually, a prophet's symbolic gestures are active, that is, the prophet *does*
something. In this instance as well, even though the gesture is character-
ized by Jeremiah's inaction – not marrying – when a thirty-year-old refuses
to marry, it sends a bold, shocking message.[2] This prophetic revelation
shows Jeremiah that everyone in "this place" will die in an act of God.

---

2. Z. Falk, "Jeremiah and Marriage," in Luria, *Studies in Jeremiah* 1, 129–51 [Hebrew].
Falk comments that "thus emerges the importance of marriage in building and
planting. The absence of marriage in Jeremiah's life imparts a stronger message

In a few years, in the time of Jeconiah, a letter from Jeremiah will accompany the first group of exiles from Jerusalem to Babylon, commanding them to "marry women and sire sons and daughters" (29:6). Later still, shortly before the fall of Jerusalem and the destruction of the Temple, Jeremiah, confined to the prison courtyard, will impart a vision of consolation: This place will yet ring out with "The sound of joy and the sound of gladness, the sound of the groom and the sound of the bride" (33:11). Jeremiah perceives the act of marriage and raising a family as a worthy, blessed act, but not in "this place." In this respect, his celibacy serves as a sign and demonstration of his curse that all who bear children in "this place" will lose them, and that grief will befall the entire community:

> For thus says the Lord: Do not enter a house of mourning; do not go to lament or bemoan them, for I have withdrawn My blessing, My love, and My compassion from this people – says the Lord. Both great and small will die in this land; they will not be buried or lamented, and no one will gash or tonsure themselves for them. No one will offer food to comfort a mourner, nor will anyone pour him a cup of consolation for his father or mother. You will also not enter a house of feasting, to sit with them to eat and drink. (16:5–8)

This is not a one-time action (like the acts of Ezekiel, for example), but the establishment of a mode of existence for a young prophet condemned to barrenness and isolation. It is one of the climactic moments of Jeremiah's tragedy. From now on, rather than follow the course of life, he pursues that of death and destruction.

DIFFERENCES BETWEEN ISAIAH AND JEREMIAH IN TALMUDIC LEGEND

At this point, we must stop and consider: Do Jeremiah's acts indicate that the fate of Israel has been sealed? Until now, he has held hope in his

---

than many speeches about the importance of marriage in Judaism – this is not just a sign of the coming destruction, but a sign about building and growth in general. The moral imparts a lesson about the fable."

heart. Has all hope now been lost, leaving only the decree of destruction? Although the prophecies of doom in this chapter seem final, for more than twenty years – throughout the reigns of the kings following Josiah (Jehoiakim and Zedekiah) – it seems that Jeremiah never stops hoping to avert destruction.

Against the backdrop of this speculation about the finality of Jeremiah's grim prophecies, we can consider the talmudic narrative of the prophet Isaiah's encounter with King Hezekiah:

> In those days, Hezekiah took deathly ill, and the prophet Isaiah son of Amoz came to him, saying: Thus says the Lord: Put your affairs in order, for you will die and not live [Is. 38:1]. What is the meaning of "you will die and not live"? "You will die" in this world, and "you will not live" in the next world.
>
> [Hezekiah] said to him: "Why all of this?" [Why is my punishment so great?]
>
> [Isaiah] answered: "For you did not try to have children."
>
> Hezekiah replied: "Because I saw through the holy spirit that my offspring would be unworthy."
>
> Isaiah said to him: "Why should you be concerned about God's secrets? You must do what you are commanded, and God will do what He wants."
>
> Hezekiah: "If so, give me your daughter for a wife. Perhaps our combined merit will help, and I will have worthy children."
>
> Isaiah replied: "You cannot change the birth of a wicked son – for it has already been decreed."
>
> Hezekiah grew irritated: "Son of Amoz, finish your prophecy and get out! For I have a tradition from my grandfather: Even with a sharp sword held to his throat, a man must not desist from prayer." (Berakhot 10a)

The homilist who compiled this intriguing dialogue sought to uplift his readers' spirits, lest they despair of mercy, or stop living life. Isaiah himself failed this test and nearly sealed a sorry fate. Hezekiah, initially in despair at the prospect of evil descendants, rebelled against the prophecy and turned to the traditions of his forefathers – never to desist from prayer.

609 BCE

The Death of Josiah

THE HISTORICAL BACKGROUND OF
JOSIAH'S JOURNEY TO MEGIDDO

Josiah devotes himself to restoring the Kingdom of Israel's glory and reconnecting the people to their Father in Heaven. Never once veering from the difficult path he has charted, he constantly searches for ways to advance his vision. Such an opportunity presents itself with the fall of the great metropolis of Nineveh. Today, with access to contemporary Babylonian historical documents, we can recreate the events of that tumultuous period.[1]

In 614 BCE, the Medes conquered the city of Assur, and the Median king Cyaxares formed an alliance with the Babylonian king Nebopolassar. In 612, an earth-shattering event took place: Nineveh, the capital and largest city in the Assyrian Empire, fell to the combined Median and Babylonian forces. This was the turning point in the war between the rising Babylonian and the crumbling Assyrian empires. The entire world paid attention to this event. Henceforth, Babylonia increasingly marginalized Assyria. The Assyrian army retreated north to Harran. In 610, the Babylonian and Median forces invaded Harran, and although Assyria called to Egypt for help, the city fell and became a Babylonian garrison.

In 609 BCE, Pharaoh Necho, who had ascended the Egyptian throne the year before, attempted to defeat the Babylonians along the Euphrates. En route, he passed through the Land of Israel, and Josiah's

---

1. See C.J. Gadd, *The Fall of Nineveh* (London, 1923).

forces met him at Megiddo. The Egyptians had little choice but to pass through Megiddo, but why did Josiah leave the Jerusalem area to confront Necho at Megiddo? It seems that Josiah was making strategic calculations based on the emerging balance of power in the region. As the king witnessed the fall of Assyria, he chose a pro-Babylonian (or at least anti-Assyrian) foreign policy. Accordingly, he sought to halt the Egyptian army's march to support the Assyrians. It is possible that there was even a treaty between Judah and Babylonia, which obligated Josiah to take action at Megiddo.[2] The king's political reckonings no doubt included his dream of reuniting the tribes of Samaria and the north with the Kingdom of Judah.

This phase of Josiah's reign is not addressed in Jeremiah's prophecies, for the prophet no longer shares the king's euphoria. Jeremiah's early prophecies supported the king's budding visions, finding them full of hope regarding the religious reformation's potential to awaken God's mercy and restore Israel's glory. Twenty years later, Jeremiah is in a very different state. He no longer speaks of imminent redemption. There is not a single mention of a meeting between the prophet and the king or his representatives. Jeremiah is not even considered. When the king needs to know God's word, he contacts the prophetess Huldah. No one is interested in the prophet wandering the streets, spouting visions of destruction and mocking the people's repentance.

THE PROPHET NAHUM ATTEMPTS TO PREVENT JOSIAH'S POLITICAL INTERFERENCE

Although Jeremiah remains silent about Josiah's mission to Megiddo, the prophecies of Nahum allude to the king's political moves. Nahum prophesies mostly about the fall of Nineveh, with nothing mentioned in the Bible regarding his prophetic background or personal life.[3]

> His warriors' shields are made red; the valiant troops are clad in scarlet; the chariots glitter with steel when they are made ready,

---

2. This possibility is suggested in A. Malamat, "The Final Wars of the Kingdom of Judah," in Y. Liver, ed., *The Military History of the Land of Israel in Biblical Times* (Tel Aviv, 1964), 296–97 [Hebrew].

3. See Menahem Bolle, introduction, in Bolle, *Nahum (Daat Mikra)*, 6 [Hebrew].

and cypress spears are brandished. The chariots rage in the streets, jostle in the squares; they flash like firelight and move as swiftly as lightning. He shouts to his officers; they stumble in their haste, rushing to the wall to set up their defenses. The floodgates have been opened, and the palace dissolves. It is set up; she is uncovered; she is carried away, and her servant girls moan like doves and beat their breasts. Nineveh is like an ancient pool whose water is draining away. "Stop! Stop!" they cry, but no one turns back. (Nahum 2:4–9)

The Book of Nahum is largely a celebration of the collapse of Assyria and the fall of Nineveh. However, it is unlikely that such a one-dimensional ode would have become part of the Bible;[4] hidden within the joy are messages for Nahum's generation and subsequent ones. Between the lines, we can find deeper prophetic significance.

During the fall of Assyria, every local leader faced the challenge of gauging the emerging balance of power and making strategic decisions about political allegiances. Nahum, stationed in the Land of Israel, primarily addresses the King of Judah, who is trying with all his might to become the king of a unified Israelite kingdom. When Josiah sees the fall of Assyria and the emergence of Babylonia, he thinks (perhaps like his great-grandfather Hezekiah) that the latter should be given allegiance as the empire of tomorrow.

Alongside his description of Assyria's fall, however, Nahum warns against involvement in imperial struggles: "Why calculate against the Lord? He completely destroys – trouble will not rise twice" (1:9). Nahum cautions Josiah not to align himself too quickly with any power other than God. By keeping a low profile, he will be able to remain on the throne and secure his kingdom.[5] Isaiah imparted a similar message, both to Ahaz regarding Assyria and to Hezekiah regarding Egypt. The

---

4. Indeed, some have attempted to categorize Nahum's prophecies as external to Israel. See the introduction to the Book of Nahum in Ze'ev Visman, ed., *Minor Prophets* 11 (*World of the Bible*) (Tel Aviv, 2002), 66 [Hebrew].

5. This interpretation is suggested in Y. Elitzur, "The Prophet Nahum, His Era, and His Mission," in Elitzur, *Israel and Scripture*, 241–46 [Hebrew].

position all true prophets is the same: Israel should take no part in the unfolding global political trends, nor should it attempt to manipulate the rise and fall of nations. For ambitious leaders like Hezekiah and Josiah, this message is difficult to accept.

A MIDRASHIC ALLUSION TO JEREMIAH'S ATTEMPTS TO PREVENT JOSIAH'S INTERVENTION

According to both Kings and Chronicles, Pharaoh Necho sets out to assist Assyria and Josiah intercepts him. In Kings, the description is brief:

> In [Josiah's] days, Pharaoh Necho, King of Egypt, went up to the King of Assyria on the River Perat [Euphrates], and King Josiah went to meet him. [Pharaoh Necho] slew him at Megiddo when he saw him, and his servants carried his corpse in a chariot from Megiddo to Jerusalem and buried him in his tomb; then the people of the land took Jehoahaz son of Josiah, anointed him, and made him king in his father's stead. (II Kings 23:29–30)

Chronicles tells the story in more detail:

> After Josiah had set the Temple in order, King Necho of Egypt went up to fight at Carchemish on the Perat, and Josiah marched out to meet him. [Necho] sent messengers to him, saying: "What is there, King of Judah, between you and me? It is not you I am attacking at this time, but the dynasty I am at war with, and God has told me to hurry. Stop opposing God, who is with me, or He will destroy you." But Josiah would not turn back from him, for he sought war; he would not listen to what Necho had said in God's name, and he went to fight him at the Valley of Megiddo. And the archers shot at King Josiah, and he told his officers, "Take me away, for I am badly wounded." So they took him out of his chariot, put him in his other chariot, and brought him to Jerusalem, where he died; he was buried in the tombs of his ancestors, and all Judah and Jerusalem mourned for Josiah. (II Chr. 35:20–24)

Neither of these descriptions explains Josiah's motives for attacking Pharaoh Necho, but it is easy to determine them. Josiah has strived to unite the kingdoms of Judah and Israel and restore the Davidic dynasty. For eighteen years, he has worked to strengthen his people's connection to God and to their land. He is blind to what Jeremiah sees in the streets of Judah and Jerusalem – his own perception of the people's repentance is clear and promising. His kingdom's time has seemingly come. With the national and religious consciousness that has crystallized within him, Josiah wishes to prevent the King of Egypt from crossing his borders. It is possible that the words of Nahum the prophet were intended to warn him against this move, but it is likely that this prophecy never reached him.

There is one piece of evidence of Jeremiah's effort to stop Josiah – a late, somewhat questionable piece of evidence, but fascinating nonetheless – recorded in the apocryphal work I Esdras. In the above verses from Chronicles, Pharaoh Necho demands that Josiah not interfere with Egypt's passage through the Land of Israel, for God has commanded him to assist Assyria in battle. Josiah, however, "would not listen to what Necho had said in God's name." According to the Book of Esdras,[6] "Josiah would not turn back his chariot from him, for he had resolved to fight him; he would not listen to *the words of Jeremiah the prophet* in God's name" (I Esdras 1:28).

Esdras finds a reference to Jeremiah in the words "in God's name" that appear in the Chronicles passage. Interestingly, the sages explain these words identically in a midrash on Lamentations: "'what Necho had said in God's name' – this is Jeremiah" (Lamentations Rabba 1:18). If so, the prophecies of Nahum were reinforced by Jeremiah.

The King of Egypt is heavily armed, with vast numbers of chariots and cavalry. He is rushing north, having covered some three hundred miles in around three weeks. He wishes to pass through Josiah's land without engaging in battle, but Josiah very much "sought war." Perhaps

---

6. This work is an extension of the canonical Ezra. It is thought to be one of the earliest apocryphal writings; some even date it prior to the canonization of the Bible. A. Kahane, *The Apocryphal Ezra*, vol. 1, (Tel Aviv, 1936), 583.

he is gambling on this war to signify to the inhabitants of the Galilee that the entire Kingdom of Israel is under his control.

There is no evidence of an actual battle between Josiah and the Egyptian king at Megiddo. It seems that Necho focuses on eliminating the king in order to put a swift end to this annoying local uprising. Without giving it further thought, Pharaoh Necho continues northward to assist Assyria.

THE TALMUDIC DESCRIPTION OF JOSIAH'S DEATH

A mishna in Ta'anit states that when the sword passes through the Land of Israel, a fast is declared. In its discussion of this mishna, the Talmud preserves this conversation between Jeremiah and Josiah:

> When [the mishna] says "sword," it goes without saying that [this word] applies to a non-peaceful sword, so [here] it refers even to a peaceful sword. For there was no sword more peaceful than that of Pharaoh Necho, and even so, King Josiah fell by it. R. Shmuel b. Naḥmani said in the name of R. Yoḥanan: Why was Josiah punished? Because he should have consulted with Jeremiah, but he did not. (Ta'anit 22b)

This tradition documents that Josiah ignored Jeremiah; he should have consulted the prophet, who certainly would have stopped him. This implies a bone of contention between the two men. The Talmud describes Josiah's error:

> What was [Josiah's] proof text? "And no sword shall pass through your land" [Lev. 26:6]. What does the word "sword" mean? If you interpret it as a non-peaceful sword, [Scripture] has already stated, "I shall bestow peace upon the land" [ibid.]. Rather, it means even a peaceful sword. But he did not know that his generation had found little favor [in God's eyes].

In one line of this passage, the Talmud conveys the vast difference between Jeremiah and Josiah. The verse in question describes the blessed days during which the people dwell in their land in peace and security.

The prerequisite for this peace is "If you follow My statutes and observe and perform My commandments" (Lev. 26:3). The blessing includes the words "I shall bestow peace upon the land...and no sword shall pass through your land." If there is peace, then what is the meaning of "no sword shall pass"? It is interpreted to mean "even a sword of peace." That is, if the people obey God's commandments, they shall dwell in such security that no foreign army shall pass through their lands, even if they have no intention of fighting Israel.

Josiah and Jeremiah may agree on the interpretation of the verse, but their interpretations of reality differ. The prophet knows the people are not truly walking in God's ways and keeping His commandments – they are merely paying lip service. The king, however, is sure that his generation had found favor in God's eyes, earning the blessings mentioned in Leviticus. He is certain that the revolution he has wrought has secured the Torah in the hearts and minds of his subjects. He is therefore overconfident as he opposes Necho, who wields a peaceful sword.

A midrash preserves the dialogue between Jeremiah and Josiah, emphasizing the people's great contempt for Josiah's inspectors when they passed from house to house, checking that every home was free of idolatry:

> "The Lord is righteous, for I rebelled against His word" [Lam. 1:18]. Who said this verse? Josiah said it....
>
> Who said: "'Stop opposing God, who is with me, or He will destroy you.' ...he would not listen to what Necho had said in God's name"? It was Jeremiah the prophet, who said to him: "My mentor Isaiah would say thus, 'And I will set the Egyptians against the Egyptians' [Is. 19:2]."
>
> Josiah responded: "Moses, your mentor's mentor, said: 'And no sword shall pass through your land' [Lev. 26:6], not even a sword of peace."
>
> But Josiah did not know that his entire generation worshipped idols.
>
> What did the scoffers of his generation do? They would put half of the [idolatrous] form on one door, and half on the other door. [Josiah] sent two wise scholars to purge their homes

of such idols. They would enter but find nothing. As they left, [the scoffers] would have them close the door, so that on the inside, the idols would be reattached. (Lamentations Rabba 1:18)

The Talmud continues with an account of Josiah's last moments:

As Josiah was dying, Jeremiah noticed that his lips were moving. Jeremiah said: Perhaps, God forbid, he is saying something unworthy out of pain. He crouched down and heard him justifying the judgment that had been passed on him. Josiah was saying: "The Lord is righteous, for I rebelled against His word" [Lam. 1:18]. At that moment, Jeremiah lamented him, saying: "The air we breathe, the anointed one of God, was trapped in their pits" [Lam. 4:20]. (Ta'anit 22b)

As the Talmud was well aware, Josiah's death raises serious theological questions. A king dedicates his life to rectifying the religious state of the nation, reinforcing national values, and bringing his people closer to serving God, yet he is killed so senselessly. Jeremiah's fears are, sadly, well-placed, as he is moved to speak from the depths of his bleeding heart. All hope seems lost. A new future that was only beginning to coalesce has already been shattered. Jeremiah bends down and hears the king he so admires affirming God's justice with his last breaths: I am the sinner, and God is righteous. At this, Jeremiah shrieks: You are the chosen one! You are the Messiah of God! The people are the corrupt ones, in whose sins you were ensnared! The chapter from which these words are taken opens with the words "How the gold has been tarnished, the finest jewel has become dull." According to the sages, Jeremiah dedicated the entire chapter to his beloved Josiah:

This chapter speaks of Josiah: "How the gold has been tarnished" – he resembled the golden base of the Menora; "the finest jewel has become dull" – his body resembled precious stones and pearls. (Lamentations Rabba 4:1)

THE EULOGY OF THE PROPHET ZECHARIAH:
YONATAN BEN UZIEL AND RABBI KOOK

The prophet Zechariah, one of Israel's most optimistic prophets, dwelled in Jerusalem in the early days of the Second Temple. He envisioned the Divine Presence returning together with the exiles who came back after Cyrus' proclamation. Among other prophecies, he described Israel gathering strength within its own land once more, and reestablishing its monarchy. He depicted later generations atoning for the sins of their predecessors:

> Then I will pour a spirit of grace and clemency on the House of David and the inhabitants of Jerusalem; and they will look toward Me regarding those whom the nations have pierced through; and they will mourn for him as for an only child; they will grieve bitterly for him as for a firstborn. The mourning in Jerusalem that day will be as great as the mourning for Hadadrimmon in the Valley of Megiddon. (Zech. 12:10–11)

These verses read like some sort of riddle. Who was pierced? Who must mourn whom, weeping as if having lost an only child or a firstborn? To complicate matters further, the comparison of Jerusalem's mourning to that of "Hadadrimmon in the Valley of Megiddon" is a mystery in itself. For generations, these verses remained incomprehensible, until the *Tanna* Yonatan b. Uziel cracked the code:

> The Aramaic translation of the Prophets – Yonatan b. Uziel recited it for the words of Haggai, Zechariah, and Malachi, and the Land of Israel shook four hundred leagues in each direction. A divine echo rang out and said: "Who is this who has revealed My secrets to men?"
>
> Yonatan b. Uziel stood up and said: "I am he who has revealed Your secrets to men. It is open and revealed to You that I revealed them not for my own honor or for the honor of my father's house, but only for Your honor, that the disputes in Israel not increase."…
>
> R. Yosef said: If not for [Yonatan b. Uziel's] translation, I would not understand what the prophet said: The mourning

in Jerusalem that day will be as great as the mourning for Ahab son of Omri, who was killed by Hadadrimmon son of Tabrimmon in Ramoth-Gilead, and like the mourning for Josiah son of Amon, who was killed by Pharaoh Necho in the Valley of Megiddo. (Megilla 3a)

According to this talmudic tradition, Yonatan b. Uziel succeeded in interpreting the eulogy of the prophet Zechariah, linking it to Ahab, King of Israel, and Josiah, King of Judah. However, this interpretation does not explain the great tremor that shook the Land of Israel upon this revelation.

The key to this earthquake can be found in the story of these two kings. Ahab is notorious as one of three kings "who have no portion in the World to Come" (Y. Sanhedrin 10:2). He filled the land with foreign gods, turned his back on the God of Israel, and even persecuted His prophets, most notably Elijah. Josiah is Ahab's antithesis. No other king of Israel or Judah receives as much specific praise as Josiah, culminating in this description in Kings:

And before him there was no king like him, who returned to the Lord with all his heart and soul and might, in accordance with the entire Torah of Moses; nor did any like him arise after him. (II Kings 23:25)

This singular description recalls the words of the *Shema*, "And you shall love the Lord, your God, with all your heart and all your soul and all your might" (Deut. 6:5). There is no higher praise for a servant of God. How can Zechariah compare the mourning in Jerusalem in a time of redemption to the mourning for these two antithetical kings?

An answer to this riddle born of a riddle can be found in "The Eulogy in Jerusalem," an essay by Rabbi Abraham Isaac Kook. A basic text of Rabbi Kook's strain of religious Zionism, this work was written in the summer of 1904, on the occasion of Theodor Herzl's death.

Rabbi Kook arrived in the Land of Israel around two months before Herzl's passing and, as the rabbi of Jaffa, was asked to eulogize the Zionist leader, who had clashed with many in the religious community.

Rabbi Kook built his eulogy around this intriguing talmudic passage, which connects the wicked Ahab of Israel with the righteous Josiah of Judah. This unusual pairing highlights the secret of their power and the missed opportunities signified by their deaths.

Ahab descended from the tribe of Ephraim, son of Joseph and grandson of Rachel. Josiah, of the Davidic line, descended from the tribe of Judah, son of Leah. The rivalry between these two dynasties originated in the days of the tribal patriarchs themselves, was resolved during the reigns of David and Solomon, and flared up again under King Rehoboam of Judah and King Jeroboam of Israel, from the tribe of Ephraim.

Joseph was the practical leader, responsible for feeding his brothers, while Judah was in charge of their spiritual welfare. The division of Israel into two kingdoms resulted in significant losses for both kingdoms – losses still felt in the time of Ahab and Josiah. Ahab was a man of action who fiercely loved his people and provided for them, but matters of the spirit were beyond him. Josiah was a spiritual leader of great vision, but his political vision was flawed. His confrontation of Pharaoh Necho at Megiddo cost him his life. His aspiration to rule over the reunited kingdoms without interference prompted him to make rash decisions. Rabbi Kook writes:

> The characteristic of nationalism was prominent in Ahab, who had great love for Israel. He followed in the footsteps of his father, Omri, who founded a city in the Land of Israel. "Scriptural commentators said: Everyone receives a portion in the World to Come. 'Gilead is mine' [Ps. 60:9] refers to Ahab, who fell in Gilead" [Sanhedrin 104b]. At the height of battle, despite being shot through with arrows, Ahab hid his injury so as not to alarm his soldiers. Such courageous spirit is derived from tremendous, abundant love. He also honored the Torah, for he outwardly preserved the nation's dignity in the eyes of Ben-Haddad. Nonetheless, he did not recognize the value of the Torah and of God's unique holiness, in which Israel's entire advantage lies. Therefore, he followed the ways of Jezebel and the despicable customs of other nations to the degree that they then prevailed over the zeitgeist.

In contrast, Josiah elevated the spiritual aspect as no king before or after him. As the text testifies, "And before him there was no king like him, who returned to the Lord with all his heart and soul and might, in accordance with the entire Torah of Moses; nor did any like him arise after him." To that end, he wanted Israel to have no relationship with the nations of the world. He therefore did not heed the words of Jeremiah, who advised him in God's name to allow the Egyptians to pass through Israel's territory.

Thus, Ahab and Josiah combine the two aspects of Joseph and Judah, the power of the Messiahs of the House of Joseph and the House of Judah. When the people are ready, the distortion of each separate dynasty will be removed, for in the times of the Messiah the two kingdoms will join together and come to fully realize the full potential of their power as a chosen nation. At that time, with this reunification, the mourning [in Jerusalem] will also reach a climax, for what was lost and the distance from true fulfillment will finally be recognized, and the mourning for both Ahab and Josiah will combine and grow exponentially. [This great mourning] will serve as a moral that [both kingdoms] must combine their powers in order to create the balance that will lead to the greatest general good.[7]

Every political leader has his strengths and weaknesses. Ahab was a responsible, mature leader concerned with the economy, national security, and politics. His administration was flawless. But he lacked spiritual values characteristic of Israel, which led him to be corrupted by his wife Jezebel's evil ways.

Josiah, on the other hand, was devoted to Israel's spiritual welfare. At the same time, he sought to realize the people's destiny as a liberated nation, independent of the nations around it. He was, in this respect, ahead of his time, defying even Jeremiah in his passion.

Only a combination of both leaders – fusing the mature, responsible political insight of Ahab with the spiritual values of Josiah – will guide the nation of Israel to a complete and secure future.

---

7. "The Eulogy in Jerusalem," *Essays of Rabbi Abraham Isaac HaKohen* [Kook], 76.

FROM ELEAZAR HAKALIR'S LAMENT FOR JOSIAH

How a wail and lament issued forth from the mighty leaders for
 him who, at the age of eight, had begun to search for God on
 his own.

The children of Ham [Egypt] passed through and encamped in
 their midst, and the merit of his righteous deeds was to no
 avail.

Among all the kings who strived to mend Israel's ways, none like
 him had arisen since the days of Moses.

But the sins of the scoffers of his generation clung to him, of those
 who concealed idols behind their doors....

He caused so many to perish on the way to the battle at the
 Euphrates in order that no sword should pass through the land
 of Ephraim.

He would not listen to the prophet who commanded to withhold
 his arms in order to let Egypt destroy itself.

Part II

The Reign of Jehoiakim (609–598 BCE)

Background

Jehoiakim's Rise to Power

A fter his brief encounter with Josiah, Pharaoh Necho speeds northward to the region of Carchemish, on the Euphrates, to assist Assyria against the Babylonians.[1] According to Babylonian chronicles, he arrives in the month of Tammuz of 609 BCE. He spends a few weeks waiting in the north, attempting to overthrow the Babylonians at Harran, then returns southward, having failed to achieve a decisive victory. From his headquarters in Riblah, Syria, he surveys the new regime in Judah. He discovers that during his sojourn in the north, the "people of the land," the local leaders, have appointed Josiah's second son, Jehoahaz, as his successor. Jehoahaz apparently shares his father's anti-Assyrian and anti-Egyptian political leanings. The pharaoh, wanting to keep Judah calm, is displeased with this arrangement. He therefore captures the new king and imprisons him in Egypt, replacing him with Josiah's eldest son, Eliakim, who seems more politically malleable. Pharaoh Necho changes Eliakim's name to Jehoiakim – an expression of a servant's patronage to his master. These events are recorded briefly in the Book of Kings:

> Then the people of the land took Jehoahaz son of Josiah, anointed him, and made him king in his father's stead. He was twenty-three years old when he was appointed, and he reigned for three

---

1. M. Cogan, *The Raging Torrent: Historical Inscriptions from Assyria and Babylonia Relating to Ancient Israel* (Jerusalem, 2008), 176–219.

months in Jerusalem. His mother's name was Hamutal, daughter of Jeremiah of Libnah. He did evil in the eyes of the Lord, as his forefathers had. Pharaoh Necho imprisoned him in Riblah, in the land of Hamath, ending his reign in Jerusalem, and he imposed on the land a fine of one hundred talents of silver and a talent of gold. Then Pharaoh Necho appointed Eliakim son of Josiah in his father Josiah's stead, and he changed his name to Jehoiakim. He took Jehoahaz away, and he came to Egypt, where he died. Jehoiakim gave the silver and gold to Pharaoh, but he assessed the land in order to give the money to Pharaoh, every man according to his assessment; he exacted the silver and gold from the people of the land to give to Pharaoh Necho. (11 Kings 23:30–35)

During this period, under Pharaoh Necho, Egypt emerges as a force to be reckoned with; Josiah had gravely underestimated its power. The first few years of Pharaoh Necho's reign consist of a long series of conquests and victories. Between 609 and 605 BCE, he dominates many strategic posts, eventually controlling all access roads in the east. Next to Carchemish, he establishes a military base that is virtually impregnable. In one Babylonian record, Nebuchadnezzar (son of the emperor, and commander in chief at the time) admits that he cannot rout the Egyptians from the Euphrates.[2] The entire Land of Israel, Syria, and the cities along the Mediterranean coast are under Egyptian control. Under these circumstances, it is hard to incriminate Jehoiakim for his submission to Egypt.

Pharaoh Necho imposes an unbearable tax on Judah – one hundred talents of silver and a talent of gold. Jehoiakim pays it by levying a progressive tax upon the population: "every man according to his assessment." We can only imagine how the people received this onerous tariff.

The true price is paid by society's lowest classes, those without a voice, who can rail against injustice without anyone hearing them. The upper classes know how to cope with the tax – by lowering the wages of their underlings, negotiating with the government, and controlling the

---

2. M. Cogan, *The Raging Torrent: Historical Inscriptions from Assyria and Babylonia Relating to Ancient Israel* (Jerusalem, 2008), 176–219.

corridors of power. The king, loyal to Egypt whether he likes it or not, does not engage with the problems of the lower classes. He is eager to establish his regime by emphasizing the traditional symbols of royalty. In the earliest days of his reign, he plans an unprecedented building project: a new palace, which requires construction materials to be imported from throughout Egypt, and whose workers come from the lowest classes of society. The financing comes from the Egyptian government in a circular motion, as Egypt plunders the nations it subdues – Judah among them.

Immediately upon ascending the throne, Jehoiakim sets a pro-Egyptian policy. Anyone who promotes a different view is summarily executed. Whoever disturbs the peace through political or social subversion finds himself persecuted by the long arm of the king. The first victim of this harsh, uncompromising policy is Uriah son of Shemaiah of Kiriath-jearim, in the Jerusalem area. Like Jeremiah, Uriah walks the streets of Jerusalem warning of impending doom: "The end of Jerusalem is nigh; do not trust the lies of the government, which is attempting to lull you into indifference." Perhaps Uriah also comments on the Egyptian regime. His words reach the king, and he is declared a traitor and sentenced to death. Uriah flees to Egypt, due to the open passages between the allied kingdoms, but the long arm of the law finds him there. As Jeremiah testifies:

> King Jehoiakim sent men to Egypt: Elnathan son of Akhbor and people with him to Egypt. They brought Uriah out of Egypt and brought him to King Jehoiakim, who smote him with the sword and cast his corpse into the graves of the common people. (26:22–23).[3]

Elnathan son of Akhbor is no random figure: He is Jehoiakim's father-in-law, the father of the king's wife Nehushtah. Elnathan's family has

---

3. A pottery shard found at Lachish (no. 3) may corroborate this story with its own tale of a messenger named Jachboriah son of Elnathan, who was sent from Jerusalem to track down a prophet. The clay tablet commands the prophet: "Beware." See S. Ahituv, *The Script and the Letter: A Collection of Inscriptions from the Land of Israel* (Jerusalem, 2005), 62 [Hebrew]; and Hoffman, *Jeremiah*, 138–39 [Hebrew].

been ensconced in Jerusalem for years. His father, Akhbor, was sent by Josiah to Huldah the prophetess to hear God's word regarding the newly discovered Torah scroll. Now, Josiah's son sends Akhbor's son to Egypt, apparently assured of the family's loyalty to the king and his policy.

This is a punishment clearly designed to humiliate. As opposed to treating Uriah as a prophet, he is cast into the beggars' graveyard. The king will not tolerate any opposition to his new policy; anyone desiring to prophesy must align his message with the pro-Egyptian, anti-Babylonian regime.

Jehoiakim seeks to improve morale by focusing on the Temple and its service. He does not follow in the footsteps of Manasseh, filling the Temple with idols, but rather turns it into Jerusalem's "insurance policy." The Temple, which had survived the onslaught of Sennacherib one hundred years earlier, would outlast the expansionist wars of Assyria, Egypt, and Babylonia. Jehoiakim strikes a winning combination: economic reliance on Egypt, spiritual and national reliance on the Temple, and a general atmosphere of compliance with the leader. What could possibly go wrong?

609–605 BCE

Jeremiah's Prophecies
of Doom

CHAPTER 22: JEREMIAH'S DEBUT AT
THE PALACE OF THE NEW KING

Josiah's death extinguishes what little hope is still flickering in Jeremiah's soul. The entire nation mourns the death of the valiant king who boosted its strength. Now that he is gone, Jeremiah does not know what God's prophecies to him will be.

Chapter 22 describes Jeremiah's descent to the king's palace at God's command. This appearance would have been described differently in the days of Josiah, who sat on David's throne in all its glory. The awkward phrasing of "O King of Judah, who sits on the throne of David" (22:2) conveys uneasiness and cynicism – as if to say, what business does a man like Jehoiakim have sitting on the throne of David?

The first lines of this prophecy do not speak of destruction, but actually express hope:

> Thus said the Lord: Do justice and righteousness; save the robbed from his oppressor; do no wrong, do no violence to the stranger, the orphan, or the widow; shed no innocent blood in this place. For if you fulfill these words, through the gates of this house will come kings to sit upon David's throne, riders of chariots and horses, he, his servants, and his people. (22:3–4)

Jeremiah says nothing here about idolatry. It seems that, technically speaking, Josiah's purge succeeded. The public domain is free of all traces of idolatry; pagan rituals are performed only in private. Now Jeremiah begins a different struggle, focusing on the social policy of the new king. As we have seen, Jehoiakim successfully dealt with Egypt's taxation by placing the financial burden upon the shoulders of "the people of the land" – the contractors, managers, bankers. These are key figures, connected to the king or his ministers, who run Jerusalem's economy and control its labor market.[1]

Jeremiah begins his speech with encouraging words: Whoever seeks justice and righteousness, whoever maintains high moral standards and relates to the downtrodden of society, will be fit to sit on the throne of the king. Moreover, the prophet determines that government stability depends on social morality. This, of course, is but a rhetorical opening, intended to draw the attention of the king (and/or his ministers) to the speaker. Is anyone in the king's household familiar with Jeremiah? Probably not. Although he has been prophesying for over twenty years, his words have not yet reached such high places.[2]

Every prophet opens his prophecies by capturing his audience's attention, and Jeremiah is no exception. He therefore begins his prophecy with a rosy depiction of the royal future. However, he quickly moves on to the flip side:

---

1. In a 1968 lecture, Y. Rosenthal noted that the scholar Abraham Menes associated the expression "the people of the land" with "the masses" (Menes was affiliated with the Jewish Labor Bund and viewed traditional sources from a radical socialist perspective). See Y. Rosenthal, "Jeremiah's Approach to the Social Problems of Our Time," in Luria, *Studies in Jeremiah* 11, 153 [Hebrew]. Others cited in *Studies in Jeremiah* reject this interpretation.
2. The sages present Jeremiah as having been close to King Josiah, but this relationship has no textual basis. The most vivid example of this imaginary bond can be found in Werfel's *Hearken Unto the Voice*, which is excellent but largely a fabrication. Rabbi Adin Steinsaltz claims that Jeremiah "certainly knew the king personally and may be assumed to have been closer to him and in sympathy with him." A. Steinsaltz, *Biblical Images* (Jerusalem, 2010), 170. Although widespread, this view remains unsupported by any biblical sources.

> But if you do not hear these words, I swear by Myself – declares the Lord – that this house will be destroyed. (22:5)

With these words, Jeremiah concludes his appeal to the king. He has had his say. The phrasing of the message renders it an irrevocable oath – if the king does not listen, the house will be destroyed. Now the prophet turns to the people grieving over the death of their beloved king, Josiah:

> Do not weep for the dead or mourn his loss, but do weep for him who has gone away, for he shall not return again and see his homeland. For thus says the Lord to Shallum son of Josiah the King of Judah, who reigned after Josiah his father, who has left this place: he will not return there again. For where he has been exiled, he will die, and he will not see this land again. (22:10–12)

Jeremiah wishes to redirect the people's grief from the father to the exiled son Jehoahaz, here called Shallum. He will never return home. In Jeremiah's eyes, the king sitting upon the throne has not truly replaced Josiah. Jehoiakim was appointed by the king of Egypt and is unworthy of the Davidic throne. To explain why, the prophet turns back to the royal household:

> Woe to him who builds his house with unfairness and his chambers with injustice, who makes his neighbor work for nothing and will not pay him for his labor. He says, "I will build myself a great palace with spacious chambers," and he cuts out windows, and it is paneled with cedar and painted with vermillion. Do you rule because you compete with cedar? Did your father not eat and drink and do righteousness and justice, so all went well for him? He defended the cause of the poor and destitute, so good was bestowed upon him, for that is to know Me – declares the Lord. But your eyes and heart are set only upon ill-gotten gains and shedding innocent blood, and upon oppression and extortion. (22:13–17)

This is but one of the wrathful prophecies that Jeremiah directs toward Jehoiakim. The prophet stands before the formidable palace that the king has built with the blood and sweat of innocents. Some years ago, archaeologist Yohanan Aharoni claimed to have found Jehoiakim's palace and fort in the excavations at Ramat Rachel:

> We did not expect a ruler of the Kingdom of Judah to have built a royal palace and fort outside the borders of ancient Jerusalem, on the road between Bethlehem and Jerusalem. Above ground level, we found massive hewn stones of a type not usually used in that period, except in palaces and luxury buildings. In the stratum from the period of the destruction of the Temple, we found the handle of a pitcher that had been sealed with a Hebrew inscription: "[belonging] to Eliakim, lad of Jokhan." [American archaeologist William F.] Albright identified the "Jokhan" of the inscription with Jokhinu, mentioned in Assyrian writings – none other than Jehoiakim's son Jeconiah, who ruled only three months before he was exiled to Babylonia. It is unusual in itself for a king to build a palace outside the city. It is evident from the few remains that were preserved that this was without a doubt a most magnificent palace, built with the most advanced architectural and artistic techniques of the period. In this context, it is fitting to cite the verses from Jer. 36:22 ff., which describe how Baruch son of Neriah brought the scroll of Jeremiah's prophecy to Jehoiakim, who flung it upon the blazing brazier. It states there that "the king sat in the winter house." "Winter house" implies that he also had a summer house. This recalls Ahab, who had a winter home in Samaria and a summer home apparently in Jezreel. It makes sense that Jehoiakim's summer home would be located among the vineyards outside the city, next to Ramat Rachel. What a unique case in the history of biblical archaeology: The cedar window panes displayed in the Israel Museum are the very panes that Jeremiah faced as he prophesied.[3]

---

3.   Y. Aharoni, "Woe to Him Who Builds His House With Unfairness," in Luria, *Studies in Jeremiah* 11, 53–67 [Hebrew].

This contention has since been criticized, but the prophecy still holds true. Somewhere, there is a beautiful palace. In its door the prophet stands, an unwelcome guest who expresses his intense pain at the falling of the "savior of God" and at the corrupt Jehoiakim's assumption of the Davidic throne: "Shall you reign, because you can compete in cedar?" (22:15).

The contrast between Jehoiakim and Josiah enrages Jeremiah and inflames his prophecy. Here the prophet proclaims the kind of rule worthy of the Davidic line: "Did [Josiah] not eat and drink and do righteousness and justice for the poor, so all went well for him? He defended the cause of the poor and destitute, so good was bestowed upon him." The prophet's concluding sentence is astounding: "for *that* is to know me – declares the Lord" (22:16). For the prophet who stands and speaks about Jehoiakim's extravagant and corrupt palace, man's service of God is measured by his social conduct.

As noted, Jeremiah did not invent this criterion. The first to know God was Abraham, about whom God says: "For I know him, that he will instruct his children and household after him to keep the way of the Lord, to do what is right and just" (Gen. 18:19). The "way of the Lord" is to do what is right and just. Following in Abraham's footsteps, Jeremiah cautions the "handlers of the Torah [who] know Me not" (Jer. 2:8) that knowledge of God equals righteousness and justice in the land. Jeremiah measures the new king by this yardstick – does he know God through his social and moral conduct, or is he estranged from Him?

Jeremiah concludes his attack on Jehoiakim with one of the harshest, most damning prophecies he has yet uttered:

> Therefore, thus said the Lord concerning Jehoiakim son of Josiah, King of Judah: None shall mourn him, [saying:] "Alas, my brother, and alas, sister"; none shall mourn him, [saying:] "Alas, master, and alas, His Majesty." He shall have the burial of a donkey, dragged and cast out of the gates of Jerusalem. (22:18–19)

Thus Jeremiah greets the new king, as the prophet girds himself for a spiritual battle to save Jerusalem from imminent destruction. From the very first days of Jehoiakim's reign, Jeremiah understands that all hope is lost, yet he does not disclose his first political forecast, which he has been harboring for over twenty years. The vision of the wind-blown tumbleweed facing northward, announcing that "From the north will disaster break loose" (1:14), remains within him, soon to be unleashed.

CHAPTERS 26 AND 7:
JEREMIAH'S DEBUT AT THE TEMPLE

It is difficult to determine exactly who heard Jeremiah's harsh prophecy against the king. There is no mention of any reaction by the king or his servants. Possibly no one at all witnessed Jeremiah standing in front of the great cedar windowpanes. Possibly, this prophecy was intended to seal the decree and condemn Jehoiakim's reign in the prophet's own heart.

From this spot, Jeremiah moves on to the entrance of the Temple itself. In all likelihood, Jeremiah has been there before – after all, by the time Jehoiakim ascends the throne, the prophet is over thirty years old. However, until now, there has been no mention of his prophetic activity in the Temple. He has been moving back and forth between the north, his home in Anathoth, and the streets of Jerusalem. During the final years of Josiah's reign, he was angrily expelled from Anathoth – the people of his hometown plotted to kill him, and he cursed them in his wrath. Now he wanders around Jerusalem, one prophet among many, another face in the crowd. He presumably lives off of the kindness of those who recognize the importance of prophecy and believe in supporting the bearers of God's word. Perhaps he has even found shelter in one of those kind people's homes, but no hint of this can be found in the text.

Jeremiah's first recorded appearance at the Temple is quite impressive. It is necessary to connect two different chapters, 26 and 7, in order to fully understand how these events unfolded.[4]

---

4. Many scholars have commented on the necessity of linking these two chapters. See S. Zalevski, "Jeremiah's Speech in the Gate of the House of God," *Bar-Ilan* 16–17 (5739): 9–31 [Hebrew]. M. Shashar suggests an interesting reading that weaves these two chapters into one plot. See M. Shashar, "On One of the Prophecies in Jeremiah," *Turei Yeshurun* 46 (5735): 28–30 [Hebrew]. I have followed his approach.

At the beginning of the reign of Jehoiakim son of Josiah, King of Judah, came this word from the Lord, saying: Thus said the Lord: Stand in the courtyard of the House of the Lord, and speak to all the cities of Judah, which have come to worship in the House of the Lord, all these words that I have commanded you to say to them; leave nothing out. Perhaps they shall hear, and each shall turn back from his evil path, and I shall revoke the evil that I plan to do to them because of the evil of their doings.

Say to them: Thus says the Lord: If you do not listen to Me, to follow My Torah, which I have given to you, to listen to the words of My servants the prophets, whom I send to you again and again, though you have not hearkened, then I shall give up this house like Shiloh, and I shall give up this city to be cursed by all the nations of the earth. (26:1–6)

Jeremiah stands in the Temple courtyard as "all the cities of Judah" flock to the Temple, probably during one of the pilgrimage festivals, when Jews are commanded to appear at the Temple. Some commentators claim that the day in question had been designated for the bereaved, broken nation to pray on account of the tragedy of Josiah's death. Nothing in the text suggests such a reading.

Religious ritual is preserved in the reign of Jehoiakim, who perceives it as a means of stabilizing the people's sense of security under his government. The people obey the king, but under the surface, two serious problems are developing. First, the religious perversions identified by Jeremiah in the days of Josiah – hypocrisy and superficiality of worship, failure of outward piety to affect internal change – have continued. Second, a violent social environment has been created, in which might makes right. Under Jehoiakim's socioeconomic policy, the law of the jungle prevails, and only the fittest survive. Jeremiah stands at the entrance to the Temple in the hope that he will awaken the hearts of those who flock to the Temple. "Perhaps they shall hear, and each shall turn back from his evil path, and I shall revoke the evil."

Jeremiah knows the royal household is undeserving, but perhaps, through renewed efforts, he will succeed in saving the Temple and Jerusalem from destruction. The only way to rouse the people is through visions of rage and doom. Jeremiah therefore spews short, staccato words of destruction. This is no fanciful, elaborate prophecy. It contains no sophisticated images or vague, elusive metaphors. It is cutting, straight to the point: The Temple is doomed like Shiloh, and the city will be cursed.

All who hear him are shocked. They may recognize him from the days of Josiah, when he wandered the streets and called for the purging of idol worship. No one paid him any attention then. But now, after the death of their righteous king, every word strikes them deeply, like a poisoned arrow, and they quickly react:

> The priests and prophets and all the people heard Jeremiah speaking these words in the House of the Lord. And as he finished speaking all that the Lord had commanded him to speak to all the people, the priests and prophets and all the people grabbed him, saying: "You will surely die! Why have you prophesied in the name of the Lord, saying that this house will be like Shiloh and this city will be destroyed so that none shall inhabit it?" And all the people gathered against Jeremiah in the House of the Lord. (26:7–9)

The Temple courtyard is teeming with festive throngs, following the king's orders to strengthen their service of God. Such religiosity gives them a sense of security in times of distress. "This house" is God's fortress; no harm can befall it. The Temple has endured for centuries, surviving political changes, hostile nations, and national crises since the days of Solomon. The prophets of Jeremiah's time all draw upon the Temple as a source of stability, declaring that "God's sanctuary will ensure our well-being," that "thus says the Lord: I will bestow peace upon this house," and using other such catch phrases to soothe and lull the people into a submissive stupor under Jehoiakim's hand. The priests dedicate themselves to Temple upkeep and service. All these factions unite forcefully against the anonymous prophet who dares to declare in the name of the Lord that "this house will be like Shiloh."

Mentioning Shiloh and Jerusalem in the same breath is tantamount to blasphemy. The terrible events that occurred in Shiloh are deeply engraved upon the national memory. The Tabernacle that stood there for hundreds of years was corrupted by the high priest's sons. Shiloh also considered itself invincible, graced with God's protection, but it was eventually trampled and reduced to ruins. No wonder the spontaneous reaction of Jeremiah's audience is to lynch him: "You will surely die!"

CHAPTER 26 CONTINUED:
JEREMIAH'S TRIAL AT THE TEMPLE GATE

Jeremiah's prophecy in the Temple courtyard stirs up a great commotion. An envoy is immediately sent to inform the government about the incident, and the "officials of Judah," the king's lackeys, come up to the Temple and settle themselves down at its new gate. The final verse of the chapter alludes to a figure who supports Jeremiah and saves him from the vicious lynch mob:

> But the hand of Ahikam son of Shaphan was with Jeremiah, refusing to deliver him into the hands of the people to kill him. (26:24)

Shaphan's family was one of Jerusalem's most pedigreed.[5] Other members of this family held positions in the Temple and its environs, and Shaphan son of Azaliah was the royal scribe who read the king the Torah scroll found by the high priest. Ahikam had already accompanied his father as part of Josiah's delegation to Huldah the prophetess. Gemariah, another of Shaphan's sons and a senior Temple functionary, became one of Jeremiah's chief patrons. And Ahikam's son Gedaliah was appointed by the Babylonians to rule over the Judeans who survived the destruction of the Temple. We are told that Ahikam came to save Jeremiah from the masses, and brought guards to keep law and order. It seems that Shaphan's family consistently seeks to strengthen the Torah while remaining at peace with foreign nations. Accordingly, they become followers of Jeremiah.[6] The ministers take charge of the

---

5. For more information on this unique family, see S. Yeivin, *Studies in the History of Israel in Its Land* (Tel Aviv, 5720), 250 [Hebrew]; and B. Luria, "Jeremiah 26 and the Family of Shaphan," *Beit Mikra* 27 II–III (5746): 97–100 [Hebrew].
6. B. Luria, "Shaphan: The King's Scribe," *Beit Mikra* 118 (5749): 261–64 [Hebrew].

situation and prevent unlawful violence, reasoning that even traitors are entitled to a fair trial:

> When the officials of Judah heard these things, they came up from the king's palace to the House of the Lord and sat at the entrance of the new gate of the House of the Lord. Then the priests and prophets said to the officials and to all the people: A death sentence for this man! He has prophesied against this city, as you have heard in your own ears!
>
> Then Jeremiah said to all the ministers and all the people: The Lord has sent me to prophesy all these words you have heard against this house and this city. Therefore, mend your ways and your deeds, and heed the voice of the Lord your God, and the Lord will relent of the evil He has pronounced against you.
>
> As for me, I am in your hands; do with me what is good and right in your eyes. Just know for certain that if you put me to death, you will bring innocent blood upon yourselves, upon this city, and upon its inhabitants; for the Lord has truly sent me to you to speak all these words to you. (26:10–15)

The judges sit at the gate, and all parties are given a fair hearing. First the prosecutors – the priests in charge of the Temple service and the prophets who police public sentiment – present their accusation: This (unnamed) man is attempting to disrupt the established order by inciting against the Temple authorities. He dares defame "this city" – as you have all heard with your very own ears!

Jeremiah pleads guilty: Indeed, I have spoken against this house and this city, but I have done so not in order to destroy, but in order to reform: "mend your ways and your deeds." To fully comprehend Jeremiah's response, we must turn to chapter 7, which opens with God's command to the prophet: "Stand at the gate of the House of the Lord." There is an obvious difference between the two chapters. In chapter 26, the prophet is commanded to stand in the courtyard of the Temple, where the masses are present. In chapter 7, he is commanded to stand at the gate, where the officers of Judah gather to hear his trial.

We may now reconstruct the events as follows: After the angry

mob attempts to lynch the prophet, the officers restore order and rescue Jeremiah from its clutches. They sit in judgment at the Temple gate
and proceed to conduct a fair trial. To the ministers' credit, the proceed-
ings appear just. The prophet is asked to repeat his prophecy, which the
priests and prophets claim was spoken against the Temple and the city.
Seeing as he is safely in the officers' custody, Jeremiah allows himself to
expand upon his prophecy and present its inner balance – the hope of
divine mercy versus the fear of destruction:

> Thus said the Lord of Hosts, God of Israel: Mend your ways and
> deeds, and I will cause you to dwell in this place. Do not trust in
> false words and say: "Here is the sanctuary of God! The sanctu-
> ary of God! The sanctuary of God!" For if you truly mend your
> ways and deeds; if you truly ensure justice between man and his
> neighbor; if you do not exploit the stranger, the orphan, and the
> widow; if you shed no innocent blood in this place; and if you do
> not follow other gods to your detriment, then I will cause you
> to dwell in this place, in the land that I gave your forefathers for
> ever and ever. (7:3–7)

After Jeremiah presents this alternate scenario (which fell on deaf ears
when he spoke it at the royal palace), he switches to condemnation. His
repetition of "the sanctuary of God" is directed against the prophets
who frequent the Temple courtyard, reassuring the people that they
shall come to no harm in God's sanctuary. These prophets play upon
the belief that the Temple is graced with the amazing ability to save all
who pass through its gates. Jeremiah wishes to shatter this myth:

> For behold, you are relying on false words to no avail. Will you
> steal, murder, commit adultery, swear falsely, burn incense to
> Baal, and pursue other gods that you have not known – and
> then come to this house, which bears My name, and claim, "We
> are saved," that you may commit all these abominations? Has
> this house, which bears My name, become a thieves' coven in
> your eyes? Behold, even I have come to see it thus – declares
> the Lord. (7:8–11)

Jeremiah's self-defense has become a foundational manifesto of Jewish consciousness. He pits the sense of security and invincibility of "this place" or "this house" against a "thieves' coven," where moral corruption violently uproots all the Torah's principles. Jeremiah's examples of transgressions all come straight from the Ten Commandments: "Will you steal, murder, commit adultery, swear falsely, burn incense to Baal, and pursue other gods that you have not known?" The people who grasp the horns of the altar, seeking sanctuary, have become estranged from the basic core of the covenant between God and Israel. Jeremiah lists both social and religious obligations, and the order in which he lists them differs from the Torah's order. Perhaps he mentions the most prevalent violations first. In Jehoiakim's time, idolatry was marginal compared to the increasingly severe social corruption.[7] This concludes Jeremiah's prophetic rejoinder to his accusers. We may now shift back to the description of the trial in chapter 26:

> Then the priests and the prophets said to the officials and to all the people: A death sentence for this man! He has prophesied against this city, as you have heard in your own ears!
>
> Then Jeremiah said to all the ministers and to all the people: The Lord sent me to prophesy all these words you have heard against this house and this city. Therefore, mend your ways and your deeds, and heed the voice of the Lord your God, and the Lord will relent of the evil which He has pronounced against you. As for me, I am in your hands; do with me what is good and right in your eyes. Just know for certain that if you put me to death, you will bring innocent blood upon yourselves, upon this city,

---

7.   Martin Buber claims that the order of these sins reflects the prophet's view of their severity: "The sins against religion come at the end, because the prophet has to proclaim just this, that God seeks something other than religion. Out of a human community He wills to make His kingdom; community there must be in order that His kingdom shall come." See M. Buber, *The Prophetic Faith* (New York, 1949), 172.
     S. Zalevski disagrees: "This list of treacherous and evil deeds progresses from the relatively minor to the severe; the worship of foreign gods is the epitome of corruption. This list culminates in the worst transgressions in order to highlight the degree and scope of corruption." Zalevski, "Jeremiah's Speech," 20.

and upon its inhabitants; for the Lord has truly sent me to you to speak all these words to you. (26:11–15)

After Jeremiah's prophecy of chapter 7, it is time for "closing arguments." The accusers – the priests and the prophets – persist in their demand for his execution: "He has prophesied against this city, as you have heard with your own ears!" (26:11). Jeremiah, too, sticks to his story: God has sent me to say exactly what you heard – if you mend your ways, He will rescind His anger; whether I live or die, it does not change God's plan. "Just know for certain that if you put me to death, you will bring innocent blood upon yourselves" (26:15). This warning reinforces his claim that the city is already awash in murder, amongst other sins. Both Jeremiah and the priests and the prophets make their case before the officials and the people. It is a public trial, and the audience, which had been on the verge of murdering the prophet in its rage, is now in a state of confusion. The judges respond to the orations of the accused and the accusers:

And the noblemen and all the people said to the priests and prophets: This man should not be condemned to death, for he has spoken to us in the name of the Lord, our God. (26:16)

The people have changed sides. They are convinced that "this man" does not deserve the death penalty, for he speaks in God's name. This turnaround gives us a glimpse into the national psyche, which is easily swayed in whichever direction the wind blows. When the closest prophets say God's sanctuary will save everyone, the masses tend to believe it. But once Jeremiah is given an audience, his words ring true. This shows the power of prophetic oration, which influenced the public mood more than anything else.

After the "court" rules in Jeremiah's favor, the elders join the trial. They support the verdict by citing an incident in prophetic history:

And some of the elders of the land arose and said to the whole gathering of people: Micah the Morashtite prophesied in the days of King Hezekiah of Judah, and he said unto all the people of Judah: Thus says the Lord of Hosts: "Zion will be plowed like

> a field, and Jerusalem will become ruins, and the Temple Mount
> like a forlorn forest." Did King Hezekiah of Judah and all of Judah
> put him to death? Did [they] not fear the Lord and beseech the
> Lord, and the Lord rescinded the evil He had pronounced against
> them? But we are bringing a great evil upon ourselves! (26:17–19)

The idea developing in Jehoiakim's administration that no one may criticize the government is foreign to the Judean tradition of free speech and
thought. As proof, the elders tell the people about Micah the Morashtite,
who prophesied a century earlier, under Hezekiah, and also warned of
Jerusalem's destruction. Micah's prophecy of Zion as a plowed field can
be found in its entirety in the third chapter of the Book of Micah. The
eldest citizens of Jerusalem have heard the tale of Sennacherib's siege
and Jerusalem's miraculous deliverance and now reiterate its lessons.
The elders recall that although Micah's prophecy was directed against
Hezekiah, it did not cross the king's mind to silence or kill the prophet
on account of his words – on the contrary, a prophecy of doom can
inspire repentance and, in turn, divine mercy. It seems that the elders
cite the case of Micah and Hezekiah in order to support Jeremiah.[8] The
elders (or perhaps the compiler of the Book of Jeremiah) also mention
the terrible fate of Uriah son of Shemaiah, who had recently spoken out
much as Jeremiah had and was killed for it. Unlike Hezekiah, Jehoiakim
tolerates no opposition, and attempts to lead the ancient "media" toward
uniformity and conformity.

CHAPTER 19 (AND THE CONCLUSION OF CHAPTER 7):
BREAKING THE CLAY BOTTLE IN THE HINNOM VALLEY

The trial is over, and Jeremiah is released. From this moment on, however,
his anonymity is gone. The prophets of Jehoiakim have marked him, the
priests watch his every move, and the elders have begun to recognize
the truth of his words. His career has taken off. His first act as a public

---

8. Y. Hoffman addresses the connections between the books of Jeremiah and Micah.
    See Y. Hoffman, "Micah the Morashtite Prophesied in the Days of Hezekiah," in
    M. Bar-Asher et al., eds., *A Gift for Sara Japhet* (Jerusalem, 2007), 287–307.

figure is to prophesy in the most cursed place in Jerusalem, a symbol of abomination and idolatry – the Hinnom Valley.

> Thus said the Lord: Go out and buy a potter's clay bottle, and take of the elders of the people and of the elders of the priests. And go out into the Valley of Hinnom, which is by the entrance to the east gate, and there you shall proclaim the words that I will speak to you. You shall say: Heed the word of the Lord, O kings of Judah and residents of Jerusalem; thus said the Lord of Hosts, the God of Israel: Behold, I will bring upon this place evil that will make the ears of all who hear of it ring. Because they have forsaken Me and estranged this place and burned incense in it to other gods – which neither they nor their forefathers have known, nor the kings of Judah – and have filled this place with the blood of innocents. They have built high places to Baal, to burn their children with fire as burnt offerings to Baal, which I have not commanded or spoken of, nor did it occur to Me. Therefore, days are coming – declares the Lord – when this place will be called Topheth or the Hinnom Valley no longer, but the Valley of Slaughter. . . .
>
> Then you shall smash the bottle in the sight of the men who have come with you. Say to them: Thus says the Lord of Hosts: Thus shall I smash this people and this city, as one smashes a potter's vessel irreparably; and they shall be buried in Topheth until there is no more room to bury. So shall I do to this place – declares the Lord – and to its inhabitants, and make this city as Topheth. The houses of Jerusalem and the houses of the kings of Judah shall be defiled like that place Topheth, because of all the houses that burned incense on their rooftops to the hosts of the heavens and poured libations to other gods. (19:1–6, 10–13)

This is the first time Jeremiah prophesies unconditional destruction. Years earlier, at more or less the start of his career, God brought him to the potter's workshop and placed a prophecy of repentance in his throat "like clay in the hands of the potter." All was still open and supple, like the clay used to form vessels. Now he is commanded to buy a finished bottle, whose clay is no longer soft and malleable but has a definite form, symbolizing unyielding finality.

For this public debut, Jeremiah takes along two groups of leaders, "the elders of the people and the elders of the priests." His opening words stress that this prophecy is unlike anything he has ever said: It will "make the ears of all who hear of it ring." This unusual expression is used in only two other places in the Bible. It appears first when Samuel prophesies about the destruction of the house of Eli (I Sam. 3). This prophecy is closely connected with the fall of Shiloh, which is also mentioned in Jeremiah's prophecies. It is used for the second time by anonymous prophets about the kingdom of Manasseh, about forty years before Jeremiah's prophecy: "Behold, I am bringing evil upon Jerusalem and Judah, which will make the ears of all who hear it ring" (II Kings 21:12). Jeremiah repeats this expression because he knows that some ears are still ringing from the earlier prophecy. He evokes the sins of Manasseh's generation, which conducted the most contemptible of pagan rituals right where they now stand – the ceremony of passing their children through fire in the name of the god Molech, "which I have not commanded, or spoken of, nor has it occurred to Me."[9]

During his reformation, Josiah purified the place: "he defiled Topheth in the Hinnom Valley, that no man should pass his son or daughter through fire" (II Kings 23:10). There is no reason to think that this pagan ritual was renewed under Jehoiakim. More likely, Jeremiah uses this site to evoke the abominations that brought on the decree of destruction in Manasseh's time. With the elders standing around him, he proclaims a name change for this place. Rather than Hinnom Valley and Topheth, it will be called "the Valley of Slaughter." To symbolize his words, he smashes the bottle. With the shards lying at his feet, he has concretized an irrevocable prophetic death sentence.

---

9. The sages even dared to use Jeremiah's words in the context of Abraham, who offered Isaac as a burnt offering: "'Which I have not commanded' – this refers to Mesha, the Moabite king, as it says, 'and he took his firstborn son, who would rule after him, and offered him up as a burnt offering' (II Kings 3:27); 'or spoken of' – this is Jephthah; 'nor has it occurred to Me' – this is Isaac the son of Abraham" (Ta'anit 3a). This is but one example of interpreting the Binding of Isaac as an attempt to set the boundaries of ritual worship.

This prophecy is so crucial in Jeremiah's eyes that it appears earlier as well, in chapter 7:

> Cut off your hair and cast it away and utter a lament on the high hills, for the Lord has rejected and abandoned His infuriating generation. For the children of Judah have done evil in My eyes – declares the Lord; they have placed their filth in the house that bears My name, defiling it. And they have built the high places of Topheth in the Valley of Hinnom, to burn their sons and daughters with fire, which I have not commanded, nor did it occur to Me. Therefore, days are coming – declares the Lord – when "Topheth" or "Hinnom Valley" shall no longer be said, but rather, "the Valley of Slaughter"; and they shall be buried in Topheth until there is no more room. The carcasses of this people shall be food for the birds of the sky and the beasts of the land, and no one will frighten them away. Then I will cause to cease from the cities of Judah and the courtyards of Jerusalem the sound of rejoicing and the sound of gladness, the sound of the bridegroom and the sound of the bride, for the land will be a ruin. (7:29–34)

CHAPTER 20: THE ENCOUNTER WITH PASHHUR AND THE FIRST PROPHECIES ABOUT BABYLONIA

Chapter 19 concludes with Jeremiah's repetition of his Topheth prophecy in the Temple courtyard. This prophecy, his first about actual destruction, is important to Jeremiah, so he repeats it to the people in the courtyard. Unlike the previous time, when he stood in the courtyard and proclaimed, "if you do not heed," this time it makes no difference whether the people obey God or not. The vessel has been shattered; Jerusalem's fate is sealed.

> Jeremiah came from Topheth, where God had sent him to prophesy, and stood in the courtyard of the House of the Lord; he said to all the people: Thus said the Lord of Hosts, God of Israel: Behold, I am bringing upon this city and all its surrounding cities all the evil of which I have spoken, for they have stubbornly not heeded My words. (19:14–15)

As with Jeremiah's previous prophecy in the Temple courtyard, his words immediately reverberate throughout the city. This time they reach Pashhur son of Immer, one of the wardens of decorum at the Temple. Not only is Pashhur the chief disciplinarian, but he also carefully monitors all that is said in the vicinity of the Temple. He is loyal to Jehoiakim and will not tolerate prophecies of doom by Jeremiah and his ilk. Because the Temple draws all sorts of people who have something to say, strict ground rules are necessary. Pashhur has the authority to keep people in line by using moderate physical force as well as the *mahpekhet* – an onsite jail or torture chamber. This is the tactic he uses with Jeremiah:

> Pashhur smote Jeremiah the prophet and placed him in the cell in the upper gate of Benjamin by the House of the Lord. (20:2)

For an entire day, Jeremiah is imprisoned in the cell, his spirit churning. For over twenty years, his first prophecy has echoed in his mind: "From the north will disaster break loose" (1:14). Now, as he sees the king and his lackey prophets pledging allegiance to Egypt, these familiar words become clear. He suddenly understands what God wants from him. Loyalty to Egypt will lead the king and his followers to annihilation. All these loyalists will fall into the hands of Babylonia. From now on, Jeremiah dedicates himself to circulating this plain and simple notion:

> The next day, Pashhur released Jeremiah from the cell, and Jeremiah said to him: God has named you not Pashhur, but Magor-missabib [Defeat All Around].
>
> For thus said the Lord: I am giving you and all your friends over to defeat; they shall fall by their enemies' sword before your eyes, and I shall give all of Judah into the hand of the King of Babylonia; he shall exile them to Babylonia and smite them by the sword. I will give all the wealth of this city, all its gains, and all it holds dear, and all the treasures of the kings of Judah I will give into the hands of their enemies, who will despoil them and

take them and carry them off to Babylonia. And you, Pashhur, and all your household shall go into captivity. You will come to Babylonia; there you will die, and there you will be buried – you and all your friends to whom you prophesied falsely. (20:3–6)

This is the first time Jeremiah explicitly invokes Babylonia. In a flash of revelation, the mystery of the identity of northern terror is solved. He now realizes that the King of Babylonia will conquer the land, overthrow the king loyal to Egypt, and plunder the city.

It is hard to remain indifferent to Jeremiah's audacious curse of Pashhur. Immediately upon his release from the cell, Jeremiah taunts the very Temple official who imprisoned and then freed him, dubs him "Defeat All Around," and curses him most damningly. We are not told of Pashhur's response, but we can fill in the blanks with the help of what Jeremiah cries out to God as he leaves the cell:

> You have seduced me, O Lord, and I was seduced; You are stronger than I and have prevailed; I am a constant laughingstock; everyone mocks me. Whenever I speak, I cry of violence and destruction; thus the word of the Lord has brought me constant shame and contempt. So I said: I will not mention Him or speak anymore in His name; but His word was in my heart like a burning fire trapped in my bones; I am weary trying to contain it – I cannot. I have heard the calumny of many, of Magor-missabib: "Denounce, and let us denounce him!" All my confidants wait for me to stumble: "Perhaps he will be seduced, and we will prevail over him and wreak our vengeance on him." (20:7–10)

Jeremiah's attack on Pashhur also stems from his loneliness and frustration, as we see in his accusation of God: "You have seduced me, O Lord, and I was seduced." All his years of prophetic isolation have resulted from God's irresistible seduction. Mockery and shame have become his lot. Though he tries to ignore the word of God, he is unable to contain himself. It bursts from him "like a burning fire trapped in my bones." The prophet cannot escape his prophecies. Many such as Magor-missabib,

Pashhur's symbolic new name, consider him a troublesome slanderer: "Denounce, and let us denounce him!"[10]... Perhaps he will be seduced, and we will prevail over him and wreak our vengeance on him." This is the powerful lament of an afflicted soul that cannot escape its prophetic visions. One of its most impudent expressions is its accusation against God: "But the Lord is with me like a mighty tyrant" (20:11). Jeremiah feels that God is abusing him. His prophecy ensnares him from within; God's word traps him and beats him mercilessly.

In his poem "With My God, the Smith," Uri Zvi Greenberg expressed this tension between prophet and God, depicting the prophet as a mass of metal struck by the smith, God, in order to generate sparks:[11]

> Like chapters of prophecy my days burn, in all the revelations,
> And my body between them's a block of metal for smelting,
> And over me stands my god, the Smith, who hits hard:
> Each wound that Time has opened in me opens its mouth to him
> And pours forth in a shower of sparks the intrinsic fire.
>
> This is my just lot – until dusk on the road.
> And when I return to throw my beaten block on a bed,
> My mouth is an open wound,
> And naked I speak with my god: You worked hard.
> Now it is night; come let us both rest.

---

10. Translator's Note: The Hebrew – *haggidu venaggidenu* – alludes to Pashhur's official title of *naggid*. Jeremiah laments that he is moving through a police state, trying to bring him down.
11. U.Z. Greenberg, "With My God, the Smith," http://www.saveisrael.com/greenberg/greenbergwith.htm.

605–604 BCE

Enter Nebuchadnezzar

POLITICAL BACKGROUND

Since 609 BCE, when Pharaoh Necho assisted Assyria in its war against Babylonia, there was ongoing conflict between Egypt and Babylonia. In 605 Nebuchadnezzar succeeds his father Nebopolassar on the throne, and his first act is to decisively rout the Egyptian forces at Carchemish, on the Euphrates. In Babylonian chronicles, this victory signifies the end of Assyria and the beginning of the Babylonian Empire. Until now, the fortress of Carchemish has blocked the Babylonians' westward and southward expansion. Now Nebuchadnezzar can extend his dominion throughout the lands of Assyria's former empire.

Within a year, he defeats the Egyptians; sailing south along the Mediterranean coast, he makes landfall at Ashkelon and captures it.[1] After this defeat, Egypt retreats beyond the wadi, where it awaits the right time to recapture its lost territories and stronghold. These events are described in II Kings: "The King of Egypt did not continue to venture out of his land anymore, for the King of Babylonia had conquered from the wadi of Egypt to the River Perat, all that had belonged to the King of Egypt" (24:7).

During this period, the Babylonians also overcome Riblah in Syria, transforming it from an Egyptian fortress to Nebuchadnezzar's campaign headquarters. According to Babylonian chronicles, the entire land of the Hittites, modern-day Syria, was conquered that same year – the first of Nebuchadnezzar's reign. It all happened very quickly.

---

1.   Malamat, "Final Wars," 301.

It takes very little imagination to picture the utter havoc wrought in Judah by the news from the north. With Egypt's defeat at Carchemish, a black cloud descends on Jerusalem, which has come to rely on Egypt. As Nebuchadnezzar rapidly advances southward, panic rises. As we will discuss below, King Jehoiakim projects a "business as usual" attitude, but the fall of Ashkelon and Egypt's retreat to its own borders have made it clear that Judah is no longer an Egyptian protectorate.

Yet just four years later, in 601 BCE, the Egyptians rebound slightly by critically routing the Babylonians at the wadi of Egypt, leading them to retreat north for two years. Egypt quickly exploits their absence to build a regional coalition, and Jehoiakim hurriedly pledges allegiance to Egypt and rebels against Babylonia once again. Hence the description of Jehoiakim's reign in II Kings:

> In his days, Nebuchadnezzar King of Babylon arose, and Jehoia-kim became subservient to him for three years, then turned and rebelled against him. (24:1)

These three years extend from the Babylonian capture of Ashkelon in 604 BCE to Nebuchadnezzar's temporary retreat northward in 601, when Jehoiakim reaffirms his loyalty to Egypt. In 597, Nebuchadnezzar con-ducts a brief campaign to put down "the rebellious city of Judah," occu-pying it on 20 Adar.[2] This conquest marks the end of Jehoiakim's reign, the brief reign and exile of Jeconiah, and Zedekiah's ascent to the throne.

CHAPTER 46: JEREMIAH CELEBRATES EGYPT'S DEFEAT AT CARCHEMISH

Chapter 46 celebrates the downfall of Egypt at the hands of Babylonia. Jeremiah emphasizes that it is the "fourth year of Jehoiakim son of Josiah" (46:2). Jehoiakim counts for little in the prophet's eyes, but he *is* the son of Josiah, the beloved king, the anointed one of God, and Jeremiah per-ceives the fall of Egypt as divine revenge for Josiah's death. The chapter portrays Egypt's arrogant march into battle. The prophet mocks the

---

2. This chronology follows Cogan, *Raging Torrent*, 134, inscription 41. The "city of Judah" refers to Jerusalem.

uniforms, helmets, and spears of the Egyptian legions, none of which will help when God declares "a day of vengeance, to exact retribution from His enemies" (46:10).

CHAPTER 4: THE EARTH QUAKES AS NEBUCHADNEZZAR APPROACHES

Immediately after his victory at Carchemish, Nebuchadnezzar embarks on a campaign to quiet the region and subdue Egypt's allies. The outcome is clear from the start: Who can resist this mighty, foreign king who has overcome the powerful Egyptian Empire? Jeremiah expresses the people's impression as the mighty army marches toward them:

> Let it be known in Judah and Jerusalem; sound and announce it; sound a horn in the land; cry out and say: Gather and let us go to the fortified cities! Raise a banner toward Zion; hurry, do not delay; for I am bringing evil from the north, and great crisis. A lion has left its lair, a destroyer of nations has set out, has left his place to lay waste to your land; your cities shall be wiped of all inhabitants. Therefore don sackcloth, lament and wail, for God has not turned back His wrath.
>
> And it will be on that day – declares the Lord – that the heart of the king and ministers shall fail, the priests will be astonished, and the prophets will be aghast. Then I said: O Lord, God, You have truly deceived this people and Jerusalem, saying: "You shall have peace"; but a sword is at their throats! (4:5–10)

The horn announces the outbreak of war, calling for an emergency assembly at the enemy's approach. "Raise a banner toward Zion" signifies the same, as reinforced by verse 21, in which Jeremiah asks, "How long will I see the banner and hear the sound of the horn?"[3] Jeremiah

---

3. There is an old Zionist lyric "Raise a banner and a flag toward Zion," which expressed – perhaps more than any other song – the moment the people became determined to return to the land of their forefathers: "who by wagon, who on foot." The modern connotations of "a banner toward Zion" are the complete opposite of the phrase's sense in this chapter of Jeremiah, in which banners warn Zion of the approaching enemy.

does not yet refer to the Babylonians by name. "A lion has left its lair" –
this is the moment he becomes aware of the imminence of destruction.
The prophet's description – the king and ministers' hearts stopping and
the priests' and prophets' astonishment – depicts the paralysis that will
strike the city when the enemy from the north approaches.

CHAPTER 6: NEBUCHADNEZZAR CONTINUES TO RISE

In the following verses, Jeremiah intensifies his description of Nebuchadnezzar's threatening advance:

> Thus says the Lord: Behold, a people advances from the land of
> the north, and a great nation stirs at the ends of the earth. They
> are armed with bow and spear; they are cruel and will show no
> mercy. The sound of them is like the roar of the sea, and they ride
> horses, prepared for war against you, O daughter of Zion. We have
> heard rumors of it, and our hands go limp. We are seized with
> terror, with trembling like a woman in labor. (6:22–24)

These verses, and others in chapters 4–6, express the terror that has
gripped the people over the impending attack. The image of a woman
trembling in labor is accurate: A woman in childbirth knows she must
first run a gauntlet of pain before she can hold her child in her arms. Yet
the metaphorical "daughter of Zion" has lost her strength, for her pangs
bring her closer not to fruitfulness and relief, but to more anguish.

This prophecy represents the antithesis of Jeremiah's celebration
of imminent redemption for Judah and Israel in Josiah's time (ch. 30).
Then, the prophet mocked those who trembled in fear: "why do I see
every man with his hands on his loins like a woman in labor?" (30:6).
Then, the tremors shaking the earth announced God's goodness and
salvation. Now that image is turned on its head; years have passed since
Josiah's promising reign, and Jeremiah's prophecies have grown bitter
and dark. He no longer sees any goodness or hope.

CHAPTER 25: DRINKING TO NEBUCHADNEZZAR

Nebuchadnezzar's ascent to the throne and the subsequent defeat of
Egypt fill Jeremiah with anxiety. For years, he has been frequenting the

Temple courtyard and the royal palace, prophesying that Babylonia would one day vanquish the empire to the south. Now, as his prophecy is fulfilled, he turns to the nation and sums up his twenty-three years of visions. For once, he does not wait for the word of God to inspire his prophecy. Here the words flow of their own accord: "words that *the prophet Jeremiah* spoke to all the people of Judah and all the inhabitants of Jerusalem" (25:2). He can no longer contain his frustration at the years of scorn and derision to which he has been subjected. Jeremiah has had to endure countless taunts that his prophecies echo emptily, unfulfilled. Before he even knew the name of Babylonia, he envisioned its legions overcoming Israel. In the first years of his career, Jeremiah described this nameless nation thus:

> They have denied the Lord and said: It is not He, and no evil will befall us; we will see no sword or famine. The prophets will turn out to be empty as the wind, for the word is not with them; thus shall befall them.
>
> Therefore, thus says the Lord, God of Hosts: Because you have spoken this word, I am making My words like fire in your mouth, and this people like wood, and it will consume them. Behold, I am bringing upon you a distant nation, O House of Israel – declares the Lord – a mighty nation, an ancient nation, whose language you do not know or understand. Its quiver is like an open grave; all are fierce warriors. It shall devour your harvest and your bread, which your sons and daughters should eat; it shall devour your flocks and herds, your vines and fig trees; with the sword it will trample your fortresses, on which you rely. (5:12–17)

We can detect Jeremiah's anguish at the people's contempt and condemnation. In the past, Jeremiah repeatedly lamented the obtuseness of his nation: "To whom can I speak so that I will testify and they will listen?" (6:10). Now, with the emergence of Babylonia, he expresses pain:

> From the thirteenth year of the reign of Josiah son of Amon, King of Judah, until today – twenty-three years – the Lord has

spoken to me. I have spoken to you constantly, but you have not listened. (25:3)

After this bitter opening, he makes his main point. He no longer portends the emergence of a nation in the north – that would not be a prophecy, but current events. His role is now to articulate the religious significance of Nebuchadnezzar's rise. Is this a fleeting episode or a new world order? Jeremiah is very clear on this; for the first time, he sets forth his political stance, which will remain with him until after the destruction of the Temple:

> I will summon all the peoples of the north – declares the Lord – and My servant King Nebuchadnezzar of Babylonia, I will bring them against this land and its inhabitants and against all the surrounding nations; I will completely destroy them and make them an object of horror and scorn, and an everlasting ruin. I will banish from them the sounds of joy and gladness, the sounds of bridegroom and bride, the sound of millstones and the light of the lamp. This whole land will become a desolate wasteland, and these nations will serve the King of Babylonia for seventy years. But when the seventy years are completed, I will punish the King of Babylonia and that nation – declares the Lord – for their sins, and the land of the Chaldeans as well; I will make it desolate forever. (25:9–12)

Jeremiah declares Nebuchadnezzar "My servant" – an unusual epithet. Throughout Scripture, this expression is reserved for those whose lives demonstrate God's presence on earth: Abraham, Moses, David, and the prophets of Israel. When Isaiah wishes to say that Cyrus will act as God's agent, he calls him "His anointed one" (Is. 45:1) or "My shepherd" (44:28). In contrast, Jeremiah calls Nebuchadnezzar by a term of endearment, not merely agency.

Some view this expression – as well as other allusions – as proof that Jeremiah supported Babylonia. However, his subsequent prophecies undermine this evidence. Rather, Jeremiah recognizes Babylonia's temporary role and prays for the nation's punishment in due time.

He is not pro-Babylonian – he is faithful to God's word, and therefore he acknowledges Babylonia's role in the fulfillment of God's will.

The prophet's job is not to tell the future, but to open the eyes of the people and their leaders to the emergent reality and to cogently and soberly sketch what will unfold. The prophet participates in real life, but from a vantage point that allows him to discern what others cannot.[4]

Very soon, the Babylonians will descend upon the land and destroy every last semblance of life there. The territory will belong to the Babylonian Empire for seventy years. Then God will wreak vengeance upon the Babylonians, and they will answer for their deeds; their empire too will be destroyed forever. Seventy years is a man's life expectancy: "The days of our years are seventy" (Ps. 90:10). The prophet's point is that the Babylonian occupation is not a passing phase, but is destined to last.

Jeremiah now symbolically illustrates his warning of the Babylonian conquest. He is commanded to take a "wine cup of wrath" and "give drink" to all the surrounding nations (Jer. 25:10):

> Jerusalem and the cities of Judah and its kings and ministers, to give them up to destruction, to decimation, to hissing and curse – as they are today. Pharaoh, King of Egypt, and his servants and ministers and all his people. And all the foreigners and all the kings of Uz; and all the kings of the land of the Philistines – Ashkelon, Gaza, Ekron, and the remains of Ashdod. Edom, Moab, and Amon. All the kings of Tyre and all the kings of Sidon; the kings of the coastlands across the sea. Dedan, Tema, and Buz, and all who cut off the corners of their hair. All the kings of Arabia and all the kings of the foreign people who live in the desert. All the kings of Zimri, Elam, and Media. All the kings of the north, near and far from each other – all the kingdoms on the face of the earth; and the king of Sheshach will drink after them. (25:18–26)

---

4. Y. Elitzur took this view in many of his lectures. For example, see his reading of Isaiah's prophecy regarding the rise of the king of Babylonia: Elitzur, *Israel and Scripture*, 209.

This drinking party "celebrates" Nebuchadnezzar's expected victory over all the kingdoms mentioned – this in only the first year of Nebuchadnezzar's reign. Before the conqueror even sets his sights on Judah, the prophet is already pouring drafts that symbolize God's wrath via the Babylonian sword. Jerusalem will be the first to drink from the cup, followed by powerful Egypt. Next Jeremiah passes the cup to the nations surrounding Judah – counterclockwise, from the south: Philistia, the Transjordanian kingdoms, Tyre, and Sidon. He then broadens the circle to more distant lands: islands near and far, the tribes of Arabia, and the nations of the far north (Elam and Media). But the last to partake of the cup will be "the king of Sheshach" – an allusion to Babylonia itself (using the *atbash* cipher).[5] Indeed, Nebuchadnezzar will have his moment; none will be able to defy him as long as God shows him favor. But Babylon's time will come, too, and the nation will drain the foul cup to its dregs.

CHAPTER 35: DRINKING WITH THE RECHABITES

Babylonia's conquest of Ashkelon shook the Judeans' world. Chapter 35 describes the meeting in Jerusalem between Jeremiah and the Rechabites, a nomadic clan that has fled the Shephelah for fear of the new conqueror. The prophet uses the Rechabites' presence to demonstrate to the inhabitants of Jerusalem what true fidelity to tradition looks like. He invites the Rechabites to one of the Temple chambers (which presumably belongs to a supporter of his) and offers them goblets of wine. They decline:

> They said: We will not drink wine, for our patriarch Jonadab son of Rechab commanded us: You and your sons must never drink wine. Nor shall you build a house, sow a field, or plant a vineyard, or have one; rather, you shall dwell in tents all your lives, that you may live long upon the land where you sojourn. (35:6–7)

The Rechabites have a centuries-old family legacy. While we may speculate about why the patriarch imposed a life of wandering upon

---

5.   Editor's Note: A Hebrew substitution cipher in which alef is replaced by tav, beit by shin, etc.

his descendants, Jeremiah is concerned not with their lifestyle itself – though he does not consider it ideal[6] – but with their strict discipline. The prophet cannot tempt them with wine, because they envision their forefather before them. Jeremiah pits the Rechabites' steely self-control against Israel's fickleness:

> The commands of Jonadab son of Rechab have been fulfilled: He ordered his descendants not to drink wine, and to this day they do not drink wine, because they obey their forefather's command – but I have spoken to you again and again, yet you have not heeded Me. Again and again I sent you all My servants, the prophets, saying: Each of you must turn from your wicked ways and reform your actions; do not follow other gods to serve them, and you will live in the land I have given you and your ancestors – but you have not paid attention or listened to Me. (35:14–15)

This is the moral that Jeremiah extracts from the story of the Rechabites. From now on, he aims to penetrate the hearts of his people in Jerusalem – perhaps they will "turn from [their] wicked ways." He wishes to exploit the frightening rise of an existential threat in order to restore Israel to its Father in Heaven.

CHAPTER 36: A FAST IN JERUSALEM, AND THE SCROLL OF JEREMIAH

Chapter 36 describes the historical processes of this period in great detail, from Jeremiah's vantage point.

The chapter opens in the fourth year of Jehoiakim's reign, which is the first year of Nebuchadnezzar's. The prophet is commanded to take a scroll and record all his prophecies, from Josiah's reign until now, from 627 through 605 BCE. He wishes to compose a document that will open the people's hearts. Jeremiah's main problem is that he has remained

---

6. I disagree with those scholars who view this chapter as an Israelite prophet's paean to ascetic nomadism, a precursor to the Dead Sea sects. See C. Abramsky, "The House of the Rechabites: Genealogy and Social Character," *Eretz Yisrael* 8 (5727): 255–64 [Hebrew].

unknown. For years, no one paid him any heed; he was overlooked in the streets of Jerusalem, and his own village rejected him. After Josiah's death, Jeremiah begins to receive *negative* attention around the Temple and the palace. The people continue blindly following the Temple prophets and priests, who feed them a fixed formula: The Temple will protect us; loyalty to Egypt is our mainstay; and fealty to the king is our future. These sound bites stifle any public discontent.

For years, Jeremiah has been trying to improve society's character and mend society's moral fabric. He has long abandoned his prophecies of doom regarding idol worship. Local leaders have weakened the crucial link between improving society and remaining on the land. They have convinced the people that their possession of the land is unassailable. Jeremiah writes his scroll for use when this wall of denial begins to crack: "Perhaps the House of Judah will hear all the evil I am planning to do to [it], so that each man will return from his wicked ways, and I will forgive their sins and iniquities" (36:3). Jeremiah clings to a single thread of hope that the people will repent and the terrible decree will be revoked.

CHAPTER 45: THE SCRIBE BARUCH SON OF NERIAH

Jeremiah assigns the actual writing of the scroll to Baruch son of Neriah, who makes his first appearance here. Baruch's official title is "scribe"; he was apparently recognized as a professional scribe who read and wrote in Hebrew and Aramaic, and probably held a government position – like Shaphan the scribe and others.[7] It is possible that Baruch had met Jeremiah at the beginning of Jehoiakim's reign, and now, four years later, he volunteers to become the prophet's personal scribe and biographer. In a chapter dedicated to him, also recorded in the fourth year of Jehoiakim's reign, Jeremiah wishes to put his new aide in his place:

> Thus said the Lord, God of Israel, to you, Baruch: You said, "Woe unto me! The Lord has added sorrow to my pain; I am worn out with groaning and find no rest." Thus you shall say to him: Thus said the Lord: I will overthrow what I have built and uproot

---

7. For more on Baruch and his status in society, see H.M.I. Gevaryahu, "Baruch Son of Neriah the Scribe," in Luria, *Studies in Jeremiah* III, 191–243 [Hebrew].

what I have planted, that entire land. Should you then seek great things for yourself? Do not seek them, for I will bring disaster on all flesh – declares the Lord – but wherever you go I will let you escape with your life. (45:2–5)

According to a rabbinic tradition dating from the second century CE, Baruch grumbles, "Why am I different from all other disciples of prophets? 'I am worn out with groaning and find no rest' – 'rest' means nothing but prophecy" (*Mekhilta DeRabbi Yishmael, Parashat Bo*).[8] According to this midrash, Baruch sought to assume the mantle of prophecy, to graduate from scribe (an important position within the monarchic hierarchy) to a role which is essentially anarchic. Jeremiah counters that there would be no purpose in Baruch's prophecy; destruction has already been decreed, and prophecy has failed to improve the people. Jeremiah deflates his colleague's prophetic aspirations, telling him: "Should you then seek great things for yourself?" (as if prophecy awards the prophet respect). What greatness can come to a prophet who merely adds another vision of imminent destruction? Instead, Jeremiah refocuses Baruch on recording and documentation. By virtue of this division of labor, many of Jeremiah's prophecies were preserved.

But there is another reason Jeremiah handpicks Baruch for this important task. His position of scribe earns Jeremiah a favorable reputation in the corridors of power. The prophet is an unwanted guest wherever he goes – he is even persecuted in his hometown. The accuracy of his prophecies regarding Nebuchadnezzar's rise to power has won him no popularity. On the contrary, it has put his life in danger. Jehoiakim is still loyal to Egypt, and such prophecies can easily be misconstrued as incitement to rebellion. A scroll written by Baruch will certainly be received more agreeably than Jeremiah's visions.

---

8. For later commentators' perceptions of Baruch as one who helped transmit the Torah from the prophets to the sages (i.e., from Jeremiah to Ezra), see N. Gutel, "The Prophetic Status of Baruch Son of Neriah," *Merḥavim* 3 (5748): 98–127 [Hebrew].

CHAPTER 36: THE SCROLL IS READ ON
A FAST DAY, KISLEV 604 BCE

> Jeremiah commanded Baruch: I am confined; I cannot go to the
> House of the Lord. So you go to the House of the Lord on a fast
> day, and read to the people from the scroll the words of the Lord
> that you wrote as I dictated. Also read them to all the people of
> Judah who come in from their towns. Perhaps their petitions will
> be accepted by the Lord, and each will turn from his wicked ways,
> for the anger and wrath pronounced against this people by the
> Lord are great. Baruch son of Neriah did everything Jeremiah
> the prophet told him to do; at the House of the Lord he read the
> words of the Lord from the scroll. (36:5–8)

The scroll is written in the fourth year of Jehoiakim's reign, which, as
stated, coincides with Nebuchadnezzar's ascent to the Babylonian throne.
Jeremiah has the scroll ready in advance, ready to be publicized as soon
as the time comes – and it comes sooner than he expects. In the middle
of the month of Kislev, the people gather from all the cities of Judah for
a public fast. To understand this fast in its historical context and in connection to the reading of the scroll, we turn to the Babylonian chronicles.
In the first year of his reign, in the month of Sivan, King Nebuchadnezzar gathers his forces and heads to the land of the Hittites. His last stop
in this campaign is Ashkelon, which he reaches in mid-Kislev, around
six months later. Characteristically, he loots and destroys this port city.

Rumors of Nebuchadnezzar's campaign and conquests reach
Judah. The Judeans spontaneously gather and decree a public fast, hoping to appeal to God and awaken His mercy. They truly wish to mend
their ways. This is the opportunity Jeremiah has been waiting for. He
hopes that in the spirit of the fast, the people will embrace his words:

> In the ninth month of the fifth year of King Jehoiakim son of
> Josiah of Judah, all the people of Jerusalem and all the people who
> had come from the cities of Judah to Jerusalem proclaimed a fast
> before the Lord. So Baruch read the words of Jeremiah to all the
> people from a scroll in the chamber of Gemariah son of Shaphan

the scribe, which was in the upper courtyard by the entrance to the new gate of the Temple. And Micaiah son of Gemariah son of Shaphan heard all the words of the Lord from the scroll. He went down to the scribes' office in the royal palace, where all the officials were sitting: Elishama the scribe, Delaiah son of Shemaiah, Elnathan son of Akhbor, Gemariah son of Shaphan, Zedekiah son of Hananiah, and all the officials. Micaiah told them everything he had heard Baruch read to the people from the scroll. (36:9–13)

Baruch reads the scroll aloud in the chamber of Gemariah son of Shaphan the scribe, right next to the gate where Jeremiah's trial was held. This location is prestigious as well as strategic, and the scroll indeed has its desired effect. In the audience is Micaiah son of Gemariah son of Shaphan the scribe. As the scroll is read, his father is meeting with the highest government officials and clerks, presumably about the new political situation. Everyone understands the significance of the conquest of Ashkelon, which is but a day's journey from Jerusalem. Micaiah bursts into his father's office and interrupts this meeting, telling all the officials what he has heard Baruch read in the courtyard of the new gate:

> Then all the officials sent Jehudi son of Nethaniah son of Shelemiah son of Cushi to Baruch, saying: "Bring the scroll from which you have read to the people and come"; so Baruch son of Neriah took the scroll and went to them. They said to him: "Sit down, please, and read it to us"; so Baruch read it to them. When they heard all these things, they looked at each other in fear and said to Baruch: "We must report all these things to the king." Then they asked Baruch: "Tell us, how did you come to write all these words – were they dictated?"
>
> Baruch replied to them: "He dictated all these words to me, and I wrote them in ink in the scroll."
>
> Then the officials said to Baruch: "You and Jeremiah, go and hide, and do not let anyone know where you are." (36:14–19)

The officials must authenticate the scroll. Baruch details how he wrote all of the prophet's words – this is a singular description of a scribe recording a speaker's words. The officials are convinced Jeremiah has broken through the façade of indifference; this is the moment he has been waiting for. Only one obstacle remains – the king's heart of steel. Anticipating failure, the officials warn Baruch to go into hiding with Jeremiah:

> After they placed the scroll in the office of Elishama the scribe, they went to the king in the courtyard and reported everything to him. The king sent Jehudi to get the scroll, and Jehudi brought it from the office of Elishama the scribe and read it to the king and all the officials standing beside him. It was the ninth month, and the king was sitting in the winter house, with a fire burning in the brazier in front of him. And as Jehudi read three or four verses of the scroll, the king cut them off with a scribe's knife and threw them into the brazier, until the entire scroll was consumed in the fire upon it. The king and all his attendants who heard all these words did not fear, nor did they rend their clothes. Although Elnathan, Delaiah, and Gemariah urged the king not to burn the scroll, he would not listen to them. The king commanded Jerahmeel, son of the king, Seraiah son of Azriel, and Shelemiah son of Abdeel to arrest Baruch the scribe and Jeremiah the prophet, but the Lord had hidden them. (36:20–26)

The officials, afraid to present the scroll to the king, leave it in the office of the scribe Elishama. But the king orders Jehudi to bring the scroll and read it aloud, word by word. This is the moment of truth. To help us fully understand the scene, the text notes that it is winter time, and the king is sitting in his winter home before a blazing fire. The people are huddled outside in the cold, fasting and praying for God's mercy, but their king prefers to sit comfortably by the fireplace, estranged from his subjects. Jehudi tentatively begins to read out the scroll – after three or four verses, the king snatches it from his hands, hacks off the offending verses, and flings the scrap into the burning brazier. His body language reveals his contempt for the words: "the king and all his attendants... showed no fear, nor did they rend their clothes." Jehoiakim is entrenched in his arrogant belief that their patron empire, Egypt, will save them from Babylonia's attack, and he has no patience for Jeremiah's prophecies.

This scene begs comparison with his father Josiah's discovery of the scroll in the Temple treasury – he hears its contents and immediately rends his clothing. This contrast illustrates the difference between a leader open to criticism and political change and a leader who is insecure and holds fast to his way of thinking, refusing to hear any alternative to his worldview.

Jeremiah has become a fugitive, hiding until the end of Jehoiakim's reign. God commands the prophet to rewrite the scroll. Jehoiakim once again becomes the target of the prophecy of doom: "Therefore, thus says the Lord about Jehoiakim, King of Judah: He will no longer sit on the throne of David, and his corpse shall be cast out into the heat by day and the frost by night" (36:30).

THE RABBINIC ACCOUNT OF JEHOIAKIM'S HEARING OF THE SCROLL

They said to Jehoiakim: Jeremiah has written a book of lamentations.

He said to them: What is written in it?

They said to him: "How deserted lies the city" [Lam. 1:1].

He replied: I am the king!

They said to him: "Bitterly she weeps at night" [1:2].

He replied: I am the king!

They said to him: "Judah has been harshly exiled" [1:3].

He replied: I am the king!

They said to him: "The roads to Zion are bereft" [1:4].

He replied: I am the king!

They said to him: "Her foes have become her masters" [1:5].

When he heard this, he rose and screamed: Who said so?!

They answered him: "For the Lord has punished her for her abundant sins" [1:5].

He immediately excised all mentions of God's name from [the book] and burned them in the fire. As it is written: "And they did not fear, nor did they rend their clothes." (Mo'ed Katan 26a)

This rabbinic retelling conveys the sages' attitude toward Jehoiakim's detachment from his people and his single-minded focus on remaining in power. They depict this scroll of laments as a first draft of the biblical Book of Lamentations, though it was composed many years prior to the actual destruction of the Temple.

Jehoiakim's reaction to the increasingly tragic verses shows his extreme arrogance and self-absorption: I am the king! Even if the streets quake at Babylonia's approach, even if they are deserted and destroyed, it does not affect me. My rule remains intact. When the fifth verse is read, the king bursts out of his chair in fury: Who dares suggest such a thing?! He is answered by the continuation of the verse: "for the Lord has punished her for her abundant sins" – it is God's will. The king's response is horrifying: He tears the scroll to shreds without the slightest reservation. He has no fear of God. Jehoiakim considers himself the supreme king, with no regard for the King of kings.

Another rabbinic tradition reinforces this view of Jehoiakim:

> The Holy One Blessed Be He wished to return the world to primal nothingness because of Jehoiakim, but when He looked at his generation, He was soothed. (Sanhedrin 103a)

The divine wrath evoked by Jehoiakim is similar to God's response to the generation of Noah and the Deluge. But the fasting and praying of the people, who in their terror gather in the dead of winter to pour out their hearts, assuages God's anger, even if He does not revoke the decree of Jerusalem's destruction.

NEBUCHADNEZZAR'S CAMPAIGN TO PUNISH JUDAH, AND THE DEATH OF JEHOIAKIM

We do not know what eventually happens to Jehoiakim, who becomes a vassal of the King of Babylonia for three years. It seems that after the conquest of Ashkelon, Jehoiakim surrendered to Nebuchadnezzar. The obvious sign of this new subservience is the tribute he must pay to Babylonia instead of Egypt. This transfer of fealty poses no problem as long as the Egyptians remain in their land, recouping their losses and steering clear of the dangerous new empire. But once Egypt rears its head again, in 601 BCE, and chases the Babylonians back up north, Jehoiakim quickly changes sides. Babylonia turns its attention to the upstart

Kingdom of Judah in order to put down this rebellion. According to Babylonian chronicles, in 598 – the seventh year of Nebuchadnezzar's reign – in the month of Kislev,

> The King of Akkad [Babylonia] gathered his forces, advanced to the land of the Hittites, and encamped opposite the city of Judah. On the second of Adar they captured the city, captured its king, and appointed a king after their own heart in his place. They extorted a heavy fine, and returned to Babylon.[9]

This historical record makes no mention of Jehoiakim – it refers to the capture of Jeconiah (see below) and the appointment of Zedekiah, a king "after [Nebuchadnezzar's] own heart." What has happened to Jehoiakim? To fill in the blanks, we must look closely at the details provided. Babylonia's punitive forces set out for Judah in Kislev. By Adar, Jeconiah has already been captured and exiled to Babylon. Capturing Jerusalem therefore takes around three months.

11 Kings reports that the reign of Jeconiah lasted three months:

> Jehoiakin [Jeconiah] was eighteen when he became king; he reigned in Jerusalem for three months; and his mother was Nehushta, daughter of Elnathan of Jerusalem. He did evil in the eyes of the Lord, like his father. At that time, the servants of King Nebuchadnezzar of Babylonia ascended to Jerusalem and besieged the city. King Nebuchadnezzar of Babylonia came to the city while his servants were besieging it. (11 Kings 24:8–11)

Clearly, by the time Nebuchadnezzar joins the siege against Jerusalem, Jehoiakim is no longer alive. According to Kings, he "lay with his forefathers," probably meaning that he was buried in the garden of Uzzah where his righteous father Josiah was buried (Jer. 22:19). If so, then Jeremiah's prediction that he would suffer a donkey's burial was not fulfilled.

---

9. Cogan, *Raging Torrent*, chronicle 41, 132.

According to 11 Chronicles, however, Jehoiakim was exiled to Babylon:

> King Nebuchadnezzar of Babylonia advanced upon him and shackled him in bronze chains to lead him to Babylon. And Nebuchadnezzar brought some of the vessels in the House of the Lord to Babylon, and he placed them in his palace in Babylon. And the rest of Jehoiakim's deeds, the abominations he committed, and all that was found against him are recorded in the book of kings of Israel and Judah. Jehoiakin his son succeeded him. (11 Chr. 36:6–8)

This version is possible only if the King of Babylonia exiled Jehoiakim and Jeconiah on separate occasions.

In his commentary on the words "And Jehoiakim lay with his forefathers" (11 Kings 24:6), Rashi tries to reconcile the two versions:

> Not in his ancestral tomb, for he was shackled by Nebuchadnezzar to be led to Babylon, and he was dragged along and died in their hands, as it says, "He shall have the burial of a donkey, dragged and cast out," and it says that Nebuchadnezzar had him shackled to be led to Babylon.

Rashi, it seems, did not want to place the wicked Jehoiakim peacefully next to his righteous father.

Another interpretation preserves Jehoiakim's character and fate in accordance with Jeremiah's prophecies:

> Nebuchadnezzar came to destroy Jerusalem; he took up his position at the wall of Antioch. The great Sanhedrin went out to meet him. [Its members] said to him: "Is it time for this house [of God] to be destroyed?" They went and said to Jehoiakim: "Nebuchadnezzar demands you!"
>
> He said to them: "That's what you do? You sacrifice a soul to save a soul? You sacrifice my soul to save your souls? It says: 'You shall not deliver a servant to his masters' [Deut. 23:16]!"

They replied: "Did not your ancestor do so with Sheba son of Bichri?"

Since he did not listen to them, they rose up and took him and lowered him down to [Nebuchadnezzar]. How did they lower him down? R. Eliezer and R. Shimon [dispute the matter]:

R. Eliezer b. R. Natan says: They lowered him down while he was still alive, as it says: "They put him into a cage with hooks" [Ezek. 19:9] – "with hooks" (*baḥaḥim*) may be read as "while alive" (*baḥayyim*).

R. Shimon says: They lowered him down when he was dead, as it says: "that his voice should never again be heard" [ibid.].

R. Yehoshua b. Levi said: I can uphold both interpretations: They lowered him down alive, but he died in their hands.

What did Nebuchadnezzar do to him? R. Yehuda and R. Neḥemia [dispute the matter]:

R. Yehuda says: They took him and marched him through all the cities of Judah. They made an example of him: They killed him, ripped open a donkey, and placed him inside. Thus Scripture states: "He shall have the burial of a donkey."

R. Neḥemia says: They took him and marched him through all the cities of Judah and killed him. Then [Nebuchadnezzar hacked off olive-size pieces of him and fed them to the dogs. Thus Scripture states: "He shall have the burial of a donkey." Where are donkeys buried if not in the guts of a dog? (Leviticus Rabba 19:6)

R. Ḥiya b. Avuya said: "This and yet another" was engraved upon Jehoiakim's skull.

R. Perida's grandfather found a skull tossed away at the gates of Jerusalem, upon which "this and yet another" was written. So he buried it, but it reemerged; again he buried it, and again it reemerged. Thereupon he said: This must be Jehoiakim's skull, of whom it is written: "He shall have the burial of a donkey, dragged and cast out of the gates of Jerusalem." Yet, [R. Perida's grandfather] reflected, he was a king, and it was not mannerly to disgrace him thus. So he took the skull, wrapped it in a shroud, brought it home, and placed it in a box.

When his wife came home and saw the shrouded skull, she brought it out and told her neighbors: "It is the skull of his first wife, whom he cannot stop thinking about." So she put it in the oven and burnt it.

When he came home, he said to her, "That was meant by its inscription, 'This and yet another.'" (Sanhedrin 82a)

This is how the sages fill in the gaps regarding Jehoiakim's death and the fulfillment of Jeremiah's prophecy. This interpretation reflects the rabbinic criticism of Jehoiakim. They considered him indifferent toward God, obsessed with his wealth, and guilty of exploiting his people.

Part III
The Reign of Zedekiah (597–586 BCE)

597 BCE

The Exile of Jeconiah

POLITICAL BACKGROUND: NEBUCHADNEZZAR
ENGINEERS A REGIME CHANGE IN JUDAH

As we read in the Babylonian chronicles, once Nebuchadnezzar learns of Judah's rebellion, he returns to Jerusalem to restore order. His campaign is designed to install a Judean leadership that will serve Babylonia's purposes. Babylonian intelligence has profiled all of Judah's potential leaders and familiarized itself with the political tensions that have prevailed since Merodach-Baladan, ancestor of Nebuchadnezzar and progenitor of the Babylonian royal line.

That same ancestor forged ties with King Hezekiah of Judah in an attempt to make strategic alliances in the Middle East. The Babylonian delegation's visit to Judah was successful, and mutual trust was established between the two kingdoms. However, Manasseh, son of Hezekiah, turned his back on his father's agreements, preferring to become a tributary of Assyria. For decades, Judah remained loyal to Assyria, until Josiah, Hezekiah's great-grandson, rebelled against that allegiance. The Babylonian ruler saw Josiah's abandonment of Assyria and anticipated a renewal of Hezekiah's alliance with Babylonia; he did not realize that Josiah's goal was complete independence. When Egypt grew powerful, it installed a king over Judah – Jehoiakim – who would toe the line of the Egyptian-Assyrian alliance against Babylonia.

Now, with Babylonia's return to greatness, Nebuchadnezzar seeks a candidate who will rule Judah to his liking – in the words of the Babylonian chronicles, "a king after [his] own heart." After Jehoiakim's death (or disappearance) in 598 BCE, the men of Judah appoint Jeconiah, the son of Jehoiakim and his wife Nehushta, Elnathan's daughter. We have encountered Elnathan before. He was part of the delegation sent to Egypt to arrest a rabble-rousing prophet. On the one hand, Elnathan is clearly loyal to the king and his pro-Egyptian, anti-Babylonian political views. On the other hand, Elnathan was among those who urged the king not to burn the scroll of Jeremiah's prophecies. The potent words Baruch read must have penetrated his heart.

In any case, Jeconiah is not suitable to be the proxy of the Babylonian king in Judah. A better candidate is found among the previous generation: Mataniah, at twenty-one years old, is the youngest of Josiah's sons and the half-brother of Jehoiakim. He is born to Hamutal, and is the brother of Jehoahaz, who was taken by Pharaoh Necho to exile in Egypt.

The time has come to turn back the clock on Pharaoh Necho's intervention. Nebuchadnezzar flips the script by installing Josiah's son as leader. He imprisons Jeconiah, Jehoiakim's son, together with his mother, Nehushta, in Babylon. Nebuchadnezzar understands that as long as there are those of Jehoiakim's mindset in the palace, there will be trouble in Judah; thus, he decides to exile the entire Judean leadership. It is important to note the difference between the mass exile of Jerusalem's inhabitants after the destruction of the Temple – when the exiles were led to Babylonia in chains, humiliated and defeated – and the "exile of Jeconiah," which was a voluntary exile:

King Jeconiah, along with his mother, his servants, his advisers, and officials, surrendered to the King of Babylonia in the eighth year of his reign. He carried off all the treasures of the Temple and the palace, and he stripped away all the golden vessels that King Solomon of Israel had made for the sanctuary of the Lord – just as God had spoken. He exiled all of Jerusalem, all the commanders and the best of the soldiers – ten thousand exiles – and all the craftsmen and artisans; only the poorest people were left in the land. He exiled Jeconiah to Babylonia, along with the king's mother, the king's wives, his officials, and all the elite of the land, from Jerusalem to Babylonia. He also exiled seven thousand of the best troops and one thousand craftsmen and artisans, all of whom were strong and fit for war; the King of Babylonia brought them to Babylonia as exiles. (II Kings 24:12–16)

According to this account, there was no real siege around Jerusalem at this point. Although Scripture states that the city was besieged (24:10), there is no description of a proper siege – no battering rams set up and no trenches dug around the city. Moreover, the events described here and in the Babylonian chronicles unfolded too quickly for there to have been an actual siege: The King of Babylonia sets out in the month of Kislev, and by the second of Adar – roughly three months later – Jeconiah has already surrendered. Considering the duration of such a march (roughly one thousand miles, with an army that could cover no more than fifteen miles on a short winter day), there seems to have been little time left to engineer a full-fledged siege.

Presumably, the Babylonians encamped around the city, spurring Jeconiah and the elites of Judah to surrender quickly and quietly and accept the terms dictated by Nebuchadnezzar. There was certainly no attempt to mount a defense. Hence Jeconiah's departure with his mother and his whole entourage. The treasurers were likely ordered to empty the treasuries of the Temple and the palace as part of the terms of surrender. These sums were insufficient for the Babylonian king, so he issued an order to strip the Temple of its golden vessels.

Jeconiah's convoy sets out for Babylonia, comprising all the senior military echelons, the upper class, and apparently the nation's spiritual leadership as well. They settle along the Euphrates, near the city of Nehardea, and begin to establish the Jewish community in Babylonia. Jeconiah retains the status of "king in exile," and does not suffer humiliation or hunger. A well-known Babylonian record from that time reports the rations that the Babylonians provided to the kings they had captured, including "Jeconiah and his five sons."[1]

---

1. This Babylonian record was published by the German assyriologist E. Weidner in 1939. The records he published were excavated in an archive of Nebuchadnezzar's in Babylonia and date to 592 BCE, five years after his exile. See A. Malamat, "The Words of Jeremiah According to External Sources," in Luria, *Studies in Jeremiah* I, 12–13 [Hebrew].

This new Judaism flourishes by the rivers of Babylonia in relative economic stability, with local leadership and ideas about the future. In another sixty years, when Cyrus calls on the Jews of Babylonia to return home, very few will heed his call. Most will be too established to consider relocating. The story of Babylonian Jewish life begins with Jeconiah.

CHAPTER 13: JEREMIAH'S PROPHECY UPON THE EXILES' DEPARTURE FROM JERUSALEM

For several years, no prophecies have passed Jeremiah's lips. Since Baruch's reading of the scroll to Jehoiakim in 594 BCE, Jeremiah has been in hiding. But during that time God commands him to perform a strange act:

> Thus said the Lord to me: Go and buy yourself a loincloth of linen, put it around your waist, and do not put it in water. So I bought a loincloth as the Lord said and I put it around my waist. And the word of the Lord came to me a second time: Take the loincloth you bought, which is around your waist, and go to Perat and hide it there in the cleft of a rock. So I went and hid it in Perat, as the Lord commanded me. (13:1–5)

This is the first time that Jeremiah is commanded to perform an act rather than speak. The silence imposed on him by Jehoiakim is replaced by an action, commissioned by God: buy a linen loincloth (essentially an undergarment), wear it, and do not get it wet.

Jeremiah is then commanded to conceal the loincloth in Naḥal Perat, near Anathoth. He knows every nook and cranny of the area, having grown up there, and there he can evade the long arm of Jehoiakim's persecution.

Some have interpreted the journey to Naḥal Perat as Jeremiah's descending to Babylonia, and been bewildered by this. Why would God command Jeremiah to go to unfamiliar Babylonia twice within a short time – once to hide the loincloth and once to retrieve it? An example of the difficulties generated by this approach is found in the commentary of Rabbi David Kimḥi (Radak):

Regarding the loincloth: It is possible that it was real and that Jeremiah in fact did what God commanded. But the great, wise, righteous teacher Maimonides wrote that this all happened in a prophetic dream.... Regarding what [the Lord] said about going to Perat to hide it there: Since it is the border of the Land of Israel, He means to say that when they leave the Land of Israel for Babylonia, their pride will be destroyed [as is subsequently explained to Jeremiah]. (Radak on 13:1)

Radak considers whether Jeremiah was commanded to actually perform this act, or whether it was all a prophetic dream, as Maimonides claims:

Just as a man can dream that he is in another land, and has married a wife there, and stayed there for some time, had a son and called him such and such, and was in a certain condition, so too such prophetic symbols that are witnessed or enacted in a prophetic vision...; they are not real things that can be perceived by the senses of the body.... Jeremiah did not leave the Land of Israel, nor did he see the Euphrates. (*Guide for the Perplexed*, II:41)

Maimonides' explanation presumably stems from the notion that Jeremiah was commanded to go to Babylonia, which does not seem at all likely. Radak's interpretation, that Jeremiah dipped the loincloth in the waters of the Euphrates, as if they were standing at the borders of the Land of Israel, is also divorced from reality. According to both explanations, the loincloth should have been dipped in the waters of the Jordan, which has always been the border of the Land of Israel.

More likely, these verses refer to Naḥal Perat, the section of the Euphrates that ran past Anathoth and is more commonly known as Wadi Qelt or Ein Perat. This identification renders Maimonides' claim – that the act does not really take place – quite unnecessary. It appears that Jeremiah is commanded to perform a symbolic action in place of speech at this time of silence.

After hiding the loincloth in the cleft of a rock along the river, Jeremiah slips back into hiding. Between this act and its continuation, "many days" pass:

> Then after many days, the Lord said to me: Arise and go to Perat, and retrieve from there the loincloth I commanded you to hide. So I went to the Perat, and I dug, and I retrieved the loincloth from the place I had hidden it. It was ruined and useless.
> The word of the Lord came to me: Thus said the Lord: Thus shall I ruin the pride of Judah and the great pride of Jerusalem. (13:6–9)

The loincloth teaches Jeremiah a lesson about the destruction of Jerusalem and the Israelite kingdom. As he looks at the ruined undergarment, he understands God's word: "Thus shall I ruin the pride of Judah." This prophecy seems to be the source of Jeremiah's frustration with and lack of faith in Jeconiah, successor to Jehoiakim. It might well have taken place during the few days between Jehoiakim's death and Jeconiah's brief reign. With these strong feelings generated by the useless undergarment (symbolizing the king), Jeremiah returns to the public sphere and to a nation reeling from exile.

Why have these particular people been exiled to Babylonia? Did the Babylonian king and his officials choose them? Were they selected for some other reason? Was there anyone who wished to go but was unable to? We do not know. But the end of the winter and the following spring must have been hard to bear. The exiled king has left behind an empty treasury, a desecrated and vacant Temple, and has taken all the artisans and elite members of society with him. The people feel orphaned and rudderless. Jeremiah stands at the gate and watches. A terrible prophecy bursts from his lips:

> Say to the king and to the king's mother: Humble yourselves, come down, for your glorious crowns have fallen from your heads. (13:18)

Jeremiah is describing the exile of Judah. King Jeconiah and his mother, Nehushta, head the convoy of exile. The prophet calls after them,

"Humble yourselves": You have lost your status; recognize your humiliation. The queen mother, wife of Jehoiakim, no doubt hates Jeremiah.
He barely knows her young son, Jeconiah, but he wishes to remove the
crown from the king's head: "your glorious crowns have fallen from
your heads." Jeremiah describes what has befallen the land at the time
of their departure:

> The cities of the south have been shut up, and none open them;
> all of Judah has been exiled, completely carried away. (13:19)

The Babylonian conquerors have not stopped in northern Israel; they
have penetrated southward, toward Egypt. The cities of the Negev are
barricaded for fear of the enemy. "All of Judah has been exiled" – the
people of Judah have already been exiled; according to one plausible
hypothesis, there was an initial round of deportations from Judah even
prior to Jeconiah's exile. Chapter 52 describes the exile of 3,023 Judeans
during the seventh year of Nebuchadnezzar's reign. Perhaps the present
verse refers to that limited exile.

Later, Babylonia continues to prey upon Jerusalem, exiling the
highest echelons of society and government. This second phase of the
exile is already part of political negotiations and a more advanced stage
of Nebuchadnezzar's master plan for the Kingdom of Judah. It therefore
takes place later, during the eighth year of his reign. The phrase "all of
Judah has been exiled" indicates that this is an exile of Judah, not just
Jerusalem.[2]

Jeremiah surveys the despair of those around him: "And if you
ask yourself: 'Why is this happening to me?'" (13:22). He remembers the
worn-out loincloth he retrieved from Perat, which can no longer conceal
his nakedness. And then he answers the people's despairing question,
why is this happening to us? "Because of your many sins, your skirt has
been uncovered, your limbs laid bare" (ibid.). Your clothes no longer
cover you. Your robes, O Jerusalem, have been peeled away, revealing
your nakedness. With this sad declaration, Jeremiah concludes his prophetic use of the loincloth. He now relates that vision to Jehoiakim's

---

2. Based on Malamat, "Words of Jeremiah," in Luria, *Studies in Jeremiah* I, 18–19.

administration, under which both the king and his subjects let false prophets lull them into blissful oblivion about any impending evil. Jeremiah looks around, knowing the people have not changed; they still refuse to accept the word of God, bringing destruction ever closer:

> Can an African change his skin, or a leopard his spots? You as well, who are so habituated in evil – can you mend your ways? So I shall scatter them like straw upon the desert wind. This is your fate, your just deserts – declares the Lord – for you have forgotten Me and placed your trust in falsehood. So I will raise your skirt over your face, and your shame will be seen. I have seen your adulterous liaisons, your lustful neighings, your shameless whoring on the hills and in the field; I have seen your vileness; woe is you, Jerusalem; will you never become clean? How much longer? (13:23–27)

CHAPTER 22: A PROPHECY ABOUT JECONIAH –
A DESPISED, BROKEN VESSEL

The scenario is a challenging one for everybody. The king and his mother are marched at the head of the convoy, fallen from grace. Jeremiah meditates upon the convoy of exiles disappearing into the distance and recalls Jehoiakim's decadent palace, about which he prophesied: "Woe to him who builds his house with unfairness" (22:13). The prophet remembers the queen mother manipulating the cruel, callous regime, in which estrangement was the norm and might made right. He has no pity for the king and his mother:

> You who dwelled nestled among cedars as if in Lebanon, how you groan when chained, trembling like a woman in labor. (22:23)

Lebanon and its cedars signify the expensive construction materials with which Jehoiakim built his palace. Jeremiah detests the woman who sat in the lap of luxury until suddenly visited by terrible pains, as if in childbirth. He expresses his contempt as an oath in God's name:

> Upon My life – declares the Lord – even if you, King Coniah, son of Jehoiakim of Judah, were a signet ring on My right hand,

I would still pull you off. I will deliver you into the hands of those who want to kill you, the hands of those you fear, the hands of King Nebuchadnezzar of Babylonia, and the hands of the Chaldeans. I will hurl you and the mother who bore you into another land, where neither of you was born, and there you both will die. They will never come back to the land to which they long to return. (22:24–27)

Next Jeremiah ridicules the young King Jeconiah, calling him Coniah. While this may be simply a different form of the name (just as Hezekiah's name is sometimes written Jehezekiah), it may also be an insulting diminutive, intended to point out the exiled king's inexperience and lack of importance:

Is this man Coniah a despised, broken vessel, a vessel no one wants? Why were he and his children taken and hurled into a land they know not? (22:28)

"A despised, broken vessel" – Jeremiah refers to a pagan idol that is easily smashed. He concludes his prophecy with a curse:

O land, land, land, hear the word of the Lord. Thus says the Lord: Record this man as if he were childless, an impotent man, for his seed shall not be accepted to sit upon the throne of David or rule in Judah evermore. (22:29–30)

These are Jeremiah's parting words to the convoy departing for Babylon. Three generations later, King Cyrus of Persia will ascend to power and allow the Jews to return to their land. Heading the returnees will be Zerubbabel son of Shealtiel son of Jeconiah. It will be the days of Haggai the prophet, whose final words contradict those of Jeremiah:

On that day – declares the Lord of Hosts – I will take Zerubbabel son of Shealtiel My servant – declares the Lord – and make you as a signet, for I have chosen you – declares the Lord of Hosts. (Haggai 2:23)

597–586 BCE

Between Two Exiles

CHAPTER 24: THE VISION OF THE
GOOD FIGS AND THE BAD FIGS

Nebuchadnezzar has installed Mataniah, Josiah's youngest son, upon
the throne, renamed him Zedekiah, and sworn him to loyalty to Babylonia. Jeremiah hopes this will be the extent of the fulfillment of his first
prophecy, "From the north will disaster break loose" (1:14), for a storm
has indeed blown in from the north, stripped the land of its leaders and
upper classes, and appointed a king "after [Nebuchadnezzar's] own heart."
Perhaps the hard times are over, and it is now time to rebuild Jerusalem
under Babylonian patronage.

A few months later, however, Jeremiah understands that Judean
society has not changed. Whereas the exiled leaders had the capacity for
leadership, their replacements come from the dregs of society, seizing the
leadership vacuum as an opportunity to accumulate power. Violence and
aggression prevail as paupers become princes overnight. Might makes
right. King Zedekiah, young, weak, and bankrupt, cannot control the
situation. That summer, Jeremiah beholds a vision:

> The Lord showed me two baskets of figs, placed before the Lord's
> sanctuary, after King Nebuchadnezzar of Babylonia had exiled
> King Jeconiah son of Jehoiakim of Judah, the officials of Judah,
> the craftsmen, and the smiths from Jerusalem and brought them
> to Babylon. One basket contained very good figs, like the first
> figs to ripen, and the other contained very bad figs, so bad they
> were inedible. (24:1–2)

Jeremiah is blessed with a sharp eye and a thorough knowledge of nature. When he beheld an almond branch, a *shakeid*, he correctly interpreted that God was watching over, *shokeid*, the fulfillment of His words. When he saw the wind-blown tumbleweed tilting from the north, he knew that "From the north will disaster break loose." Now, as summer ends, he sees two baskets of figs. He contemplates their symbolism, and when asked what he sees, he focuses on the differences between them: "The good figs are very good, and the bad figs are so bad they are inedible" (24:3). God then explains the significance of this vision:

> Thus said the Lord, God of Israel: Like these good figs, I will look favorably upon the exiles of Judah whom I sent away from this place to the land of the Chaldeans. I will watch over them kindly, and I will bring them back to this land. I will build them up and not tear them down; I will plant them and not uproot them. I will give them the insight to know Me, that I am the Lord; they will be My people, and I will be their God, for they will return to Me with all their heart.
>
> But like the bad figs, which are so bad they are inedible – says the Lord – so will I deal with King Zedekiah of Judah, his officials, and the remnant of Jerusalem, whether they remain in this land or live in Egypt. I will make them abhorrent and an offense to all the kingdoms of the earth, a disgrace, an example, a byword, and a curse wherever I banish them. I will send the sword, famine, and plague against them until they are eliminated from the land I gave them and their ancestors. (24:5–10)

All at once, Jeremiah resumes his role as prophet of doom who cannot live in peace with his surroundings. He views the land's inhabitants as inedible "bad figs" and the new community in Babylonia – consisting of those same upper echelons of leadership he fought with during Jehoiakim's reign – as "good figs," Israel's only hope of salvation and renewal. Those left in the land will die in shame, but those in Babylonia will return seventy years later.

This is a new phase of Jeremiah's prophecy. He now understands that the exile of Jeconiah was but the precursor to a larger, more painful exile that is shortly to befall the inhabitants of the land. Jeremiah must help maintain Zedekiah's loyalty to Babylonia, in order to keep Nebuchadnezzar from destroying Jerusalem and the Temple. This becomes his final mission.

THE JEWS OF ISRAEL AND BABYLONIA
ACCORDING TO THE PROPHET EZEKIEL

After the exile of Jeconiah, the Jewish people live in two different centers.[1] The Babylonians recognize the stature of Jeconiah and his government-in-exile in Babylonia. Zedekiah, his uncle, is recognized as the king in Jerusalem. The two kings are similar in age: Jeconiah, Jehoiakim's eldest son, was born in 615 BCE and Mataniah/Zedekiah, Josiah's youngest son, in 618. Both were raised in the palace; they may even have been close to one another.

We glimpse what becomes of those exiled to Babylonia through the prophecies of Ezekiel, who walked the banks of the rivers of Babylonia at that time. In all likelihood, Ezekiel himself was exiled along with Jeconiah, especially as the prophet refers to *"our exile"* (Ezek. 39). Ezekiel's prophecies in Babylonia occur throughout the years of Zedekiah's reign in Jerusalem and beyond the destruction. Thus, combining the prophecies of Ezekiel and Jeremiah affords us a clearer picture of Jewish society in the two centers. Let us start with Ezekiel:

> And the word of the Lord came to me: Son of man, your brothers, your brethren, your next of kin, and all the House of Israel are they to whom the inhabitants of Jerusalem have said: "Stay far from the Lord; this land has been given to us as an inheritance." (Ezek. 11:14–15)

Usually, prophets repeat the word of God rather than that of His opponents. Yet Ezekiel's prophecy to his fellow Jews in Babylonia quotes the opposition, the Jews of Jerusalem. These people believe the God of Israel

---

1. This section was influenced entirely by Y. Elitzur's article "Two Prophets Versus Four Factions," in Elitzur, *Israel and Scripture*, 219–29, also available at http://www.daat.ac.il/elitzur/maamarim/shney.asp [Hebrew].

dwells only in the Land of Israel. Accordingly, closeness to God depends not on Israel's deeds, but rather on its location. Ezekiel, far from the land but close to God, rejects this belief and cites God's words:

> Say then: Thus said the Lord, God: Though I have distanced them among the nations, and though I have scattered them among the lands, I will be unto them a miniature sanctuary in the lands to which they have come. (11:16)

In Ezekiel 33, those remaining in the Land of Israel again claim its sole ownership:

> Son of man, those who dwell upon these ruins of the Land of Israel are saying: Abraham was but one man, and he inherited the land, and we are many, so the land has been given to us as an inheritance. (33:24)

This is the same claim, but this time those still living in the land wish to ride on the coattails of their forefather Abraham.

It is difficult to identify the speakers due to the opening phrase, "those who dwell upon these ruins." If they are already dwelling upon ruins – i.e., the destruction has already occurred – then what is the meaning of the prophecy that "those who are in the ruins shall fall by the sword" (33:27)? Haven't the people already been destroyed and exiled? If we accept Y. Kaufmann's reading in his *History of the Religion of Israel*, the prophecy about "those who dwell upon these ruins" preceded the actual destruction. The claim that "the land has been given to us as an inheritance" was made in the aftermath of Jeconiah's exile, by those who remained; they are called "those who dwell upon these ruins (*yoshvei haḥarevot*)" only to set up Ezekiel's next prophecy – "those who are in the ruins shall fall by the sword" (33:27).[2] This reading criticizes the people of Jerusalem who were not exiled; they claim an absolute and exclusive right to the land, not recognizing that this right depends entirely on their behavior. Aren't you ashamed, Ezekiel asks,

---

2. Kaufmann, *History of the Religion of Israel* III, 522.

to claim the land of God, when you have already turned it into a place of infamy?

> So say to them: Thus said the Lord, God: You consume blood, you lift your eyes toward your idols, and you shed blood – and yet you will inherit the land? (33:25)

Ezekiel lists a number of sins, combining pagan ritual with the social corruption spreading through Jerusalem despite Josiah's reforms. Just as Jeremiah imagines the exiled community in Babylonia without experiencing it firsthand, Ezekiel imagines Jerusalem as rife with all sorts of aggression – murder, abomination, lechery – and yet its inhabitants expect to inherit it.

Ezekiel also describes the Jews exiled to Babylonia, who strive to remain close to God. These people are represented in the first verse of chapter 20: "Some of Israel's elders came to inquire of the Lord." A careful reading of the entire chapter, which is a historiosophical statement, informs us that the Babylonian exiles want mainly to rebuild the Temple by the rivers of Babylon, a "Jerusalem of Nehardea." These Jews understand that a connection with God transcends geography. They believe the prophecies of their not returning home for a long time. Therefore, they wish to become entrenched in this foreign land until the end of the exile. Ezekiel also looks upon this group unkindly, answering its inquiry unequivocally:

> For only upon My holy mountain, the high mountain of Israel – declares the Lord, God – there in the land shall all of Israel serve Me; there shall I accept them, and there I shall require your offerings and the choicest gifts of all your holy sacrifices. Like a sweet fragrance I shall desire you when I extract you from the nations and gather you in from the lands where you have been scattered, and I shall be sanctified in the eyes of the nations through you. And you shall know that I am the Lord when I bring you to the soil of Israel, to the land I swore to your forefathers. (20:40–42)

Here, then, is Ezekiel's full picture – God cannot truly be served by the people of Jerusalem, who put their faith in mere sticks and stones, or by well-meaning Babylonian Jews, who wish to build a Temple outside the Promised Land. The Land of Israel is the sole Jewish homeland, but settling there guarantees nothing. "At His will He gave it to us, and at His will He took it from us and gave it to them."[3]

Thus far we have encountered two factions: one remaining in the Land of Israel, convinced of its security, and one entrenched in exile. Jeremiah's statements indicate yet another faction in Babylonia, one seeking to rebel against Nebuchadnezzar and end the exile.

CHAPTER 29: JEREMIAH'S LETTER
TO THE JEWS OF BABYLONIA

After Jeconiah's exile and Jerusalem's subjugation to Babylonia, King Zedekiah sends a delegation to Nebuchadnezzar. We do not know the nature of the mission Zedekiah delegates to Elasah son of Shaphan and Gemariah son of Hilkiah, his envoys. Jeremiah sends a message along with them to the leaders of the Jewish community in Babylonia:

> These are the words of the scroll that Jeremiah the prophet sent from Jerusalem to the elders of the exiles and to the priests and prophets and to all the people Nebuchadnezzar had exiled from Jerusalem to Babylonia – after the departure from Jerusalem of Jeconiah, the king's mother, the king's officials, the ministers of Judah and Jerusalem, the artisans, and the smiths – with Elasah son

---

3. This is a paraphrase of Rashi's first comment on the Torah, in which he explains why the Torah opens with stories of the patriarchs and not with the commandments:

> "He declared to His people the power of His deeds, to give them the inheritance of the nations" (Ps. 111:6). In case the nations of the world say, "You are thieves, for you have conquered a land not your own," [the Jews] can reply: "The whole world belongs to God. At His will He gave it to you, and at His will He took it from you and gave it to us."

Rashi's words have become a mantra for all who wish to prove the Jews' rightful ownership of the Land of Israel. But Rashi is saying the exact opposite. No nation has true rights to the land. The People of Israel are responsible for bringing God's word to His chosen land through their actions. As Ezekiel says, if their deeds are unworthy, "will you inherit the land?" (33:25). See D. Statman, "The Right to the Land," in P. Leiser and Z. Mazeh, eds., *Seeking Peace* (Tel Aviv, 2010), 236–47 [Hebrew].

of Shaphan and Gemariah son of Hilkiah, whom King Zedekiah of Judah had dispatched to King Nebuchadnezzar of Babylonia, to Babylonia. (29:1–3)

The contents of the letter appear after this lengthy introduction. The epistle is no less than a full-length, precise description of the life God expects His people to lead in exile: They should live normal lives, raise families, work the land, and, above all, inquire about and pray for their hometown: "for its well-being shall guarantee your well-being" (29:7). Thus far, Jeremiah's words are constructive, positive. Then he criticizes the prophets in Babylonia, who have been stirring up the people with contravening prophecies:

> For thus said the Lord of Hosts, God of Israel: Do not let the prophets and diviners in your midst deceive you, and do not listen to the dreams you dream. For they prophesy to you falsely in My name; I have not sent them – declares the Lord…. So hear the word of the Lord, all you exiles whom I have cast out of Jerusalem to Babylonia: Thus said the Lord of Hosts, God of Israel, about Ahab son of Kolaiah and Zedekiah son of Maaseiah, who prophesy lies to you in My name: I will deliver them into the hands of King Nebuchadnezzar of Babylonia, and he will put them to death in your presence. All the Judean exiles in Babylonia will use them as a curse: "May the Lord treat you like Zedekiah and Ahab, whom the King of Babylonia roasted in fire." For they have done outrageous things in Israel; they have committed adultery with their neighbors' wives, and in My name they have uttered lies, which I did not authorize; I know it and am a witness to it – declares the Lord. (29:8–9, 20–23)

Jeremiah names the false prophets who compete with him in shaping public opinion – Ahab son of Kolaiah and Zedekiah son of Maaseiah – and who agitate for immediate return to the Land of Israel. Evidently Jeremiah assesses their impact as significant, as he takes drastic measures to turn them into a curse among the exiles. He also accuses them of adultery, but this accusation is certainly based on rumors rather than on Jeremiah's direct knowledge.

Let us now attempt to understand the situation from the perspective of Jeremiah's disputants. Instead of reading the official organ of the "Babylonian Accommodation Party," headed by Jeremiah, let us read an editorial by the "Land of Israel Loyalist Party," chaired by Ahab and Zedekiah. These patriotic prophets cannot reconcile themselves to seventy years of exile. They want to return to Zion at all costs and cannot fathom the notion of living, marrying, raising families, or farming in an alien, impure country. Without the Land of Israel, they argue, life is not worth living. Their heroes are Caleb and Joshua, who resisted the defeatism of the other spies and insisted that the Israelites could conquer the Promised Land, and whose motto was "Let us go up at once… for we are well able to overcome it" (Num. 13:30).

When Jeremiah calls on these prophets to get used to Babylonian life, their opposition becomes more entrenched. They would rather die in the king's furnaces than live on his soil! This party has already generated a considerable following and established ties back home. When Jeremiah's letter arrives, urging accommodation, Shemaiah the Nehelamite, a leader of this faction, hastily dispatches a sharply worded complaint to the wardens of law and order in the Temple. Jeremiah offers evidence of this complaint:

> Tell Shemaiah the Nehelamite: Thus said the Lord of Hosts, God of Israel: Because you sent letters in your own name to all the people in Jerusalem, to the priest Zephaniah son of Maaseiah, and to all the other priests, saying: "The Lord has appointed you priest in place of the priest Jehoiada, to be in charge at the House of the Lord of every prophesying maniac, to put him into stocks and neck irons. So why have you not reprimanded Jeremiah of Anathoth, who poses as a prophet among you? He has sent this message to us in Babylonia: It will be a long time – build houses and settle down; plant gardens and eat their produce." (29:24–28)

Shemaiah's message to the priest in charge of the Temple is scathing. The sender is clearly convinced that the recipient is on his side. In fact, he cannot imagine anyone in Jerusalem (aside from the crazy prophet from Anathoth, of course) exhorting the exiled Jews to grow accustomed to Babylonia; it flies in the face of all logic, all morality, all faith – everything! A people in exile must constantly renew its passion for its homeland and not let defeatists weaken it.

Shemaiah is obviously well-known, for the priest indeed summons Jeremiah to a hearing about the letter he has sent: "And Zephaniah the priest read the letter to Jeremiah the prophet" (29:29). Jeremiah immediately responds to Shemaiah with a terrible prophetic curse:

> The word of the Lord came to Jeremiah: Send this message to all the exiles: This is what the Lord says about Shemaiah the Nehelamite: Because Shemaiah has prophesied to you, though I did not send him, and has persuaded you to trust in lies, thus said the Lord: I will certainly punish Shemaiah the Nehelamite and his descendants; he will have no one left among this people, nor will he see the good I will do for My people – declares the Lord – because he has preached rebellion against the Lord. (29:30–32)

The picture that emerges from this correspondence is clear: Those who live in Jerusalem toe the party line that "this land is ours." Whoever remains in the land is protected by God; nothing can change this formula.

This stance has a strong following in Babylonia as well. The faction led by Shemaiah, Ahab, and Zedekiah has stirred up anti-Babylonian unrest. The King of Babylonia has become aware of these movements and has begun liquidating their leadership.

Yet Jeremiah remains worried. He continues to condemn this movement, but his is a hard prophecy to accept; it is not easy to convince a people that its promised inheritance will be given to foreigners for seventy years.

Where does King Zedekiah stand in this dispute? At the start of his reign, he certainly is not so bold as to defy his Babylonian patron. But as the months pass, with the King of Babylonia focused on his own kingdom, Zedekiah begins listening to those around him, urging him to shed the Babylonian yoke again.

CHAPTER 27: 594 BCE –
A SUMMIT OF REGIONAL RULERS

Chapter 27 opens with "At the beginning of the reign of Jehoiakim son of Josiah," but it is clear to anyone who reads the chapter in context that the name "Jehoiakim" should be emended to "Zedekiah." The content of the chapter undoubtedly reflects the beginning of Zedekiah's reign, and more precisely, his fourth year on the throne.[4]

During this year, a summit is held in Judah for representatives of (almost) all of the nations in the area – Edom, Moab, Ammon, Tyre, and Sidon. It is not difficult to guess the main topic of the meeting. It is a tense time. Babylonia has finally returned to the north, and Egypt is trying to mount a comeback and tempt the surrounding nations into a coalition against Nebuchadnezzar. The gathering is held in an attempt to formulate a strategic consensus of the nations in the region. No representatives from Syria are present, as it is still under Babylonian rule.

Jeremiah, that rustic prophet, stages a production before the assembled. He places five yokes – the kind used to drive animals as they work the field – around his neck. As the leaders gather in Jerusalem, he sends them the yokes, thereby delivering his prophetic message: Submit to the yoke of Babylonian leadership. A prophecy accompanies his "gifts":

> Thus said the Lord to me: Make for yourself yokes and bars, and bear them upon your neck. And you shall send them to the King of Edom, the King of Moab, the King of the Ammonites, the King of Tyre, and the King of Sidon via the envoys who have come to Jerusalem, to King Zedekiah of Judah. Order them to tell their masters: Thus said the Lord of Hosts, God of Israel – thus you shall say to your masters: I created the earth, and man and beast

---

4. Traditional exegetes do not address this issue, since they deal not with the milieus of the prophets, only with the general lessons of their prophecies. In the *Daat Mikra* commentary on the Book of Jeremiah, M. Bolle engages in apologetics to avoid amending Scripture. He claims that "it appears that this prophecy was said twice… but appears in the Book of Jeremiah only once." Y. Hoffman shows (in *Jeremiah*) that in the Septuagint this chapter has no introductory verse at all, and the title it eventually received resulted from its proximity to the previous chapter, which (correctly) opens at the beginning of Jehoiakim's reign.

upon the earth, with My great strength and outstretched arm, and I gave it to him whom I deem proper. And now I have given of these lands to My servant King Nebuchadnezzar of Babylonia; I have also given him mastery over the beasts of the field. All the nations shall serve him, his son, and his grandson, until the time comes for his own land, and then many nations and great kings shall make him serve. (27:2–7)

Jeremiah keeps returning to his most deeply held principles: God controls geopolitics, and He has chosen Nebuchadnezzar to rule the world at this time. This decision cannot be revoked, and anyone who rebels against it is in fact rebelling against God. As long as Zedekiah was isolated in Judah, Jeremiah was relatively calm; the king would not dare rebel. But now, as representatives of the neighboring nations urge Zedekiah to form an Egypt-led alliance, and the patriotic faction within the Temple and in Babylonia agitate to throw off the Babylonian yoke, Jeremiah again endeavors to prevent this tragic mistake. He does not stop at declarations of God's will, but cautions the nations in general, and the King of Judah in particular:

> Any nation or kingdom that does not serve King Nebuchadnezzar of Babylonia and bow its neck under the Babylonian king's yoke, I will punish that nation with the sword, famine, and plague – declares the Lord – until I destroy it by his hand. So do not listen to your prophets, diviners, interpreters of dreams, mediums, or sorcerers who tell you: "Do not serve the king of Babylonia." They prophesy lies to you, which will only remove you far from your lands; I will banish you, and you will perish. (27:8–10)

It seems that the exiled Jews are not the only ones with prophets calling for rebellion against Babylon. Every nation has its prophets. The emerging regional political consensus is not to remain subject to the King of Babylonia. This is no fringe phenomenon, but the conventional wisdom of pundits throughout the area.

This approach seems logical enough. After all, Egypt has a strong foothold in the region and is entrenched in its own land. Babylonia has all the trappings of a flash in the pan whose dominance will end as quickly as it began. Only the most venerable kingdoms can survive the era. So the best bet is to gather under Egypt's banner once again.

Jeremiah continues screaming at the King of Judah, the priests, the people – at anyone and everyone: Do not listen to those who claim they speak the word of God – they are lying! His repetition of the same messages indicates the depth of his distress. He rails against the zeitgeist and the conventional wisdom. He repeatedly uses the phrase "declares the Lord" to convince his audience that all his statements are the literal word of God. But this tactic only underscores his powerlessness in the face of statements by other prophets, who complacently call on their kings to depend on Egypt.

Jeremiah's desperation knows no bounds. He sees Jerusalem, its people, and the Temple teetering on the edge of the abyss – and for no reason. He is certain that whoever remains loyal to Nebuchadnezzar will survive in his land, and that whoever rebels will be exiled and executed. Cursed with this knowledge, a heartrending cry bursts from his lips:

> Serve the King of Babylonia and live! Why should this city be destroyed?! (27:17)

CHAPTER 28: CONFLICT BETWEEN TWO PROPHETS

Jeremiah tries to spread his word to every corner of Jerusalem. He wanders around the city with a yoke on his neck like an oversized necklace. Everybody already knows what he has to say. He calls out again and again: "Serve the King of Babylonia and live!" But by now public opinion has been won over by Egypt's reemergence as a power. Babylonia may come and go, but the Nile will flow forever. This is the refrain throughout Judah. Many prophets prophesied in Jerusalem, all agreeing with the party line, which demands that Judah free itself from the Babylonian yoke. The nationalist Jews of Babylonia grow stronger, inspiring hope. Jeremiah is alone against the world, holding fast to his prophetic message. He has no doubts about the veracity of his prophecy – until an unfortunate encounter in the Temple.

In the fifth month of that same year, the fourth year, early in the reign of King Zedekiah of Judah, the prophet Hananiah son of Azzur of Gibeon said to me in the House of the Lord, in the presence of the priests and all the people: Thus said the Lord of Hosts, God of Israel: I have broken the yoke of the King of Babylonia. In another two years I will bring back to this place all the articles of the Lord's house that King Nebuchadnezzar of Babylonia removed from here and took to Babylonia. I will bring back to this place King Jeconiah son of Jehoiakim of Judah and the entire Judean exile to Babylonia – declares the Lord – for I will break the yoke of the King of Babylonia. (28:1–4)

As Hananiah begins his oration, Jeremiah recognizes that this is no ordinary foe. Not only is his style identical to Jeremiah's – anyone can do that – something else about this speech throws Jeremiah into a tizzy: This man has taken a risk by setting a deadline for his prophecy's fulfillment. This is not the typical sedative offered by the garden-variety sycophantic prophets to lull the people to sleep. This time, a prophet has dared to stand by the Temple and announce that in just two years King Jeconiah will return from exile with the looted articles of the Temple. Hananiah is essentially telling the reigning king to start packing his bags. Babylonia's days are numbered – two years are but the blink of an eye.

Jeremiah seeks God's answer to this challenge and tries to discern how to respond to this prophet, but he cannot find the words. With no better option, he responds meekly:

Jeremiah the prophet said to Hananiah the prophet in the presence of the priests and all the people assembled at the House of the Lord. And Jeremiah the prophet said: Amen, may the Lord fulfill the words of your prophecy to return the vessels of the House of the Lord and the entire Babylonian exile to this place. (28:5–6)

This is an obvious mistake on Jeremiah's part. An important rule in public debate is never to concede your opponent's claim. As soon as Jeremiah utters the word "amen," he exposes his lack of confidence. Hananiah speaks confidently, while Jeremiah speaks hesitantly. Hananiah therefore emerges as the victor in the eyes of the priests, the people, and perhaps even in Jeremiah's own eyes. Jeremiah's despondency intensifies, and he attempts to clarify, for his audience and for himself, how to decide between the two prophecies. Is it even possible to determine which of these men speaks the truth, and which is delusional?

The Torah provides a simple device for distinguishing between true and false prophets:

> You may say to yourself: How shall we know the word that the Lord has not spoken? If what a prophet proclaims in the name of the Lord does not take place or come true, that is a message the Lord has not spoken; that prophet has spoken presumptuously, so do not fear him. (Deut. 18:21–22)

According to the Torah, sometimes there is no choice but to wait and see. As long as an alleged prophecy is not idolatrous, a prophet's credibility cannot be known until his words are borne out. Furthermore, even true prophecy can go unfulfilled. Prophecies of doom against Israel (or even the whole world) can be overturned by God's mercy. This is precisely why Jonah tried to evade prophesying to Nineveh.

Perhaps this is the source of Jeremiah's anxiety in his debate with Hananiah: You, Hananiah, claim that in two years, Babylonia will fall and peace will prevail in the world. On the other hand, I say that if we rebel, there will be complete destruction. If you speak the truth, your prophecy must come true, because it is positive, whereas mine, a prophecy of doom, may or may not come true if God wishes to show mercy to His people. Jeremiah expresses this dilemma thus:

> Nevertheless, listen to what I have to say to you and all the people: The prophets of old who preceded you and me have prophesied war, disaster, and plague against many countries and great kingdoms. But the prophet who prophesies peace will be recognized as one truly sent by the Lord only if his prediction comes true. (28:7–8)

There is nothing to do but wait and see, claims Jeremiah. Hananiah, however, claims victory, and in a dramatic climax to their debate, he intervenes in Jeremiah's prophetic presentation:

> Hananiah the prophet removed the yoke from around Jeremiah the prophet's neck and broke it. And Hananiah said in the presence of all the people: Thus said the Lord: So shall I break the yoke of King Nebuchadnezzar of Babylonia, in two years, from around the necks of all the nations. So Jeremiah the prophet went on his way. (28:10–11)

This is a knockout blow. Jeremiah leaves the ring completely defeated, with a broken yoke and a broken heart. All his prophecies have been undermined. His wordless departure speaks volumes to the crowd.

Hananiah's prophecy offers a fascinating case study. The talmudic rabbis consider that he may have been a true prophet:

> One who prophesies that which he did not hear, like Zedekiah son of Kenaana, and one who prophesies what was not said to him, like Hananiah son of Azzur, who would hear things from Jeremiah the prophet as he prophesied in the upper market, and then go and repeat his words in the lower market. (Tosefta, Sanhedrin 14:4)

The rabbis attempt to define a false prophet. A mishna in Sanhedrin asserts that some prophets are put on trial for their prophecy: one who invents a prophecy without having actually received it, and one who prophesies what another prophet heard. An example of the first category is Zedekiah son of Kenaana, who stages a prophetic performance in the presence of the kings of Israel and Judah before they battle Edom. As an example of the second category, the rabbis offer Hananiah son of Azzur, "who would hear things from Jeremiah the prophet as he prophesied in the upper market, and then go and repeat his words in the lower market." How can this be? Jeremiah uttered the exact opposite of Hananiah's prediction! This contradiction is addressed in the Talmud itself:

Jeremiah stood in the upper market and said: "Thus says the Lord of Hosts: Behold, I shall break the bow of Elam" [49:35]. Hananiah reasoned *a fortiori*: If concerning Elam, which merely assisted Babylonia, God said: "Behold, I shall break the bow of Elam," then it should certainly be true of the Chaldeans! He went to the lower market and said: "Thus said the Lord of Hosts…I will break the yoke of the King of Babylonia."

R. Papa said to Abbaye: Didn't he repeat this prophecy to his colleague [i.e., Jeremiah]?

Abbaye responded: Since Hananiah deduced this conclusion logically, it was as if Jeremiah had said these words. (Sanhedrin 89a)

Evidently, the rabbis felt that Hananiah's words had some substance. The rebellion against Babylonia was not absurd; there was much logic in it.

After Jeremiah leaves the Temple and goes on his way, riddled with self-doubt, he receives another divine vision, instructing him to encounter Hananiah once more. This meeting takes place not in public, but in private:

Go tell Hananiah: Thus said the Lord: You have broken wooden bars, but in its place you have made iron bars. For thus said the Lord of Hosts, God of Israel: I will place an iron yoke on the necks of all these nations, to make them serve King Nebuchadnezzar of Babylonia, and they will serve him; I have even given him mastery over the wild beasts. Then the prophet Jeremiah said to the prophet Hananiah: Listen, Hananiah! The Lord has not sent you, yet you have persuaded this nation to trust in lies. Therefore, thus said the Lord: I shall cast you off the face of the earth – this year you will die, because you have preached rebellion against the Lord. In the seventh month of that year, Hananiah the prophet died. (28:13–17)

No one else heard Jeremiah's curse. Though Hananiah indeed died, his prophecy did not die with him, and the people still believed in it. Hananiah probably died a hero's death, meriting an honorable burial.

CHAPTER 14: JEREMIAH'S DOUBTS REGARDING FALSE PROPHETS

Both Jerusalem and Babylonia swarm with prophets who shape public opinion. Their prophecies do not foretell the future, nor can they be easily authenticated. They are pundits and prognosticators, blessed with a crystal-clear view of the world and attempting to convince their audiences to think likewise. In the media today, commentators often interpret the same data in diametrically opposite ways. The prophet, however, experiences his prophecy from within – there is no real distinction between his logic or emotions and his prophetic inner voice.

Constantly clashing with opposing prophets, Jeremiah tries to define true prophecy, which emanates from God. When he parts from Hananiah, his heart is broken – there are indeed prophets of stature calling for a course of action at odds with what Jeremiah has been suggesting. He feels lost and misguided, unable to determine who is right. In chapter 14, he lashes out at God, apparently after his defeat in his debate with Hananiah:

> But I said: Alas, Sovereign Lord! The prophets keep telling them: You will not see the sword or suffer famine; indeed, I will give you lasting peace in this place.
>
> Then the Lord said to me: The prophets are prophesying lies in My name; I have not sent them or ordered them or spoken to them; they prophesy to you false visions, divinations, idolatries, and the delusions of their own minds.
>
> Therefore, thus said the Lord: Concerning the prophets who prophesy in My name, and I did not send them; who say: No sword or famine will touch this land – those very prophets will perish by sword and famine. (14:13–15)

In his pain, Jeremiah tells God of the prophets who call for rebellion against Babylonia, and God responds that their words are false. Of course, this is what Jeremiah himself shouts out from morning to night, but the constant grating of their words has taken its toll on the true prophet. He is plagued with self-doubt.

Babylonia Raids Judah

POLITICAL BACKGROUND

The summit of the nations of the region, as noted, gravely deliberates the question of allegiance to Egypt or Babylonia. It is clear to everyone that the situation suggests a pro-Egyptian and anti-Babylonian policy. The summit takes place in 594 BCE. Two years later, an event transpires that creates a favorable climate for this shift in policy. Psammetichus II, King of Egypt, dies and is succeeded by his son Apries. The new king's goal is to restore Egyptian glory after the Babylonian debacle. His charisma reinvigorates the region, the coalition allies with Egypt, and the Judean rebellion against Babylonia finally breaks out.

Nebuchadnezzar takes his time before embarking on his campaign to quell and punish. The rebellion of a vassal state against its empire is not the same as the taking up of arms against an occupying force (as in the Hasmonean and Bar Kokhba revolts, for example). In this case, the rebellion takes the form of the vassal state's refusal to pay its annual dues. At first it may seem like a mere delay, but eventually it becomes clear that the vassal has risen up against the empire. For the Babylonians, such a move is unforgivable. A delegation had previously been sent to restore order during the brief reign of Jeconiah. The exile of Jeconiah and Zedekiah's installation on the throne were designed to ensure that the leader of Judah was not of the rebellious type. Apparently, this was not enough; more drastic measures are necessary.

In 588 BCE, Nebuchadnezzar launches a punitive campaign against Judah. The course of the campaign has not been recorded, but snippets from Scripture and archaeology can help us piece together the events.

As in most long-distance campaigns, Nebuchadnezzar takes a roundabout route to Judah. He sets out from his encampment at Riblah in Syria, passing through Lebanon and then sailing to Ashkelon, a city he conquered in 605 BCE. Judah has prepared for military engagement by building fortifications and outposts in the area around Lachish, west of Jerusalem. History had taught the rulers of Judah that even northern enemies usually travel by sea and ascend to Jerusalem through the cities of the Shephelah. The first fortified cities the enemy will encounter are Azekah and Lachish. The Babylonians advance at full strength, apparently crushing everything in their path. The inhabitants of Judah and Jerusalem huddle together in their fortifications, knowing deep down that they don't stand a chance. According to Jewish tradition, the siege begins on the tenth of Tevet in the ninth year of Zedekiah's reign (588 BCE). King Zedekiah and his men still hope Egypt will rise to their assistance, and they send delegations asking for help. After all, they are part of a coalition built around the new Egyptian king, Apries.

The Babylonian army advances rapidly toward Jerusalem. The city elders still recall their grandparents' tales of the horrific invasion of Sennacherib, just over a century earlier (701 BCE). History seems to be repeating itself, but with Babylonia replacing Assyria, Nebuchadnezzar replacing Sennacherib, Zedekiah replacing Hezekiah, and Jeremiah replacing Isaiah. The names are different, but the story is the same.

Then, just before all is lost, they hear the news – an entire Egyptian army is sailing to Tyre. The Egyptians have declared war and opened a northern front against Babylonia. Nebuchadnezzar's army has no choice but to defend itself; his forces leave the Judean front and head toward Tyre. For several months, battle rages between Babylonia and Egypt, and there is a lull in Judah. The people hope God has answered their prayers and removed the enemy from Jerusalem, just as He answered them in the days of Hezekiah and Sennacherib.

But their hope is short-lived. A few months later, on the tenth of Tevet, the siege of Jerusalem begins. This time, the objective is clear: to lock down the city and let its people wither away. The siege is impenetrable and inescapable.

THE DESCRIPTION IN THE BOOK OF KINGS

> In the ninth year of his reign, in the tenth month, on the tenth
> day, King Nebuchadnezzar of Babylon and all his army came to
> Jerusalem, encamped upon it, and built towers around it. The
> city was besieged until the eleventh year of King Zedekiah's reign.
> (II Kings 25:1–2)

This is the traditional description, in which the siege lasts a year and a
half, until the month of Tammuz, 586 BCE. The author of Kings makes
no mention of the lull while Babylonia deals with Egypt in the north.
Rather, the siege is mentioned generally, as a precursor to the destruction.

CHAPTER 37: THE KING'S FIRST
APPEAL TO THE PROPHET

> King Zedekiah sent Jehucal son of Shelemiah and Zephaniah son
> of Maaseiah the priest to Jeremiah the prophet, saying: Please
> pray for us to the Lord, our God. (37:3)

The situation is rough. Jerusalem trembles as the Babylonians approach.
It has no chance of surviving against this mighty empire. All the prophets
from the school of Hananiah son of Azzur, who promised and prophesied the impending fall of Babylonia, are struck dumb and flee underground. No one imagined that the prophecies of Jeremiah, of all people,
would come to fruition. Rumors of the fall of the cities of the Shephelah
have reached Jerusalem, leaving it in turmoil. The elders of the city, the
Temple priests, and the rest of the people gather to fast and pray, in the
best Jewish tradition.

As if the frightening political situation were not enough, God
has turned the heavens to iron; there has been no rain for two winters.
Cisterns run dry, and the city's water supply is depleted. It is clear to all
that only God's mercy can bring relief.

King Zedekiah, Josiah's youngest son, was raised on his father's
righteous knees. He knows that the Torah's promises of peace and

prosperity depend on obedience to God. Following in his father's footsteps, he has forbidden all foreign worship in Jerusalem. At this point, he makes a decision. He sends delegates to Jeremiah, inviting him to lead a communal prayer for God's mercy. This invitation recalls Zedekiah's great-grandfather Hezekiah's invitation to Isaiah for similar purposes before the fearful invasion of the Assyrian king Sennacherib in 701 BCE:

> [Hezekiah] sent Eliakim, who was in charge of the palace, Shebna the scribe, and the elders of the priests, covered in sackcloth, to Isaiah son of Amoz. They said to him: Thus said Hezekiah: This day is a day of strife and rebuke and disgrace, as when children are about to be born but there is no strength to deliver them. Perhaps the Lord, your God, will hear all the words of Rab-shaken, sent by his master, the Assyrian king, to blaspheme the living God, and will punish him for his words that the Lord, your God, has heard – O pray for the remnant who is left! (11 Kings 19:2–4)

For years, Isaiah had been locked in an ideological struggle against Hezekiah. Although Hezekiah was a righteous king, he did not heed the prophet's warnings to refrain from political involvement with foreign empires. When Assyria invaded Judah, destroyed entire cities, and stood on Jerusalem's doorstep, Hezekiah begged Isaiah – whose prophecies were sadly proven right – to pray on the city's behalf. The Book of Kings describes the poignancy and intensity of the king's and the prophet's combined prayers, and the miracle that immediately followed – Assyria's hasty retreat in a single night.

Now, 112 years later, Zedekiah hopes to reenact that course of events. He calls to Jeremiah and asks him to pray on their behalf. He sends two clerks, one from the palace and one from the Temple. He is convinced that because Jeremiah is a true prophet, faithful to his God and devoted to his people, he will not stand by idly, but will join them in their desperate supplications.

CHAPTER 14: THE DROUGHT –
GOD SILENCES JEREMIAH'S PRAYERS

> Over these I weep, my eyes, my eyes stream with water
> For far from me is the comforter, restorer of my spirit
> My children are forlorn, for the enemy has prevailed. (Lam. 1:16)

The king's plea to Jeremiah does not come out of nowhere. All of Jerusalem stands in prayer. The memory of centuries of supplication to God in times of crisis is seared into the national consciousness. Joshua son of Nun prostrated himself before God after the defeat at Ai (Joshua 7); all the tribes of Israel ascended to Bethel to weep and pray after falling into the hands of the Benjaminites (Judges 20); Samuel cried out to God on Israel's behalf before battle with the Philistines (1 Sam. 7); King Solomon prayed and designated the Temple as a center for prayer in times of distress, that Israel may "pray to You and petition You in this house" (1 Kings 8:33). And during Jehoiakim's reign, we saw how the people gathered for a fast at the Temple in the dead of winter. That was immediately after the Babylonians had conquered Ashkelon in 605 BCE, and Jeremiah had seized the moment and enlisted Baruch the scribe to read aloud the scroll of his prophecies, in an attempt to appeal to the people (Jer. 36).

Now, fifteen years later, the nation stands on the brink of even worse disaster. The Babylonians are marching toward Jerusalem, and nothing can stand in their way. Where is Jeremiah? Chapter 14 contains Jeremiah's dialogue with God about the droughts He has brought upon Judah. At first glance, this chapter could be taken from almost any prophetic work; in the Land of Israel, every generation suffers a drought at one time or another. Such is the uniqueness of Israel's climate. Man's dependence on rain creates an awareness of the connection between heaven and earth.[1] But reading between the lines of this chapter yields

---

1. For further discussion, see my book *Etnaḥta: Readings of the Weekly Portion* (Tel Aviv, 5769), 445–48 [Hebrew].

hints that its events occurred precisely on the eve of the Babylonian invasion of Jerusalem:[2]

> The word of the Lord that came to Jeremiah concerning the droughts: Judah mourns; her gates languish in gloom to the ground, and a cry rises from Jerusalem. The nobles send their servants for water; they go to the cisterns but find no water; they return with their vessels unfilled; dismayed and despairing, they cover their heads. The ground is cracked because there is no rain in the land; the farmers are dismayed and cover their heads. Even the doe in the field deserts her newborn fawn because there is no grass. Wild donkeys stand on the barren heights and pant like jackals; their eyes fail for lack of grass. (14:1–6)

The verses poetically describe a drought at the frontier of the desert, from the perspective of someone deeply connected to nature. The prophet sees the youngsters sent by their elders to bring water, only to return empty-handed; he sees the plight of the farmers; he sees the does abandoning their fawns and wild asses panting like wild dogs. The whole world pines for rain.[3]

The next passage contextualizes this particular drought. The nation fears that God has abandoned the land:

> Although our sins testify against us, do something, O Lord, for the sake of Your name, for we have often rebelled; we have sinned against You. O Hope of Israel, its Savior in times of distress, why are You like a stranger in the land, like a traveler who stays only a night? Why are You like a paralyzed man, like a warrior power-

---

2. This reading of the chapter, including the possibility that it deals with the events immediately prior to the Babylonian invasion, is based on B. Oppenheimer's article "On Matters of the Drought," *Hagut BaMikra* 5 (5748): 33–51 [Hebrew].
3. An extensive description of all the phenomena of a drought as seen through the eyes of a naturalist can be found in Hareuveni, *New Light*.

less to save? You are among us, O Lord, and we bear Your name;
do not forsake us! (14:7–9)

This is one of the earliest, clearest examples of a traditional Jewish fast-
day prayer. Jeremiah, it seems, does not compose the prayer as much as
draw it from the lips of the people themselves. It begins with a confes-
sion of sin: "our sins testify against us … we have sinned against You," but
quickly moves on to supplication: "why are You like a stranger?" The
people express their insecurity about their future in the land, saying
perhaps: If we are Your people, and we trust in You, how can You allow
another people, worshippers of other gods, to take control of our land?
How can You, Master of the land, be like a traveler passing through?

Until now, the Judeans have believed that God dwells in Zion.
This conviction has given them a sense of security that the land is their
birthright. The sound of Nebuchadnezzar's thundering horses has
shaken this foundation. The worshippers conclude with a declaration
of loyalty to God: "You are among us, O Lord, and we bear Your name;
do not forsake us!"

Initially, God rejects the people's supplication:

> Thus said the Lord to this people: They greatly love to wander;
> they do not restrain their feet; so the Lord does not accept them;
> He will now remember their wickedness and punish them for
> their sins. (14:10)

The expression "to this people" indicates that God is not inclined to
answer their prayers or respond to their tears. They are a rash people –
now they indeed scurry to the Temple to pray, but later they are liable
to run to worship other gods. God's short, sharp rejection amounts to
the fact that "the Lord does not accept them."

This concludes the first part of the public prayer and God's reply.
Then comes a dispute between the prophet and God:

> Then the Lord said to me: Do not pray on behalf of this people.
> Though they fast, I do not hear their cry; though they offer burnt

offerings and grain offerings, I do not want them; rather, I will destroy them with sword, famine, and plague. (14:11–12)

The prophet hears the final verdict: "Do not pray on behalf of this people." But like Moses, who prostrates himself before the Lord after the sin of the Golden Calf, and like all the prophets of Israel, who suffered the shame of their people's iniquities, Jeremiah struggles against God's decree not to pray:

> But I said: Alas, Sovereign Lord! The prophets keep telling them: You will not see the sword or suffer famine; indeed, I will give you lasting peace in this place. (14:13)

Jeremiah attempts to defend his people. For years, prophets such as Hananiah son of Azzur force-fed them the line that God "will give lasting peace in this place." Such claims would never have been made during the reigns of Josiah or even Jehoiakim. Only in the days of Zedekiah was Jeremiah forced to confront prophets who fomented an anti-Babylonian platform. They lulled the people to sleep with worthless promises like "You will not see the sword or suffer famine." The people are not at fault, protests Jeremiah. Blame lies on those prophets who have been feeding them lies!

But God is not appeased. Though He concedes that the prophets are at fault, the people still have free choice:

> Then the Lord said to me: The prophets are prophesying lies in My name; I have not sent them or ordered them or spoken to them; they prophesy to you false visions, divinations, idolatries, and the delusions of their own minds.
>
> Therefore, thus said the Lord: Concerning the prophets who prophesy in My name, and I did not send them; who say: No sword or famine will touch this land – those very prophets will perish by sword and famine. And the people to whom they are prophesying will be thrown out into the streets of Jerusalem because of the famine and sword – there will be none to bury

them, their wives, their sons, and their daughters – for I will pour their evil upon them. (14:14–16)

This is unprecedented in the Bible. The prophet beseeches God as the people's defender, yet God refuses to hear him. The prophet fails. The gates of mercy remain impenetrable. Death stands at the door. Jeremiah envisions the city's near future, and it breaks his heart:

Say this to them: Let my eyes overflow with tears night and day without ceasing; for the virgin daughter of my people has suffered a grievous wound, a crushing blow. If I go into the country, I see those slain by the sword; and if I go into the city, I see the ravages of famine – both prophet and priest wander the land but do not know it. (14:17–18)

Jeremiah is grimly accurate – the battle is not in the city, but in the open areas of the Shephelah foothills. Inside Jerusalem, the people hunger for food and thirst for water. The siege has not yet fallen upon the city, but the wells have already dried up, and new crops have not sprouted in the field. The prophet cries out to God:

Have You rejected Judah completely? Do You revile Zion? Why have You afflicted us incurably? We hoped for peace, but no good has come; for a time of healing, but there is only terror. We acknowledge our wickedness, O Lord, and the guilt of our ancestors; we have indeed sinned against You. For the sake of Your name, do not despise us; do not dishonor Your glorious throne; remember Your covenant with us, and do not abrogate it. Can any of the worthless gods of the nations bring rain? Do the skies themselves send down showers? No, it is You, O Lord, our God, so we hope in You, for You do all this. (14:19–22)

Jeremiah accuses God of annulling His covenant. In the terrible curses of Leviticus, God limits the curse He will visit upon the land should Israel sin:

Yet, despite all this, when they are in enemy territory, I shall not
reject them or revile them so as to wipe them out, breaching My
covenant with them. (Lev. 26:44)

God clearly states the conditions of His covenant: I shall not reject them
or revile them. I may grow angry, punish, become furious, and exile –
but I shall never break the covenant. God has promised never to wipe
His people out. Now, facing famished, humiliated Jerusalem, Jeremiah
screams at God: "Have you rejected Judah completely? Do you revile
Zion?" Jeremiah disregards God's instructions not to pray for the people.
We acknowledge the wickedness that caused our downfall, but are the
gates of prayer truly locked?

Jeremiah's appeal receives no answer. He is left with a question
mark and his broken heart. Trapped by his own prophecy, he is forced
to reject the king's appeal; he will not pray on the people's behalf.

CHAPTER 21 AND THE BEGINNING OF CHAPTER 34: JEREMIAH'S REPLY TO KING ZEDEKIAH'S DELEGATES

Jeremiah's reply to Zedekiah appears not in the chapter describing the
war on Judah, but in chapter 21:

> The word that came to Jeremiah from the Lord when King
> Zedekiah sent to him Pashhur son of Malchiah and the priest
> Zephaniah son of Maaseiah, to say: Please inquire of the Lord
> on our behalf, for King Nebuchadnezzar of Babylonia is attack-
> ing us – perhaps the Lord will perform wonders for us, so he will
> withdraw from us. (21:1–2)

From these delegates' first words, the king's expectations are clear. He
hopes to reproduce the miracle that saved Jerusalem from the wrath of
Sennacherib: "perhaps the Lord will perform wonders for us."

> Jeremiah said to them: Tell Zedekiah: Thus said the Lord, God
> of Israel: I am about to turn your own weapons of war against
> you, with which you are fighting the King of Babylonia and the
> Chaldeans besieging you outside the wall, and I will gather them

inside this city. I Myself will fight against you with an outstretched hand and a mighty arm, furiously, angrily, and very wrathfully. I will strike down the inhabitants of this city – man and beast; they will die in a great plague. Then – declares the Lord – I will give King Zedekiah of Judah, his officials, and the people, and the city's survivors of the plague, sword, and famine, into the hands of King Nebuchadnezzar of Babylonia, into the hands of their enemies, and into the hands of those who want to kill them. He will put them to the sword; he will show them no mercy, pity, or compassion.

And tell the people: Thus said the Lord: I set before you the path of life and the path of death: Whoever remains in this city will die by sword, famine, or plague, but whoever leaves and surrenders to the besieging Chaldeans shall live; he will have his life as spoils. For I have determined to do this city harm and not good – declares the Lord – it will be given into the hands of the King of Babylonia, and he will burn it with fire. (21:3–10)

Jeremiah ignores the request to pray, instead sending the king and the people a prophetic portent of doom. The first part is addressed to the king and his courtiers, and the second part to the people. The king and his proxies do not know why Jeremiah has refused their request; they have no idea that God is staying the prophet's hand. To them, Jeremiah simply does not love his people as much as Isaiah, who acquiesced to Hezekiah's plea and enlisted in the effort to stop Assyria. Jeremiah, in contrast, intensifies his doom-saying. He watches the military buildup in Jerusalem, the bravery of the soldiers, their devotion to the cause – and it all seems futile. God is about to turn their own weapons of war against them as the battle reaches the city's streets. Jeremiah knows there will be a catastrophe. And after the initial massacre when the Babylonians breach the city, the leaders – the king and his entourage, and the rest of the survivors – will be delivered into the hands of the King of Babylonia, who will slaughter them mercilessly.

The second part of the prophecy addresses the people as they quake in terror before the Babylonians. Jeremiah instructs them unambiguously: Surrender. Give yourselves up to the Babylonians. He does not beat around the bush: "Whoever leaves and surrenders to the besieging Chaldeans shall live."[4]

Jeremiah generates an atmosphere of defeat among the people. His words hit home and many indeed throw themselves to the mercy of the Babylonian king:

> The remainder of the people in the city – those who surrendered to the King of Babylonia and the remnant of the population – were exiled by the commander Nebuzaradan. (II Kings 25:11)

In the list of exiles at the end of the Book of Jeremiah, we find that a group of people indeed went into exile – apparently willingly – before the destruction. This list includes those who were not connected to the main exile: "In the eighteenth year of Nebuchadnezzar, from Jerusalem, 832 people" (Jer. 52:29). That year (587 BCE, Nebuchadnezzar's eighteenth year in power), the destruction had not yet taken place; this is an earlier exile. According to II Kings 25:8, the destruction occurred in Nebuchadnezzar's nineteenth year. Moreover, the number of exiles listed (832) makes no sense in the context of Jerusalem's destruction. Apparently, this figure refers to deserters who opposed Zedekiah's bellicosity and surrendered to the Babylonians for ideological reasons.[5] This theory is supported by Zedekiah's own words. As the Babylonians tighten their siege of Jerusalem, Jeremiah suggests that the king give himself up. Zedekiah is not afraid of his brethren in Jerusalem, but he is "concerned lest I be given to the Jews who surrendered to the Chaldeans, and they will torture me" (Jer. 38:19). Zedekiah's fears are well-placed. Those who capitulated despise the king and are still incensed over his military adventurism. Jeremiah requests permission to see Zedekiah personally and repeat God's words to him:

> The word that came to Jeremiah from the Lord, while King Nebuchadnezzar of Babylonia, all his army, all the kingdoms of the land

---

4. Regarding the interpretation of the Hebrew verb *nafal* as "surrender," see I. Ephal, "To the Chaldeans You Fall," *Eretz Yisrael* 24 (5754): 18–19 [Hebrew].
5. See A. Malamat, "Words of Jeremiah," in Luria, *Studies in Jeremiah* III, 173.

he ruled, and all the nations were fighting against Jerusalem and all its surrounding towns: Thus said the Lord, God of Israel: Go to King Zedekiah of Judah and tell him: Thus said the Lord: I am about to deliver this city into the hands of the King of Babylonia, and he will burn it down. You will not escape his grasp but will be captured and handed over to him; you will see the King of Babylonia with your own eyes, and he will speak with you face to face; and you will go to Babylonia. Yet hear the word of the Lord, King Zedekiah of Judah! Thus said the Lord concerning you: You will not die by the sword. You will die peacefully: Just as burnings were made for your ancestors, the kings who ruled before you, so they will make a fire in your honor; they will lament, "Alas, master!" I Myself make this promise – declares the Lord.

Jeremiah the prophet told all this to King Zedekiah of Judah in Jerusalem, while the army of the King of Babylonia was fighting against Jerusalem and the remaining cities of Judah – Lachish and Azekah – for these fortified cities remained of the cities in Judah. (34:1–7)

At God's command, Jeremiah asks to speak to Zedekiah directly, not to the delegation sent to him. The king's representatives cannot refuse the prophet's request. These are mad, mad times. The Babylonian army is already encroaching upon Jerusalem and its surrounding cities. While the final siege leading to the destruction has not yet commenced, the military threat to the city and the kingdom is very real. In the midst of all this, after asking Jeremiah to pray on the city's behalf, Zedekiah makes time to hear him out. The king knows Jeremiah's political opinions well, but he still hopes the prophet's great love for Jerusalem will move him to prayer. But Jeremiah bitterly disappoints him. Perhaps Zedekiah has already heard the rumor that Jeremiah is advocating surrender and defection. Still, the king agrees to see him, to honor this stubborn prophet. Rather than throwing him out as a traitor, he is willing to meet with him privately.

Jeremiah does not sugar-coat his forecast for the days ahead: The city will be taken by the King of Babylonia, who will burn it to the ground. You, King Zedekiah, will be seized, brought to Nebuchadnezzar and then led to Babylonia. The prophet offers one slight comfort: "You will die peacefully...they will lament, 'Alas, master!'" This prophecy is the polar opposite of the fate Jeremiah prophesied for Jehoiakim: "None shall mourn him, [saying:] 'Alas, master...' He shall have the burial of a donkey" (22:18–19). Jeremiah wishes to communicate to the king that the impending destruction is not his fault. Political pressure and media influence on public opinion left him with no choice – the rebellion was virtually forced upon him.

At the conclusion of Jeremiah's prophecy, the text immediately switches back to the harsh reality on the ground, the worst battle Jerusalem has ever faced. All of Judah's fortified cities have fallen, with the exception of Lachish and Azekah. "The army of the King of Babylonia was fighting against Jerusalem and the remaining cities of Judah – Lachish and Azekah – for these fortified cities remained of the cities in Judah."

In 1935, a British excavation of Tel Lachish shed surprising light on this verse. In a well-preserved room by the city's gate, in an archaeological stratum from the time of the Babylonian conquest, archaeologists discovered an archive of some twenty letters, written in ink on ostraca (pottery shards), which became known as "the Lachish letters."[6] This unprecedented discovery included the correspondence conducted during those fateful days. Most of the letters were sent by a clerk or minor official named Hoshaiah, stationed outside Lachish, to his superior, Joash, stationed at Lachish. The letters are written in paleo-Hebrew. Some document the Judean kingdom's final days. In letter 4, lines 10–13, the clerk writes to his commanding officer: "And may (my lord) be apprised that we are watching for the fire signals of Lachish according to all the signs that my lord has given, because we cannot see Azekah." Apparently, Hoshaiah was stationed at a vantage point between Azekah and Lachish, tracking the signals sent out by these two fortified cities, bonfire by night and smoke by day. The letters thus complement the account in the Book of Jeremiah. The prophet reports that of all of Judah's fortified cities, only Azekah and Lachish remained; soon afterward, the Lachish

---

6. S. Ahituv, *Echoes from the Past: Hebrew and Cognate Inscriptions from the Biblical Period* (Jerusalem, 2008), 60–85.

letters report that Azekah too has fallen – its fires have been extinguished, and only those of Lachish can still be seen.

The Babylonian army approaches from the sea (as noted, large armies preferred to invade Jerusalem by sea, from the west, as it was safer and easier). The troops drop anchor at Ashkelon, which Babylonia conquered in 605 BCE. The armies march through the Shephelah and crush all of Judah's defensive outposts along the way, until only Lachish and Azekah remain outside of Jerusalem.

The connection between the Lachish letters and the verse in Jeremiah sheds a harsh but clear light on the Babylonian war on Judah. The campaign advanced toward Jerusalem with virtually no resistance. Despite the grand coalition between the nations of the region, Judah was left to face the great empire of the north alone. Perhaps this explains the verse from Lamentations: "All her allies betrayed her, became her enemies" (Lam. 1:2). At this point, Judah's entire army has mobilized for war. There is a mass enlistment. Simultaneously, King Zedekiah sends urgent appeals to Egypt for reinforcements, as we will see below. The year is 588 BCE, the siege of Jerusalem has begun, and most of Judah's cities have already fallen.

CHAPTERS 34 AND 37 CONTINUED:
A LULL IN THE SIEGE, A RETURN TO NORMALCY

After reporting that Lachish and Azekah have survived (for the moment), chapter 34 becomes disjointed. Suddenly, during the course of the war, King Zedekiah announces that the time has come to fulfill the mitzva of freeing one's Hebrew slaves:

> The word came to Jeremiah from the Lord after King Zedekiah had made a covenant with all the people in Jerusalem to proclaim freedom, to emancipate everyone's Hebrew slaves and bond-women; no one was to hold a fellow Hebrew in bondage. So all the officials and people who entered into this covenant agreed that they would emancipate their male and female slaves and no longer hold them in bondage; they agreed, and set them free. But afterward they changed their minds and took back the slaves they had freed and enslaved them. (34:8–11)

To understand this event, we must look at another passage, in chapter 37:

> Pharaoh's army left Egypt, and the Chaldeans besieging Jerusalem heard, and they withdrew from Jerusalem. (37:5)

Babylonia has attacked Judah and is approaching Jerusalem. Zedekiah turns to his pro-Egyptian coalition partners for help. Pharaoh Apries advances his army toward Tyre in order to gain a dominant position on the sea in the north. When Nebuchadnezzar becomes aware of Egypt's advance, he abandons the campaign to take Judah and devotes all his forces to the war with Egypt in the maritime cities. Once again, as during Sennacherib's campaign against Hezekiah 120 years earlier, Jerusalem is threatened with obliteration, and at the last minute, the enemy army retreats. It is easy to imagine the mood in Jerusalem; the people have placed their faith in the holiness of the Temple and believed it will serve as their fortress and shelter in times of crisis.

This background explains the emancipation and reenslavement of the slaves. As Nebuchadnezzar marches on Judah, Zedekiah enlists all able-bodied men, slaves included. He therefore emancipates the latter so they can fight – an accepted practice in many ancient nations.[7] The moment Babylonia withdraws its army from Judah and turns northward to face Egypt, the landowners all reclaim their slaves.

Jeremiah's reaction is harsh. He lambastes the landowners, the leadership, the priests, and the people of Jerusalem – God's sword will flash against all of them, via none other than the recently departed Babylonians:

> I will deliver them into the hands of their enemies, the hands of those who want to kill them. Their corpses will become food for the birds of the heavens and the beasts of the earth. I will deliver King Zedekiah of Judah and his officials into the hands of their

---

7. Y. Hoffman, "The Law as a Stabilizing Literary Medium," *Beit Mikra* 47 (5762): 2–10 [Hebrew]. See also Y. Rosenson, "Jeremiah and the Liberation of the Slaves," *Shmaatin* 144 (5761): 64–71 [Hebrew].

enemies, the hands of those who want to kill them, the hands of the army of Babylonia's king, which has withdrawn from you. I will give the order – declares the Lord – and bring them back to this city; they will fight against it, take it, and burn it down, and I will make the towns of Judah an uninhabited wasteland. (34:20–22)

What ridicule Jeremiah suffers now! All his curses, all his prophecies of doom and destruction, come crashing down amid the joy engulfing Jerusalem. It seems that Jerusalem will survive forever. We can only imagine the smug looks on the faces of Zedekiah and his messengers, whom Jeremiah has told that he will not pray for the city. The prophet who predicted the city's destruction and the exile of its king, who called for surrender to the Babylonians, must now look on as Jerusalem dances in the streets and on the rooftops. He feels that God is frustrating and tormenting him, saving His people despite their sins. At this moment, a prophecy bursts from his lips, an answer to those officials who asked him to pray for the safety of Jerusalem:

> Then the word of the Lord came to Jeremiah the prophet: Thus said the Lord, God of Israel: Say thus to the King of Judah, who sent you to inquire of Me: Pharaoh's army, which has marched out to support you, will go back to its own land, to Egypt. Then the Chaldeans will return and attack this city; they will capture it and burn it down.
>
> Thus said the Lord: Do not delude yourselves, thinking: The Chaldeans will leave us. They will not! Even if you were to defeat the entire Chaldean army that is attacking you, and only wounded men were left in their tents, they would come out and burn this city down. (37:6–10)

Jeremiah stands his ground, intensifying and expanding on his prophecy. For him, the destruction is a foregone conclusion. Even if only a few Babylonians remain, they will fulfill God's words and burn the city.

EZEKIEL 17: EZEKIEL CRITICIZES
ZEDEKIAH'S PLANS OF REBELLION

Rumors of the rebellion in Judah and Nebuchadnezzar's campaign to quell it have reached the ears of the exiled community in Babylonia. No doubt, the party of Shemaiah the Nehelamite and those who have dedicated their lives to promoting the gospel of national liberation, such as Ahab and Zedekiah (who are later burned to death by Nebuchadnezzar), encourage these rumors and fan the local flames of rebellion. Ezekiel also hears of the events and articulates a prophecy dripping with cynicism about King Zedekiah's hubris:

> Son of man, ask a riddle and present a parable to the House of Israel. Say: Thus said the Lord, God: A great eagle, with large wings, long feathers, and full of plumage of many shades, came to Lebanon and seized the top of a cedar. He broke off the highest branch and brought it to the land of Canaan, to a city of merchants there. He took of the seed of the land and planted it in fertile soil, where much water flowed.... It sprouted and became a low, measly vine, whose tendrils turned toward him and whose roots were under him; so it became a vine that produces branches and leafy boughs. But there was another great eagle with large wings and full plumage, and the vine now sent out its roots toward him and stretched out its branches to him for greater irrigation than the bed where it was planted – though it had been planted in good soil by abundant water – so it would produce branches, bear fruit, and become a splendid vine. Say: Thus said the Lord, God: Will it thrive? He will uproot it and strip it of its fruit so that it withers; all its new growth will wither; it will not take a strong arm or many people to pull it up by the roots. It has been planted, but will it thrive? It will wither when the east wind strikes it – wither away in the plot where it grew. (17:2–10)

To decipher this riddle, we must first understand its specifics. A large and impressive eagle tears off a cedar bough and brings it to Canaan. There, the eagle takes from the seed of the land and plants it in well-irrigated soil. The seed grows into a lowly, rather pathetic vine that barely produces offshoots, although it has been placed in nourishing soil. Along comes another eagle, and the vine eagerly stretches its roots out toward it, pleading for the eagle to water it, despite its abundant water source. God asks about this vine: Will it thrive? Will the eagle that planted it tolerate this rejection of its own water source in favor of another eagle's irrigation? Won't it just yank the ungrateful, withering vine from its roots?

The prophet explains that this parable represents recent historical events. The seed replanted in foreign soil by many waters represents Jeconiah, who was relocated to Babylonia by Nebuchadnezzar, the mighty eagle. He goes on to describe Zedekiah, vassal of the Babylonian king, "whose tendrils turned toward him and whose roots were under him":

> Then the word of the Lord came to me: Say to this rebellious people: Do you not know what these things mean? Say to them: The King of Babylonia has gone to Jerusalem and carried off her king and her nobles, bringing them back with him to Babylonia. And he has taken a member of the royal family and made a treaty with him, placing him under oath. He has also carried away the mighty of the land, that the kingdom be brought low, unable to rise again, surviving only by upholding its treaty. But [the king] has rebelled against him by sending his envoys to Egypt to be given horses and a large army. Will he succeed? Will he who does such things escape? Will he break the treaty and yet escape? As surely as I live – declares the Lord, God – he shall die in Babylonia, in the land of the king who enthroned him, whose oath he despised and whose treaty he broke. Pharaoh, with his mighty army and great horde, will not help him in war, when ramps are built and siege works erected to destroy many lives. He despised the oath by violating the covenant. Because he gave his hand in pledge and yet did all these things, he shall not escape.
>
> Therefore – thus said the Lord, God – as surely as I live, I will repay him for despising My oath and violating My covenant. I will spread My net for him, and he will be caught in My snare; I will bring him to Babylonia and execute judgment on him there, because he was unfaithful to Me. (17:11–20)

Ezekiel is not interested in the political aspect of Zedekiah's rebellion – rather, he focuses on the breach of his covenant. One who violates a covenant is unworthy of God's protection. Like Jeremiah in Judah, Ezekiel upon the rivers of Babylonia envisions Jerusalem's end even as the people of Jerusalem rejoice at what appears to be their salvation from the enemy.

CHAPTER 37: 587 BCE – JEREMIAH ATTEMPTS TO ABANDON JERUSALEM

> When the Chaldean army had withdrawn from Jerusalem on account of Pharaoh's army, Jeremiah started to leave Jerusalem for the territory of Benjamin, to slip out of there among the people. But when he reached the gate of Benjamin, a sentry there, whose name was Irijah son of Shelemiah son of Hananiah, arrested him, saying: "You are deserting to the Chaldeans!" Jeremiah replied: "That is a lie; I am not deserting to the Chaldeans!" But he would not listen to him; instead, Irijah arrested Jeremiah and brought him to the officials. They were angry with Jeremiah and beat him and imprisoned him in the house of Jonathan the scribe, which they had made into a prison. Jeremiah was put into a vaulted cell in a dungeon, where [he] remained a long time. (Jer. 37:11–16)

The lull in the Babylonian campaign allows many Jerusalemites to venture out of their homes and join a steady stream of people leaving the city. Jeremiah attempts to melt into the crowd – "to slip out of there among the people."[8] He cannot bear the mockery and scorn he has suffered ever since the Babylonian withdrawal from Judah. He is stuck with his prophecies of doom and destruction, while all around him people sing songs of salvation, just like in the days of Hezekiah. The blessing that "God has kept us alive and sustained us" is heard everywhere.

It is not clear where Jeremiah intends to go to escape further humiliation. Perhaps he will return to his hiding place in the days of Jehoiakim's persecution. But as he attempts to make his exit, he is spotted by one of the king's men, Irijah son of Sheleimah son of Hananiah. Irijah

---

8. See Ephal, "To the Chaldeans," 19–20.

recognizes Jeremiah from his prophecies calling for Judah to submit and therefore perceives him as public enemy number one. The sentry puts two and two together. Given Jeremiah's prediction of Babylonian victory, he must now be collaborating with the enemy. The officer assumes that he is not slipping out through the gate of Benjamin for a breather, like the rest of the throng, but is going to surrender to the Babylonians, like so many hundreds of Jews before him. He is suspected of treason, not merely desertion.

The clerk hands Jeremiah over to his superiors, who attempt to beat all traitorous thoughts out of him. A sound thrashing and a stint in the dungeons ought to silence all his predictions of destruction. The "long time" in the dark dungeons marks a new stage in the ever-declining events of Jeremiah's troubled life.

CHAPTER 37: JEREMIAH LAUNCHES AN APPEAL IN THE PRISON COURTYARD

It is difficult to determine the length of the lull in Judah while the Babylonians are fighting up north. In the meantime, the Jews rebuild their fortifications and repair what was destroyed, replenishing the cities' defenses. Endless days pass for Jeremiah in the "house of Jonathan the scribe" next to the dungeon. We learn about his experience there – including the "pit house" and the "vaults" (probably dark, locked, underground storage spaces)[9] – only from his conversation with King Zedekiah, who eventually summons him for a private audience:

> King Zedekiah sent for him, and he took him and asked him secretly, in his house: Is there any word from the Lord? Jeremiah answered: There is …. You will be given into the hands of the king of Babylonia. And Jeremiah then said to King Zedekiah: How have I sinned against you and your servants and this people, that I have been placed in prison? And where are your prophets, who prophesied to you, saying: The King of Babylonia will not come upon you or this land? Now, please hear me, Your Majesty; let my supplication please be accepted before you. Do not put me

9. Based on H. Rabin's explanation of this verse in *Jeremiah* (*World of the Bible*), 173–74.

back in the house of Jonathan the scribe, or I will die there. So King Zedekiah issued a command, and they placed Jeremiah in the prison yard (*ḥatzar hamatara*), and a loaf of bakers' bread was given to him each day, until all the bread in the city had run out. So Jeremiah settled in the prison yard. (37:17–21)

This intimate meeting takes place as the Babylonians are finishing up their Tyre campaign and returning to Jerusalem. Jeremiah once again taunts the king: "And where are your prophets, who prophesied to you, saying: 'The King of Babylonia will not come'?" During the lull, these prophets have celebrated their victory over him, while he sits alone, rotting in the dungeons. He pleads with Zedekiah to improve his conditions.

The answer he gives to the king upon his inquiry as to God's word has not changed, nor will it change. "You will be given into the hands of the King of Babylonia." This is an irrevocable decree. The king takes Jeremiah's words seriously and has him transferred to better, safer conditions. He is moved from the improvised makeshift prison of the house of Jonathan the scribe (where there was no supervision over the prison guards, who could harass the prophet at will) to the prison courtyard, where he is under the king's protection, receiving regular rations and living in decent conditions. This courtyard was probably a restricted area within the city walls. Rabbi Joseph Schwarz describes the place in his book, *Descriptive Geography and Brief Historical Sketch of Palestine*:

> The Prison Gate (Neh. 12:39), the site of which can be accurately determined even at present by means of a tradition which defines the position of the prison, the grotto of Jeremiah, or otherwise called the Archer's Court – *ḥatzar hamatara*: it was situated near the Bab al Amud. To the east of this gate were the towers Meah and Chananel of Nehemiah 12:39.[10]

---

10. J. Schwarz, "The Walls of Jerusalem," in Schwarz, *Descriptive Geography and Brief Historical Sketch of Palestine*, trans. I. Leeser (Philadelphia, 1850). In the Middle Ages, they identified the prison courtyard within the vicinity of Zedekiah's cave, between the Flower Gate and Damascus Gate. The Prison Gate was blocked off by Schwarz's time and is recognizable only from the outside.

Wherever this courtyard may have been, it leads us to the final stretch of Jerusalem's story.

CHAPTERS 38 AND 39: JEREMIAH CONTINUES
TO AGITATE AND IS THROWN INTO THE PIT

As Babylonia draws ever closer to Jerusalem, Jeremiah's message does not change. The Chaldeans take a long time to build their siege ramp,[11] while the people of Jerusalem desperately search for a way out. The prophet keeps urging anyone who will listen: "Give yourselves up to the Babylonians!" Despite his preferential treatment in the prison yard, he continues to agitate, trying the patience of local leaders, who wish to keep up morale:

> Shephatiah son of Mattan, Gedaliah son of Pashhur, Jucal son of Shelemiah, and Pashhur son of Malchiah heard what Jeremiah was telling all the people: Thus said the Lord: Whoever remains in this city will die by sword, famine, or plague, but whoever goes over to the Chaldeans will live; he will have his life as spoils and live. Thus said the Lord: This city will certainly be given into the hands of the army of the King of Babylonia, who will capture it. Then the officials said to the king: This man should be put to death; he is discouraging the soldiers who are left in this city, as well as all the people, with these words; this man seeks not the good of these people but their ruin. (38:1–4)

Finally, someone has the courage to say it explicitly – Jeremiah does not seek the welfare of his people! He seeks only their ruin and should be put to death! These officials have been waiting a long time for permission to kill the prophet. This aging prophet simply does not let up.

One person mentioned here is Gedaliah son of Pashhur – almost certainly the same Pashhur who placed Jeremiah in the stocks decades

---

11. See I. Ephal, *The City Besieged: Siege and Its Manifestations in the Ancient Near East* (Leiden, 2009). He explains the technical aspects of the building of the ramp in the biblical period. Ephal bases his article on the Assyrian ramps at Lachish, but the technical aspect of the Jerusalem ramp was certainly similar.

earlier. His son, one of the highest officials in the city, has inherited his father's distaste for the man who cursed his family. The king, never a strong figure, feebly grants Gedaliah and his cronies their wish:

> And King Zedekiah said: Behold, he is in your hands, for the king cannot hold you back. (38:5)

Without further ado, they take action:

> They took Jeremiah and flung him in the pit of Malchiah, the king's son, which was in the prison yard; they lowered him down with ropes; there was no water in the pit, only mud, and Jeremiah sank down in the mud. (38:6)

The Judean officials do just what Joseph's brothers did – why dirty your hands with killing when you can fling your victim into a pit? Most probably, they choose to kill him this way because Jeremiah is no longer an unknown figure. As Babylonia advances on Jerusalem, many recall his warnings and begin to believe him. Therefore, he cannot be openly executed. By lowering him into the mud, his executioners can easily cover their tracks.

In a backhanded way, the text draws attention to the empty wells of Jerusalem by confirming that this pit is empty of water, containing only mud. The well is not in use, so no one, the officials think, will ever discover how they eliminated the traitorous prophet. However, they fail to notice Ebed-melech the Cushite (a servant of the king, of Ethiopian origins),[12] who serves his masters but, like all good servants, remains invisible to them:

> Ebed-melech the Cushite, a eunuch, was in the palace when they flung Jeremiah into the pit (the king was sitting at the gate of Benjamin). So Ebed-melech left the palace and spoke to the king: Your Majesty, these people have perpetrated evil in all they have done to the prophet Jeremiah; they have cast him into the pit, and he

---

12. Many armies in the region had servants from Ethiopia. See Hoffman, *Jeremiah*, 177.

shall die of hunger when there is no more bread in the city. So the king commanded Ebed-melech the Cushite: Take thirty men from here and raise him out of the pit before he dies. Ebed-melech took the men to the king's palace and brought them beneath the treasury; he took rags and worn-out clothes from there and lowered them down to Jeremiah in the pit with ropes. Ebed-melech the Cushite said to Jeremiah: Please put these rags and old clothes under your arms to pad the ropes, and Jeremiah did so. Then they pulled Jeremiah up with the ropes and raised him out of the pit, and Jeremiah returned to the prison yard. (38:7–12)

This servant of a different color and class notices Jeremiah's plight and takes great pains to rescue him from the depths of the pit. Jeremiah utters a prophecy of gratitude to this sensitive man who, despite his enslavement, has not lost his humanity:

Go and tell Ebed-melech the Cushite: Thus said the Lord of Hosts, God of Israel: I am about to fulfill My words against this city – words concerning disaster, not prosperity; at that time, they will be fulfilled before your eyes. But I will rescue you on that day – declares the Lord; you will not be given into the hands of those you fear. I will save you; you will not fall by the sword, but will escape with your life, because you trusted in Me – declares the Lord. (39:16–18)

By virtue of his faith in God, Ebed-melech the Cushite earns the protection of the Lord of Hosts, God of Israel.

Jeremiah is now summoned to what will be his final meeting with the king:

Then King Zedekiah sent for Jeremiah the prophet and took him to the third entrance to the House of the Lord. The king said to Jeremiah: I am going to ask something of you; do not withhold anything from me. Jeremiah replied to Zedekiah: If I give you an answer, will you not kill me? And even if I did give you counsel, you would not listen to me. So King Zedekiah swore this oath to Jeremiah in secret: As surely as the Lord who has given us breath lives, I will neither kill you nor hand you over to those who want to kill you.

Then Jeremiah said to Zedekiah: Thus said the Lord, God of Hosts, God of Israel: If you surrender to the officers of the King of Babylonia, your life will be spared, and this city will not be burned down; you and your family will live. But if you do not surrender to the officers of the King of Babylonia, this city will be given into the hands of the Chaldeans, and they will burn it down; you will not escape them. (38:14–18)

Jeremiah remains steadfast in his vision. The city has already fallen into Babylonian hands, but it need not be burned down. If you, the king, surrender yourself to Babylonia, the city will be saved and you will live. If you remain besieged in Jerusalem, the city will be razed and you will not be able to flee. There is no sense in trying to hold out – needless death and destruction will result. This is your last chance, warns the prophet. But the king is paralyzed with fear, unable to take action. He has already been convinced by Jeremiah's prophecy, but he cannot face what will await him if he hands himself over to Nebuchadnezzar. He is frozen with terror, forced into passivity.

King Zedekiah said to Jeremiah: I am concerned lest I be given to the Jews who surrendered to the Chaldeans, and they will torture me. (38:19)

Sensing that the king is irresolute, Jeremiah feels he still has a chance to win him over. He tries desperately to encourage him to surrender:

Jeremiah said: They will not hand you over; if you obey the Lord by doing what I tell you, then it will go well with you, and your life will be spared. But if you refuse to surrender, this is what the Lord has revealed to me: All the women left in the palace of the King of Judah will be brought out to the officials of the King of Babylonia, and those women will say to you: "They misled you and overcame you – those trusted friends of yours; your feet are sunk in the mud; your friends have deserted you." All your wives and children will be brought out to the Babylonians, and you yourself will not escape their hands but will be captured by the King of Babylonia; and you will cause this city to be burned down. (38:20–23)

Zedekiah too is desperate, yet he cannot act on Jeremiah's prophecy. He knows his ministers suspect that he is wavering and possibly about to surrender. He therefore asks Jeremiah to keep their conversation secret:

Then Zedekiah said to Jeremiah: Do not let anyone know about this conversation, and you shall not die. If the officials hear that I talked with you, and they come to you and say: Tell us what you said to the king and what the king said to you – do not hide it from us, or we will kill you, then tell them: I was pleading with the king not to send me back to Jonathan's house to die there.

All the officials did come to Jeremiah to question him, and he told them everything the king had ordered him to say. So they said no more to him, for no one had heard [his conversation with the king].

And Jeremiah remained in the prison yard until the day Jerusalem was captured. (38:24–28)

CHAPTER 32: PURCHASING A FIELD IN ANATHOTH

The word that came to Jeremiah from the Lord in the tenth year of King Zedekiah of Judah, which was the eighteenth year of Nebuchadnezzar. The King of Babylonia's army was then besieging Jerusalem, and Jeremiah the prophet was confined to the prison yard at the palace of the King of Judah....

Jeremiah said: The word of the Lord came to me, saying: "Hanameel, son of your uncle Shallum, will come to you and say: 'Buy my field at Anathoth, because as the closest relative it is your duty to redeem it by purchase.'" Then, just as the Lord had said, my cousin Hanameel came to me in the prison yard and said: "Please buy my field at Anathoth, in the territory of Benjamin,

> since it is yours to inherit by right and yours to redeem – buy it
> for yourself." And I knew this was the word of God. (32:1–2, 6–8)

In this chapter, Jeremiah shares one of his innermost secrets. He has
been prophesying for forty long and lonely years, since he was a teen-
ager (by simple calculation, he is now in his fifties). We have followed
him through many challenges and obstacles, including trials that caused
him to doubt his own visions and lose the will to prophesy. But until
now, he has never questioned the institution of prophecy itself. Even in
his humiliating confrontation with Hananiah son of Azzur seven years
earlier, Jeremiah merely prayed that Hananiah's vision would come
true. But here, something else happens. He receives a prophecy that his
cousin from Anathoth will come to sell him a field, for he has the right of
first refusal. When his cousin arrives, Jeremiah is taken by surprise and
exclaims, "And I knew this was the word of God." What can this mean?
Did Jeremiah need to prove that his vision was from God? The commentators entirely negate this suggestion. For example, Abrabanel writes:

> Although he said, "And I knew this was the word of God," this
> does not mean…that Jeremiah initially doubted whether the
> prophecy that had come to him was the word of God, for the
> prophets had no doubt about their prophecy, and the prophecy
> itself was self-evidently a prophecy based on the intensity of feel-
> ing. (Abrabanel on Jer. 32:8)[13]

Y. Hoffman's simple reading of the verse seems preferable. Hoffman
demonstrates that for many years, Jeremiah has indeed been preoccu-

---

13. Other commentators also refuse to countenance any hint of doubt in the prophet's
    words. Radak, for example, explains that by "I knew from God that I will buy it,"
    he means to say that God did not command him about buying, just that Hanameel
    would come to him. The Malbim says exactly this: "He was not sure about the
    exact interpretation of the word of God, who said 'pay.'" Also, in *Daat Mikra*, the
    interpretation is like this: "that he knew that Hanameel did not know that there was
    another element to what he was doing." All of these uphold the thesis that Jeremiah
    feels no doubt.

pied with discerning the truth of his prophecy.[14] The grim reality of his imprisonment just moments before the destruction, with his prophecies heralding national disaster, leads him to think that a message of God suddenly announcing that his cousin is coming to sell him a field is but a surreal hallucination. Much earlier in his career, the people of his hometown conspired against him when he openly questioned the authenticity of Josiah's reformation. For decades he has had no contact with his relatives; he no doubt wonders about them from time to time. Now, as he sits in the prison yard, protected from his enemies yet aware of the destruction that would descend at any moment, he worries that it is not God speaking, but his own voice. Why would God command him to purchase a field just before the entire land is to be destroyed? Why torture him? In the past, he has tried to distinguish between true and false prophecies. Now he tests his own thoughts. Could this really be God's word?

When he sees his cousin, Jeremiah quickly regains his composure and takes immediate action:

> So I bought the field from Hanameel, my cousin from Anathoth. I weighed out the money for him, seventeen shekels of silver. I signed and sealed the deed, had it witnessed, and weighed out the silver on scales. I took the deed of purchase – the sealed copy containing the order and conditions, as well as the unsealed copy. Then I gave the deed of purchase to Baruch son of Neriah son of Mahseiah in the presence of my cousin Hanameel, the witnesses who had signed the deed of purchase, and all the Jews sitting in the prison yard. In their presence I gave Baruch these instructions: Thus said the Lord of Hosts, God of Israel: Take these documents, the sealed and unsealed copies of the deed of purchase, and put them in a clay jar, so they may last a long time.
>
> For thus said the Lord of Hosts, God of Israel: Houses, fields, and vineyards will again be purchased in this land. (32:9–15)

---

14. Y. Hoffman, "And I Knew This Was the Word of God," *Beit Mikra* 42 (1997): 198–210 [Hebrew]. Interestingly, Hoffman's take on this verse is not mentioned in his *Jeremiah*.

Jeremiah ensures that his purchase will be properly documented well into the future. The weighing of the silver, the recording of the deed of purchase, and its signing and sealing in the presence of witnesses all seem to have been standard practice in those days. Yet this purchase includes the transfer of the deed from the purchaser, Jeremiah the prophet, to his confidant, Baruch son of Neriah son of Mahseiah, in the most public manner possible, in the presence of his cousin, the witnesses listed in the deed itself, and all the Jews in the jail yard. After the transaction has been concluded, Jeremiah commands Baruch to place both the sealed and unsealed deeds in "a clay jar, so they may last a long time" (32:14).

Let us explain some technical terms here. The "sealed" copy is the upper part of the scroll, listing the details of the purchase along with the impetus for the sale – in this case, the commandment to redeem a family homestead – and the rules governing the transaction. This document is recorded and signed by witnesses, then rolled up and bound, so it cannot be reopened. Then the entire deed is rewritten, on the same piece of parchment, and left unsealed. Whenever it is necessary to demonstrate ownership, the scroll is produced, with the unsealed portion displayed. If there are legal problems, the judge may open the sealed document and check its contents. The sealed part of the scroll prevents forgery while the open part allows for its use as evidence of ownership.[15]

Once his transaction with Jeremiah has been completed, Hanameel takes his leave. He is surely pleased to have earned some extra money during what was undoubtedly an unprecedentedly steep downturn in the local real estate market. He considers the stupidity of his crazy cousin, who has fallen prey to his swindle, and takes his leave.

For his part, Jeremiah now demands to know why he was commanded to purchase a field in his hometown, opening up old wounds, on the eve of the land's destruction:

> After giving the deed of purchase to Baruch son of Neriah, I prayed to the Lord: Ah, Lord, God, You have made heaven and

---

15. According to A. Wolf and R. Gabbai Friedson, "The Sealed and the Unsealed," in *Mattot 5765*, weekly Torah portion sheet 215 of the Israel Ministry of Justice, Department of Jewish Law [Hebrew].

earth by Your great power and outstretched arm – nothing is too great for You. You show kindness to the thousandth genera- tion but bring the punishment for the parents' sins into the laps of their children after them – O great and mighty God, whose name is the Lord of Hosts, whose purposes are great, and whose deeds are mighty, whose eyes observe the ways of all mankind, rewarding each person according to his conduct and as his deeds deserve. You have performed signs and wonders in Egypt to this day, in Israel and among all mankind, and have gained renown to this day. You rescued Your people, Israel, from Egypt with signs and wonders, with a mighty hand and an outstretched arm, and with great terror. You gave them this land You had sworn to their ancestors to give to them, a land flowing with milk and honey. They came in and took possession of it, but they did not obey You or follow Your law; they did not do what You commanded them to do, so You brought all this disaster on them. See how the siege ramps are built up to take the city, and the city, because of the sword, famine, and plague, is in the hands of the attack- ing Chaldeans – as You said, so it was, and so You see. Yet You, Sovereign Lord, said to me: Buy the field with silver, and have the transaction witnessed – while the city is in the hands of the Chaldeans! (32:16–25)

Jeremiah accuses God of tormenting him. By now he is alone. No one is with him. Until now, he has been surrounded by witnesses, signatories, and curious onlookers. Everyone created the atmosphere, but now he grapples alone in his distress. He has been swindled by his cousin; that's a small problem. He is more troubled about the illogic of God's com- mand. God, the all-powerful, nothing is beyond You. You have sealed the fate of Your children for destruction; the ramp has come to destroy the city. The city already lies in starvation. It is clear that Your word has come true. So what do You want from me now? What is the purpose of this evil purchase?

God answers Jeremiah point for point, but in reverse order. Indeed, the verdict is final: The Chaldeans will destroy the city due to the sins of Israel, Judah, and Jerusalem. All that Jeremiah has prophesied for forty years – about their idolatry, corruption, and estrangement from God – has come to pass. The decree has been sealed. But, says God, there is something else I wish to teach you:

> But now, thus said the Lord, God of Israel, about the city that you say has been given to the King of Babylonia through sword, famine, and plague: I will surely gather them from all the lands where I banish them in My furious anger and great wrath; I will bring them back to this place and cause them to live in safety. They will be My people, and I will be their God. I will give them one heart and one path, that they may always revere Me, and that all may go well with them and their children after them. I will make an everlasting covenant with them: I will never stop doing them good, and I will inspire them to fear Me, never turning away from Me. I will rejoice in doing good for them and will assuredly plant them in this land with all My heart and soul.
>
> For thus said the Lord: As I have brought all this great calamity on this people, so I will give them all the prosperity I have promised them. Fields will be bought in this land of which you say, "It is a desolate wasteland, without people or animals; it has been given into the hands of the Chaldeans." People will buy fields for silver, and deeds will be signed, sealed, and witnessed in the territory of Benjamin, in the villages around Jerusalem, and in the towns of Judah, the hill country, the Shephelah, and the Negev; for I will bring them back from captivity – declares the Lord. (32:36–44)

CHAPTER 33: THE PROPHECY OF CONSOLATION, INTENSIFIED

In the depths of his despair, Jeremiah is revisited by a prophecy of consolation from the beginning of his career. In the early days of Josiah's reign, Jeremiah wandered the streets of Jerusalem, prophesying that God would raise up a scion of the House of David, a faithful shepherd, who would gather all the scattered remnants of Israel from the north, and then they would dwell in their land in peace and security. At the time, the prophet was sure that this vision was about to be fulfilled –

blossoming like the almond branch he was shown – and that Josiah was the great hope. Now he is an adult well past fifty and has borne the suffering and frustration of a much older man. Yet his prophecy about the field in Anathoth transports him back to his childhood and hometown – back to the faith that animated his first revelations. On the eve of Jerusalem's destruction, Jeremiah hears God speaking words of comfort:

> Thus said the Lord: There will yet be heard in this place, about which you say, "It is a desolate wasteland, without people or animals," in the towns of Judah and the streets of Jerusalem, desolate of people, inhabitants, and beasts: The sound of joy and the sound of gladness, the sound of the bridegroom and the sound of the bride, and the voices of those who cry, "Give thanks to the Lord of Hosts, for the Lord is good; His kindness endures forever!" when they bring a thanksgiving offering in the House of the Lord; For I will restore the captivity of this land as of old – said the Lord. (33:10–11)

This is the mirror image of the terrible curse that Jeremiah cast upon the people of Anathoth (ch. 11). Then, when he had just accepted the verdict of a celibate life, his prophecy was interpreted as the seal of Israel's destruction. Now, after all those bitter years, he repeats these same words, but inverted – as consolation. All these years after Josiah's fall at Megiddo, after Jerusalem has deteriorated and reached the brink of destruction, Jeremiah utters a prophecy abstract and distant, but eternal:

> Behold, days are coming – declares the Lord – when I shall uphold the good word I spoke about the House of Israel and the House of Judah. In those days and at that time, I will raise up a true scion of David, and he will do what is just and right in the land. In those days, Judah shall be saved, and Jerusalem shall dwell in security and be called "The Lord is our righteousness." (33:14–16)

The Destruction of Jerusalem

POLITICAL BACKGROUND

The situation in Jerusalem continues to deteriorate. People are fleeing from the city and surrendering to the Babylonians; refugees attempt to enter the city seeking refuge among their countrymen; hunger ravages its inhabitants. Military discipline is beginning to break down – some soldiers desert to the open areas held by the Edomites in the southern Hebron hills (Edom's entry into the area will be discussed below). Others head westward, to the Shephelah. Only a few remain to defend the disgraced city and its humiliated king.

On the ninth of Tammuz, 586 BCE, the Babylonians breach the northern wall of Jerusalem. It is not entirely clear what happens immediately afterwards. The remaining fighters flee or are captured; the remaining Jerusalemites – mostly the lower classes – watch helplessly as Babylonian soldiers march through the streets and the Temple. Only a month later, on the tenth of Av, does Nebuzaradan, the chief of the guards, arrive and begin the systematic destruction of the city: "He burned the House of the Lord, the king's palace, and all the houses of Jerusalem. He burned down every important building with fire. The walls all around Jerusalem were smashed by the entire Chaldean army" (II Kings 25:8–10). The residents of the city are rounded up for a deportation victory march. A long convoy of exiles, chained to one another in heavy shackles, are led from Jerusalem through the gate of Benjamin northward across Samaria, eastward across the Jordan, and from there northward to Babylonia itself. Unlike the exile of Jeconiah, in which the Jews were led out under decent conditions, having somewhat agreed to their fate, this time Babylonia wishes to annihilate Judah as punishment for its breach of a treaty with the superpower.

It is summer. Nebuzaradan does not drag the poorest class – the thousands of villagers around Jerusalem – on his victory march. Instead, he appoints over them a Jewish official who has been loyal to Babylonia, Gedaliah son of Ahikam, from the family of Shaphan the scribe. Gedaliah is charged with reorganizing the survivors and governing a region still licking its wounds. He sends word to all the Jews still in hiding all around Jerusalem to come to his headquarters at Mizpah, in the territory of Benjamin, whence they will spread out to the abandoned villages nearby, harvest the grapes, and tend to the fig trees. Come fall, they will be able to harvest the olives and try to resume some sort of normal routine in the wake of the terrible disaster that has befallen them.

Gedaliah's position is shaky from the start. The Babylonians have appointed him local governor, but he has not been awarded much authority, certainly nowhere near as much as Zedekiah received when appointed King of Judah. The Babylonians may have even voided Judah's status as a distinct geographical region, appending it instead to the province of Samaria, where Gedaliah is in charge of Judean affairs only.

Soon after Gedaliah's appointment, he is assassinated by a band of soldiers who have escaped across the Jordan River and enlisted the aid of the Ammonite King Baalis, part of the Egyptian coalition. This band is headed by Ishmael son of Nethaniah, a member of the Davidic dynasty. It is possible that Ishmael wishes to continue the rebellion against Babylonia with the help of the Transjordanian nations; perhaps he thinks the remnants of Judah and Benjamin will rally around him and maintain the struggle for the land. As Ishmael and his men make their way back to Transjordan after murdering Gedaliah, they are attacked by a group of soldiers led by Johanan son of Kareah. Ishmael makes it back to his Ammonite protector by the skin of his teeth.

Now the stunned survivors find themselves at a crossroads. The Babylonian government will soon find out about the assassination of their governor, and punishment will follow. Where are they to turn? Should they trust Egypt to welcome them, or can they safely assume that the Babylonians have satisfied their desire for revenge and surrender to them completely? The survivors are split. Some, including Jeremiah, exile themselves to Egypt, while others remain in Benjamin. Four years later, Babylonia returns to the area for another punitive campaign, this time against the rebellious Transjordanian nations of Ammon and Moab. Another wave of deportations is organized for them, and the remaining residents of Judah are included in it. This marks the end of the First Temple era and the Israelite settlement of Jerusalem until the return of Zerubbabel and High Priest Joshua in the wake of Cyrus' proclamation in 539 BCE.

CHAPTER 39: KING ZEDEKIAH'S FLIGHT AND CAPTURE

Where is King Zedekiah throughout all this? As soon as the city is breached, he flees. We do not see him fighting until his last breath, leading his troops into battle like the valiant kings of his lineage. Zedekiah is simply not made of the same stuff; we have already seen his fear of surrendering to Babylonia, lest he end up in the hands of the Jews who have already defected. He believes Jeremiah but is paralyzed, unable to take action. He can muster the courage neither to surrender nor to fight. Trapped, he attempts to flee eastward, probably aiming to take shelter in Ammon. Although the Ammonite army has not come to his assistance, he is counting on political asylum from an ally in Egypt's coalition. Jeremiah describes Zedekiah's escape route (a similar description can be found in 11 Kings 25):

> Then all the officials of the King of Babylonia came and took up seats in the middle gate: Nergal-sharezer, Samgar-nebo, Sarsechim Rab-saris, Nergal-sharezer Rab-mag, and all the other officials of the King of Babylonia. When King Zedekiah of Judah and all the soldiers saw them, they fled; they left the city by night via the king's garden, through the gate between the double walls, and he headed toward the Arabah. But the Chaldean army pursued them and overtook Zedekiah in the plains of Jericho. They captured him and took him to King Nebuchadnezzar of Babylonia at Riblah, in the area of Hamath, where he put him on trial. (39:3–5)

The description opens with a calm meeting of Babylonian officials within the breached gate of Jerusalem. The war is over. The hunger and exhaustion of the Jerusalemites have done their work; the King of Babylonia has not had to sacrifice a single soldier for the capture of Jerusalem. The Book of Lamentations describes the starvation and death that bloodied the city streets.

Jeremiah records how the king escapes from his palace together with a group of soldiers, "via the king's garden, through the gate between the double walls." The escape route must have been planned; the king must have known he had no other hope of survival. A rabbinic tradition mentions a tunnel through which Zedekiah attempted to escape:

> He commenced his flight through a tunnel that led to Jericho through an aqueduct. He was exhausted, so his children went first. Nebuzaradan saw him, seized him and his ten sons, and sent them to Nebuchadnezzar. (*Pesikta Rabbati* 26)

Some have attempted to identify the tunnel based on Jeremiah's description of its location "between the double walls." Hezekiah's water tunnel too was dug out "between the double walls" (Is. 22:11). It ran from the Gihon Spring, just outside the city wall, to the Pool of Siloam (Shiloah), inside the wall – about half a kilometer in length. This tunnel was designed to secure the city's water supply during Sennacherib's siege, but it could just as easily have offered a way out of the city. Zedekiah keeps an eye on this route, and once the Babylonians occupy the city he takes his remaining troops, slips under the wall that the Babylonians had broken through, and turns toward the plains of Moab to seek refuge in Ammon.[1]

Zedekiah's arrest, punishment, and exile are briefly described later in the chapter:

> The King of Babylonia slaughtered the sons of Zedekiah at Riblah before his eyes; the King of Babylonia also slaughtered all the nobles of Judah. Then he put out Zedekiah's eyes and chained him in bronze shackles to take him to Babylonia. The Chaldeans set

---

1. As suggested by Y. Medan, "The King's Garden, Through the Gate Between the Double Walls," *Al Atar* 3 (5758): 79–85.

fire to the royal palace and the people's homes, and they smashed the walls of Jerusalem. Nebuzaradan, chief of the guards, exiled to Babylonia the people who remained in the city, along with those who had defected, and the rest of the people. (Jer. 39:6–9)

WHO DESTROYED JERUSALEM?
DIFFERENT SCRIPTURAL TRADITIONS

II Kings 25: Nebuzaradan, Chief of the Babylonian Guards

In II Kings, the destruction is described almost laconically in chapter 25, the single chapter devoted to it. It opens with the siege of the tenth of Tevet, continues with the breach of the city on the ninth of Tammuz and Zedekiah's capture on the plains of Jericho, and ends with Nebuzaradan entering Jerusalem and burning it down. With that, "Judah was exiled from its soil" (v. 21). Here the actual destruction of Jerusalem is attributed to Nebuzaradan, the chief of the guards, who successfully accomplished his mission.

A similar account appears in Jeremiah 39. This tradition represents the consensus of Jewish historiographers.

Psalms 137 and Jeremiah 49: The Edomites

Another bona fide account tells of the Edomites arriving in the area of Judah during the siege, settling the southern Hebron hills, and serving as auxiliaries to Nebuzaradan's army of destruction. The most explicit source of this tradition is Psalms 137, composed from the perspective of the Babylonian exiles: "By the rivers of Babylon, where we sat and indeed wept as we remembered Zion." This psalm is best known for the exiles' oath: "If I forget you, O Jerusalem...." But the subsequent verses are not nearly as well-known:

> Remember, O Lord, what the Edomites did on the day of Jerusalem's fall, when they said: Destroy! Destroy it to its foundations! Daughter of Babylonia, doomed to destruction, praised is he who repays you, visiting upon you what you visited upon us. Praised is he who seizes your infants and dashes them against the rock! (137:7–9)

The exiled Jews swear revenge against the Edomites, who rejoiced at the fall of Jerusalem and made sure it was razed to the ground. To comprehend the enormity of this rage, we must understand the history of Edomite-Israelite relations.[2]

The connection between these two nations began, of course, with the struggle between Jacob and Esau in their mother's womb (according to Jewish tradition, Esau is the progenitor of Edom). After Jacob fled from home in fear of his brother and stayed with Laban for twenty years, a climactic reunion is described in Genesis 32. On parting, Jacob promises to visit his brother someday in Seir, which is Edom.

En route to Canaan, the Israelites were commanded not to provoke the inhabitants of Seir, for "I gave Mount Seir to Esau as an inheritance" (Deut. 2:5). Therefore, Israel sought their permission to cross their land: "Please let us pass through your land" (Num. 20:17). Seir's reaction was short, sharp, and to the point: "You shall not pass through me, lest I come out to meet you with a sword!" (20:18). The Israelites tried to negotiate, but Edom would not budge: "Edom came toward them with many people and a strong hand" (20:20). The text offers no reason for Edom's refusal, though presumably it was merely the natural reaction of a nation entrenched in its land and seeking to prevent any foreign entity from taking control. Indeed, the Edomites had much to lose. Their southern territory was full of quarries and mines. Its geographical layout created natural fortification that granted them control of the trading routes to the north and east. The Israelites thus detoured to the north and east, crossing into Canaan from the land of Moab.

Centuries later, the two rivals met again. King David sent his general, Joab son of Zeruiah, to conquer Edom. His interests were clear: Copper mines and trade routes are major draws for anyone with imperial designs. From the little information the verses offer us, we can ascertain that David's army massacred the Edomites, wiping out every male. Only

---

2. B. Luria, "The Historical Background to Jeremiah's Prophecy About Edom," in Luria, *Studies in Jeremiah* 1, 155–78 [Hebrew]. Luria describes the process by which the Nabateans moved into Edomite territory as the Edomites took the southern Hebron hills. He limits his discussion to the days surrounding the destruction, but I wish to hold a panoramic lens to the relations between Israel and Edom, brothers and rivals.

Hadad, an Edomite prince, managed to escape to Egypt, where he was granted political asylum. Edom thus became a vassal of David's kingdom: "He placed garrisons throughout Edom, and all Edom became servants to David" (II Sam. 8:14). The Edomites constantly attempted to regain their independence and remove Judah's yoke.

One of the most shocking events in the history of this fraught relationship occurred during the reign of King Amaziah of Judah. Scripture describes how Amaziah killed ten thousand Edomites and led another ten thousand captives to the rocky cliffs atop the Edomite city of Selah (possibly today's Petra), where he cast them down to their deaths (II Chr. 25:12). This was no act of war, but an act of vengeance. We can imagine how the Edomites preserved the memory of this atrocity from generation to generation, until they were finally presented with the opportunity to take revenge.

During the reign of Jehoiakim, when Egypt established a regional coalition against Babylonia, Edom joined in and supported the rebellion. Together with the other nations of Transjordan, Edom convinced Jehoiakim to rely on their combined defenses. Ammon and Moab remained faithful to the alliance, but Edom backed out.

There is historical evidence that around the same time, the Nabateans conquered Edomite territory, pushing the Edomites toward the land of Judah. Nebuchadnezzar welcomed the appearance of the dispossessed Edomites, enlisted them as an auxiliary force, and allowed them to settle in the ghost towns of Judah. We can imagine the Edomites reveling in the ruins of Jerusalem, demolishing whatever houses still stood and gleefully taking over the abandoned territories.

Rereading Psalm 137, we might suggest that the Judeans suffered more from their humiliation at the hands of the Edomites who took over their homes than from the actual destruction. We can also better understand the call for revenge. It aims to remind Edom of the horrific events of Amaziah's reign. Your day will come, warn the displaced Jews in Babylonia. "Praised is he who repays you, visiting upon you what you visited upon us."

The southern Hebron hills become Edom's territory. When the exiled Jews finally return home, they find that Judah's borders have shrunk. Only under the Hasmonean king John Hyrcanus in the second century BCE does Judah finally reconquer the area:

> Hyrcanus took also Dora and Marissa, cities of Idumaea [Edom], and subdued all the Idumaeans; he permitted them to stay in that country if they would circumcise themselves and uphold the laws of the Jews...from then on, they were Jews. (Josephus, *Antiquities* XIII, 9:1)

King Herod himself descended from those Edomite converts. This is the story of Edom within the Jewish collective memory.

Jeremiah also has a score to settle with Edom – he too witnesses the Edomites eagerly entering the towns south of Jerusalem during the siege of the city. Chapter 49 of his book is dedicated to Edom. There he bemoans this nation's lost wisdom and describes the punishment it will one day receive for its abuses. He portrays the wretchedness of the Edomites who come like paupers to glean the grapes remaining on the vine after the harvest:

> If grape harvesters came to you, wouldn't they leave a few grapes? If thieves came in the night, wouldn't they steal only what they wanted? (49:9)

Such is Jeremiah's opinion of Edom. He continues, describing its arrogance and its inevitable downfall:

> For I shall make you the smallest of nations, the most despised among man. Your monstrous nature and the pride of your heart have deceived you, O dwellers in the cleft of the rock, who occupy the hilltops. Should you build your aeries as high as the eagle's, from there I will bring you down. (49:15–16)

Ezekiel 9: Angels of Destruction Destroy
the City and Protect Its Righteous

The prophet Ezekiel was not overly interested in reality. He sat by the Chebar River in Babylonia and beheld visions that joined heaven and earth. Reading his prophecies, one wonders where the prophet stands – among his people in their political situation, or among the angels. One of the harshest descriptions of the destruction appears in a short chapter in the Book of Ezekiel and depicts God's messengers destroying the city. Clearly, this chapter is written with the religious consciousness that everything that occurs in the world is God's will:

> Then He called loudly in my presence: "Come near, you who are charged with executing judgment on the city, each with his weapon of destruction in his hand." And I saw six men coming from the direction of the upper gate, which faces north, each with a deadly weapon in his hand; with them was a man clothed in linen, a scribe's inkwell at his side; they came in and stood beside the bronze altar. (Ezek. 9:1–2)

The prophet hears "a loud call" directing him to send his soldiers to battle. It is a description of an angelic army preparing for battle. Six warriors come "from the direction of the upper gate," armed with weapons. Among these angels of destruction is a singular figure armed only with an inkwell. He is clothed in linen, and the reader immediately understands that he is the guardian angel amidst the angelic destroyers. Before the latter set about their task, two more steps are necessary:

> Then the Glory of the God of Israel rose up from the cherub, upon which it had been, to the threshold of the Temple. It called to the man clothed in linen, who had the scribe's inkwell at his side. And the Lord said to him: Go through the city of Jerusalem, and put a mark on the foreheads of those who moan and groan over all the abominations done within it. (9:3–4)

First, Ezekiel envisions the Divine Presence, the *Shekhina*, the "Glory of the God of Israel," abandoning its usual perch – in the inner sanctum of the Temple – and ascending to the Temple threshold. This is God's first stop in His departure from His Temple, and the origin of the rabbinic legend of "ten stations in the *Shekhina's* exile during the destruction."[3]

---

3. This is an ancient rabbinic tradition found in the introductory section of Lamentations Rabba and in Rosh HaShana 31a. To understand how the tradition regarding the *Shekhina's* exile during the destruction of the First Temple evolved into a description

It is also the reader's first indication of the events about to unfold. The *Shekhina* leaving the city cannot be a good sign.

Next, God turns to the linen-clad angel and instructs him to make a mark – a *tav*, which would have resembled an X in ancient Hebrew orthography – on the foreheads of all "who moan and groan over all the abominations" going on in Jerusalem. This vision is clearly informed by the Bible's description of the destroying angel passing through Egypt and skipping over the houses marked with the blood of the Passover sacrifice. The marking of foreheads here corresponds to the marking of the homes in Exodus and serves the same purpose: to distinguish between God's children and His enemies. In contrast to the Egyptian episode, however, here God's enemies are Jerusalem's sinful inhabitants. Unlike Jeremiah, Ezekiel did not experience the spiritual revolution of Josiah, and all his prophetic criticism focuses on idol worship in the city. Entrenched in his prophecies about religion, he ignores the political reality that so concerns Jeremiah. In Ezekiel's eyes, the destruction is God's way of avenging Himself on His enemies – in this case, His own sinful children. For some time now, Ezekiel has perceived Jerusalem as having been rendered insignificant. (See Ezekiel 24, which he prophesied on the tenth of Tevet, when the siege began in Jerusalem.)

Once the linen-clad angel has marked those worthy of protection and rescue, God activates the angels of destruction:

> He said to the others, in my presence: "Follow him through the city and kill; do not spare or pity. Slaughter old men, young men and maidens, women and children, but do not go near anyone who bears the mark; begin at My sanctuary"; so they began with the elders, who were in front of the Temple. Then He said to them: "Defile the Temple, and fill the courts with the slain – go!" So they went out and began to smite the city. (9:5–7)

---

of the ten-step exile of the Sanhedrin during the destruction of the Second Temple, see D. Henshke, "From Usha to Yavneh: The Transformations of a Tradition," *Jewish Studies, An Internet Journal* 2002: 1–9 [Hebrew].

The destruction is well under way, yet Ezekiel makes no mention of Nebuzaradan (who does not even appear in the Book of Ezekiel, though the prophet lived in Babylonia) or his soldiers. Jerusalem and its Temple were destroyed by God's angels alone. They begin in the Temple, where the idolatry was most painfully apparent. This description contradicts everything we have learned about Josiah's reformation, which purged the Temple of idol worship.

Ezekiel envisions the destroying angels slaughtering their way through the city, until even he, who has scorned and condemned Jerusalem, cannot bear it anymore:

> During the killing, when I was left alone, I fell on my face and cried out: Alas, Sovereign Lord! Will You destroy the entire remnant of Israel in this outpouring of Your wrath upon Jerusalem? And He said to me: The sin of the House of Israel and Judah is exceedingly great; the land is full of bloodshed, and the city full of injustice, for they said: The Lord has forsaken the land; the Lord does not see. So I will not spare or pity, but I will bring down on their own heads what they have done. (9:8–10)

Ezekiel implores God to leave some remnant of Israel. He fears that no one has been marked for salvation and none will survive the onslaught. At that moment, the angel in linen returns and reports that he has carried out his mission:

> And then the man clothed in linen, who had the scribe's inkwell at his side, returned to report: I have done all You have commanded me. (9:11)

How can the cry of the prophet who is left alone be reconciled with the report of the linen-clad man that he has marked those who deserve protection? Ezekiel must live with this contradiction. For him, the city has been flattened to its foundations by the destroying angels, and only he remains (dwelling, in the vision, in heavenly Jerusalem).

A TALMUDIC SUBVERSION OF "THE MAN CLOTHED IN LINEN"

In the hands of the talmudic rabbis, this chapter of Ezekiel undergoes a drastic transformation. The sages take considerable artistic license in aggadic literature, and when they meet "the man clothed in linen," they cannot tolerate the idea that Jerusalem's righteous are marked for survival:

> God never uttered a good decree and then recanted, except in this instance. It is written: "And the Lord said to him: Go through the city of Jerusalem, and put a mark (*tav*) on the foreheads of those who moan and groan over all the abominations done within it."
>
> God said to Gabriel: Go put an ink mark on the foreheads of the righteous, so they will be spared by the destroying angels, and place a blood mark on the foreheads of the wicked, so the destroying angels will overpower them.
>
> The attribute of justice said to God: Master of the World, what's the difference between those and those?
>
> He said to it: These are completely righteous, and those are completely wicked.
>
> It said before Him: Master of the World, these could have protested and did not!
>
> He said to it: I know full well that had they protested, they would not have been heeded.
>
> It said before Him: You know, but did they?
>
> Thus it says: "'Slaughter old men, young men and maidens, women and children, but do not go near anyone who bears the mark; begin at My sanctuary'; so they began with the elders, who were in front of the Temple." R. Yosef taught: Read not "My sanctuary" (*mikdashi*) but "My sanctified" (*mekudashai*) – the people who have observed My Torah in its entirety, from *alef* to *tav*. (Shabbat 55a)

The attribute of justice changes God's verdict, convincing Him that even those who moan and groan do not deserve the mark of life. These righteous people are sealing themselves off as the world around them collapses. This sort of behavior does not merit the spark of life. This is a sort of "Noah's ark," where man saves himself alone. *Après moi, le deluge!* Such behavior is unacceptable for the People of Israel in the Land of Israel. In this land, "All of Israel is responsible for one another" (Sifra, *Parashat Beḥukkotai* 7:5). The moaners and groaners ought to be washed away in the same waters that drown the wicked. Audaciously, the rabbis alter the end of this story. In their demand for mutual responsibility, they erase the marks of life from the foreheads of the righteous.

CHAPTERS 39–40: JEREMIAH'S ROLE DURING AND AFTER THE DESTRUCTION

We last left Jeremiah in the prison yard, under the watchful eye of the king. When the Chaldeans enter the city, all the inmates presumably break out and scatter in all directions. Jeremiah, however, does not budge. Chapter 39 describes how Nebuzaradan receives orders from Nebuchadnezzar to protect the prophet, entrusting him to the care of Gedaliah son of Ahikam, the new local governor:

> King Nebuchadnezzar of Babylonia had given orders about Jeremiah to Nebuzaradan, chief of the guards: Take him and look after him; do not harm him, but do whatever he asks for himself. So Nebuzaradan, chief of the guards, Nebushasban Rab-saris, Nergal-sharezer Rab-mag, and all the other officers of the King of Babylonia sent and had Jeremiah taken out of the prison yard, and they turned him over to Gedaliah son of Ahikam son of Shaphan to take him back home; thus he dwelled among the people. (39:11–14)

This matter-of-fact description ignores Jeremiah's major dilemma, detailed in chapter 40: Should he go down to Babylonia or stay in Judah?

> The word that came to Jeremiah from the Lord after Nebuzaradan, chief of the guards, had released him from Ramah, when he had him bound in chains among the exiles of Jerusalem and Judah, on their way to exile in Babylonia. The chief of the guards took Jeremiah and said to him: "The Lord, your God, decreed this

disaster upon this place. The Lord has brought and done as He said He would – because you all sinned against the Lord and did not obey Him.... But today I am freeing you from the chains on your wrists. Come with me to Babylonia if you wish, and I will look after you; if you do not want to, there is no need; look, the whole country lies before you; go wherever seems good and right in your eyes." But before [Jeremiah] could respond, [Nebuzaradan] said: "Go back to Gedaliah son of Ahikam son of Shaphan, whom the King of Babylonia has appointed over the towns of Judah, and live with him among the people; or go anywhere you please" – then the chief of the guards gave him provisions and a present and sent him away. So Jeremiah went to Gedaliah son of Ahikam at Mizpah and lived with him among the people who were left in the land. (40:1–6)

Unless we combine these two accounts,[4] we must assume that Jeremiah's story unfolds in two stages. The first stage occurs when the wall is breached. Presumably, the prison guards run for their lives, leaving the inmates free to bolt. But where does Jeremiah want to go? Who wants him? Who still cares what he has to say? One noble family, that of Shaphan the scribe, has been his patron for decades. At the beginning of his career, during his debut in the Temple courtyard, he was saved by Ahikam son of Shaphan the scribe when everyone wanted to lynch him (end of ch. 26). Baruch son of Neriah read out Jeremiah's scroll of prophecies in the office of Gemariah son of Shaphan (ch. 36). The family was known for opposing the rebellion against Babylonia and supporting Jeremiah's prophecies. No doubt, the next generation has followed this tradition. Thus, Jeremiah finds himself under the capable patronage of Gedaliah son of Ahikam son of Shaphan. It makes sense that Gedaliah, who has publicly opposed the rebellion in Jerusalem and Judah, finds safe

---

4. As Radak suggests in his commentary after raising the issue of the repetition of Jeremiah 39:14. J. Klausner writes similarly in *The History of the Second Temple 1*, 56 n. 22 [Hebrew]. Most scholars see two distinct and opposing narratives. See M.Z. Segal, "The Prophet Jeremiah in the Days of the Destruction," in H. Gevaryahu, B. Luria, and Y. Mehlmann, eds., *A Volume in Honor of A. Biram* (Jerusalem, 5716), 100–105 [Hebrew].

haven in Mizpah (in the Benjamin area) as soon as the wall is breached, even before the Temple is destroyed.[5] While Jeremiah can theoretically stay safe with Gedaliah in Benjamin, the prophet's heart goes out to his brethren. Therefore, after Jerusalem is put to the torch and chain gangs of exiles are marched to Riblah on their way to Babylonia, Jeremiah leaves his sheltered haven under Gedaliah's protection. The following midrash describes these events most poignantly:

> R. Aḥa said: Nebuchadnezzar gave Nebuzaradan three instructions concerning Jeremiah [39:12]: "Take him and look after him" – him, not his nation; "do not harm him" – do nothing bad to him, but do as you please with his nation; "but do whatever he asks for himself" – but not on behalf of his people. (Lamentations Rabba, petiḥta 34)

According to this midrash, Babylonian intelligence has informed the heads of state that the only man who actively tried to prevent the rebellion and struggled to promote loyalty to Babylonia was Jeremiah. The time has now come to reward him, and an order is issued to ensure his safety and welfare. Jeremiah rejects all this protection; he insists on sharing his people's suffering. Wherever they go, he will go, and if they are shackled, he will shackle himself to them:

> Jeremiah would see a chain gang of youths in metal collars and place his head among theirs. Nebuzaradan would come and remove him. He then would see a chain gang of old people and would stick his neck among theirs. Again, Nebuzaradan would come and remove him. (ibid.)

According to midrashic tradition, Nebuzaradan pleads with Jeremiah to remove his shackles, for the chief of the guards himself will pay the price if Jeremiah is mistreated. The textual basis for this midrash appears in chapter 40, which, as we have seen, describes Jeremiah as "bound in chains among the exiles of Jerusalem and Judah, on their way to exile in

---

5. As suggested by Segal, "Days of Destruction," 102–3.

Babylonia." He has *chosen* to join the convoy. But the chief of the guards instructs him to leave the exiles and invites him to travel comfortably to Babylonia, as befits a loyal subject under the king's protection. Alternatively, he may stay in the Land of Israel and return to Gedaliah's protection. (Nebuzaradan's statement "*Go back* to Gedaliah" implies that Jeremiah has been there already but ran away to join the convoy.) "So Jeremiah went to Gedaliah son of Ahikam at Mizpah and lived with him among the people who were left in the land."

The following midrash offers a dark view of Jeremiah's lonely journey back to Benjamin:

> On his way back he found severed fingers scattered along the mountain paths. He gathered them up, caressed them, embraced them, kissed them, and wrapped them in his garments. He said to them: O my children, didn't I warn you? (ibid.)

Jeremiah witnesses all his prophecies of doom coming to pass. He walks alone through his people's graves, picking his way through the ruins of Judah to join the broken nation gathering under the temporary leadership of Gedaliah son of Ahikam.

> Over these I weep, my eyes, my eyes stream with water
> For far from me is the comforter, restorer of my spirit
> My children are forlorn, for the enemy has prevailed. (Lam. 1:16)

The Murder of Gedaliah

When a leader is murdered while holding high office, normal life cannot continue.... Gedaliah son of Ahikam was the great hope of renewal and rebuilding. His assassination by the rival faction, led by Ishmael son of Nethaniah, brings about the destruction after the First Temple and a holocaust upon the nation. Judah is emptied of its inhabitants.... There is no doubt that Rabin's assassination was a travesty for this nation and its hopes of living in peace.... It is the greatest catastrophe that could befall a nation and its homeland.

(Haim Haimoff, *Murder, and the Land Became Desolate,*
Tel Aviv, 2001)

Gedaliah son of Ahikam returned to the Jewish collective consciousness following the murder of Prime Minister Yitzchak Rabin on November 4, 1995. The political assassination of a leader sued for peace in a war-ridden land led to the resurrection of the character of Gedaliah , as concerned Israelis drew parallels between the biblical murder, and its disastrous consequences, to what might become of the modern Jewish state.[1]

---

1. In the wake of the Rabin assassination, the Israeli movement Gesher ("Bridge") declared the Fast of Gedaliah (3 Tishrei) as a day of dialogue. Prof. Uriel Simon devoted an entire article to the connection between Gedaliah and Rabin in his

Although the desire to tragic historical events is understandable, we should not be quick to make such analogies. Gedaliah was the leader of a poor, downtrodden national remnant. His leadership in the wake of the destruction of the First Temple was that of a low-ranking bureaucrat. Gedaliah was appointed not to determine foreign or defense policy, but to restore order to the shattered remains of a conquered people. It is a gross error to claim that the assassination of Gedaliah led to the destruction. This murder was undoubtedly symptomatic of a violent society and extreme political factionalism, but to suggest that, if not for the assassination, the Jewish people would have dwelled securely upon their soil is no more than a delusionional.

THE ACCOUNT OF THE ASSASSINATION
IN THE BOOK OF KINGS

At first glance, the story of Gedaliah's murder has nothing to do with Jeremiah. The surviving remnant does not seek his counsel until much later in the story, as we will see.

The assassination is outlined briefly in ii Kings:

> When all the army officers and their men heard that the King of Babylonia had put Gedaliah in charge, they came to Gedaliah at Mizpah: Ishmael son of Nethaniah, Johanan son of Kareah, Seraiah son of Tanhumeth the Netophathite, Jaazaniah son of the Maachite, and their men. Gedaliah swore to them and their men, saying: Do not be afraid of serving the Chaldeans. Settle down in the land and serve the king of Babylonia, and it will go well with you.
>
> In the seventh month, however, Ishmael son of Nethaniah son of Elishama, who was of royal blood, came with ten men and struck Gedaliah, and he died, along with the Judeans and Chaldeans who were with him at Mizpah. So all the people, from the

book *Seek Peace and Pursue It* (Tel Aviv, 2002), 218–26 [Hebrew]. Tracing attitudes toward Gedaliah since the founding of the State of Israel, we discover that he has not always been this popular (to put it mildly). A history of Israeli literature on Gedaliah can be found in Eli Eshed, "The Murder of a Governor in Judah," http://bit.ly/eshedgedaliah.

least to the greatest, as well as the army officers, fled to Egypt in fear of the Chaldeans. (25:23–26)

For the author of Kings, what stands out about the story is that Gedaliah's assassins are of royal lineage. In their opinion, the war against Babylonia is not yet over; Judah will yet remain under Davidic rule, not under some foreign occupier or his lackey. But after the murder, everyone flees to Egypt in fear of the Chaldeans. Thus, the curtain falls on Jewish life in the Land of Israel.

CHAPTER 40: THE PEOPLE GATHER IN MIZPAH UNDER GEDALIAH'S LEADERSHIP

The Book of Jeremiah devotes more than two long, detailed chapters (the latter part of ch. 40 through ch. 42) to the story of Gedaliah's assassination. The author knows every detail, including dates and names, allowing us to reconstruct the event.

Before recounting the murder itself, we become acquainted with its main characters. Chapter 40 describes the ingathering of soldiers from the fields to Mizpah, Gedaliah's headquarters. These include Ishmael son of Nethaniah, Kareah's sons Johanan and Jonathan, and others. Gedaliah tries to reassure them that the struggle is over, that Babylonia has finished its punitive campaign against Judah, and that there is nothing left to do but submit to the yoke of Babylonia and carry on with life. These attitudes sum up what Jeremiah has been prophesying ever since Nebuchadnezzar's rise to power twenty years earlier.

Gedaliah attempts to unify the remnant of Israel without a king or a Temple. The Jews who had fled to Transjordan (Moab, Ammon, and Edom) also gather to Gedaliah:

> They heard that the King of Babylonia had left a remnant in Judah.... So all the Judeans returned from all the places to which they had been scattered; they came to Judah, to Gedaliah in Mizpah, and harvested an abundance of wine and summer fruits. (40:11–12)

Scripture does not mention how much time passes before all the refugees gather at Mizpah. Gedaliah is assassinated in the "seventh month," so the reader is inclined to think that this gathering occurs immediately after the destruction. That is, the Temple is burnt in Av (the fifth month), but by Elul (the sixth month), the refugees from the surrounding areas have emerged from their hiding places and the lands of their asylum, having heard that the king has left a remnant in Judah. The transition is extremely abrupt. However, there are several indications that these events unfolded over a longer period.[2]

CHAPTER 40 CONTINUED: THE ASSASSINATION

Refugees stream into Mizpah from all directions. Naturally, as the new community acclimates, it divides into rival factions. Thus, Johanan son of Kareah, the leader of a group of army officers, informs Gedaliah of an assassination attempt plotted by Ishmael son of Nethaniah and the King of Ammon. Political logic would take such a warning seriously, as Ammon is the leading supporter of rebellion against Babylonia in Transjordan. But Gedaliah naïvely does not believe Johanan and his faction. He dismisses his concerned guests without even engaging in dialogue with them. Undeterred, Johanan, the leader of the army, approaches Gedaliah privately and asks his permission to discreetly eliminate Ishmael: "No one will know it – why should he strike you down and cause all the Judeans who have gathered to you to scatter and the remnant of Judah to perish?" (40:15) The chances of gathering the remnants a second time are virtually nonexistant, argues Johanan. We have suffered destruction and deportation, yet you are succeeding here. Should all this be lost because of this man's machinations? Once again,

---

2. Y. Hoffman writes: "Noting the month without the year leads the reader to assume that the affair took place in the same year as the destruction…. This may imply that Gedaliah governed for three months at most, between the fourth and seventh months." Y. Hoffman, "On the Method of the Narrator in the Gedaliah Affair," *Iyyunei Mikra Ufarshanut* 5 (5760): 118 [Hebrew]. Hoffman himself prefers the view that Gedaliah governed for about five years. In 582 BCE, there was another deportation from Judah to Babylonia – perhaps in reaction to the assassination.

A summary of opinions about the year of the murder – which seems to favor the view that the assassination took place several years after the destruction – can be found in T. Ganzel, "The Fast of Gedaliah: Its Continued Observance and Significance for the Restoration Period," *Shnaton – An Annual for Bible and Ancient Near Eastern Studies* 20 (2010): 51–69 [Hebrew].

Gedaliah tersely responds: "You speak falsely about Ishmael" (40:16). Gedaliah trusts his men.

The reader knows nothing about Ishmael except that he is of royal stock, but this is sufficient to suggest that he has a rebellious streak and schemes to restore an independent and sovereign Davidic monarchy. Gedaliah overlooks this. He understands that his community has divided into two rival factions – one led by Johanan and the other by Ishmael – and refuses to allow one to violently eliminate its rival. As the story unfolds, it seems that he tries the opposite tack, attempting to draw Ishmael into his inner circle.

The murder takes place when Ishmael and ten of his men come to Mizpah to dine with Gedaliah. That they dine together suggests that Gedaliah was trying to become closer to Ishmael or cement an alliance with him (implicitly rejecting Johanan's leadership). Biblical precedents for this interpretation include Abraham breaking bread with Melchizedek following the battle of the kings (Gen. 14) and Laban sitting down to eat with Jacob after concluding a treaty with him (ibid. 31).

In the middle of the banquet, the guests arise and murder their host and all his men. The verse documents the motive: "because the King of Babylonia put Gedaliah in charge of the land" (Jer. 41:2). In Ishmael's eyes, Gedaliah symbolizes Israel's unconscionable submission to foreign rule. In his zeal to restore the Davidic line, Ishmael cannot accept the leadership of a commoner under the patronage of the nation that destroyed the capital and exiled the holy nation.

The murder of Gedaliah and his entourage at the hands of Ishmael's ten men indicates just how unsuspecting the governor was. Even the Chaldeans present – a permanent garrison of Babylonian soldiers who undoubtedly kept a close eye on Gedaliah – were murdered at the banquet. There were no survivors in all of Gedaliah's headquarters.

CHAPTER 41: A SECOND MURDER AND ITS MOTIVE

A second killing spree follows, and it is worse than the first. Gedaliah's murder, in all its violence, resulted from political motives and national pride. The "sequel" is nothing but bloodlust (see Jer. 41:4–9). An eighty-person procession arrives from Shiloh, Shechem, and Samaria, "with their beards shaven, their clothes torn, and their skin gashed, bearing grain offerings and frankincense to bring to the House of the Lord" (41:5). Word of the destruction has reached Samaria, and in the seventh month, people embark on a pilgrimage to mourn God's defiled altar. Ishmael goes out to meet them as though he too were mourning, and invites them to rest at Gedaliah's headquarters:

> As they entered the city, Ishmael son of Nethaniah and the men who were with him slaughtered them and threw them into a pit. But ten of them said to Ishmael: Don't kill us! We have wheat, barley, oil, and honey hidden in a field. So he desisted and did not kill them with the others. The pit into which Ishmael threw all the bodies of the men he had killed along with Gedaliah was the one King Asa had made as part of his defense against King Baasha of Israel – Ishmael son of Nethaniah filled it with corpses. (41:7–9)

These verses describe the most sickening, bloodthirsty, and murderous act in all of Scripture. Only Jehu son of Nimshi's murder of all of Jezebel's prophets of the Baal comes close. Scripture does not conceal Ishmael's ignominy; not only does he callously massacre innocent masses, he spares those who can satisfy his greed. Ishmael is no prince, but a lowly, contemptible murderer.[3]

Nevertheless, as distasteful as it is, there seems to have been a "rational" motive for this massacre, based on Ishmael's presentation as a royal figure: "The pit into which Ishmael threw all the bodies of the men he had killed along with Gedaliah was the one King Asa had made as part of his defense against King Baasha of Israel – Ishmael son of Nethaniah filled it with corpses." This expository note takes us back to the wars between the kingdoms of Judah, led by the Davidic line, and Israel, descendants of the House of Saul. King Asa reigned in Judah soon after the split into two kingdoms and during the first of the wars between them. I Kings describes the war between Asa and Baasha:

> There was war between Asa and King Baasha of Israel all their days. King Baasha of Israel rose up against Judah and fortified

---

3. See Hoffman, "Gedaliah Affair," 114–15.

Ramah to prevent anyone from coming and going to King Asa of Judah. (15:16–17)

So began the centuries-long war between Ephraim and Judah. In Judah's national memory, King Baasha of Israel built Ramah – a fortification against Judah. After securing the political backing of Aram, Asa strengthened his borders by fortifying Geba and Mizpah. Mizpah thus symbolized the Judean attempt to prevent the Israelite kingdom from encroaching on its territory.

From then on, there was almost complete acrimony between the Davidic line and the inhabitants of Samaria. When Josiah wished to gather Israel's scattered remains, the exiles of Samaria, and reunite the kingdoms, he first had to convince his own royal family. The royals were divided over this issue – half dreamt of a kingdom reunited, while the other half advocated an isolationist and exclusivist Davidic dynasty. Josiah managed to win the people over to his side and sent word to Ephraim. The men of Ephraim accepted this message of reconciliation, gave up their temples in Bethel and Dan, and returned to Jerusalem.

But Jerusalem never fully welcomed them. For some, the exclusivist impulse had become too entrenched. Moreover, a century and a half earlier, King Tiglath-Pileser of Assyria had resettled the depopulated region of Samaria with peoples from Mesopotamia. Many of the remaining Israelites intermarried with these new groups, who had accepted the Israelite religion. Exclusivist elements within Judah would not countenance a renewed alliance with the assimilationist Samaritans.[4]

The first massacre is born out of vengeance and the drive to defend David's honor. The second massacre springs from the resentment boiling

---

4. This isolationist and exclusivist attitude of the "seed of Israel" toward the local population is generally discussed in the context of the return of the Jews under Zerubbabel at the beginning of the Second Temple era. Judah was thus divided into two rival factions: those who adhered to the local deity and those exiled with Jeconiah, who were concerned with preserving their traditional religious identity. See D. Rom-Shiloni, "Exiles and Those Who Remained: Exclusivity Strategies in the Early Sixth Century BCE," *Gift for Sara Japhet*, 119–38 [Hebrew]. I contend that those of royal lineage still had a score to settle with Ephraim, and Ishmael son of Nethaniah settled it most callously.

in the veins of this Davidic scion when he sees the people of Samaria, of Ephraim, coming to mourn Jerusalem. Ishmael son of Nethaniah has been raised on tales of strife between Judah and Israel. He vividly recalls the stories of Ephraim's attempts to conquer Judah, and the coalition formed by Israel and Aram to wage war against it. The time has come to settle accounts. Ishmael fills the pit dug by his distant forebear Asa with the bodies of the descendants of Baasha, who tried to eradicate the line of David; the tribe of Judah has the last laugh.

CHAPTER 41 CONTINUED: THE AFTERMATH OF THE ASSASSINATION

The verse after the second massacre describes, in painstaking detail, how Ishmael takes control over the surviving remnant:

> Ishmael captured all those who remained in Mizpah – the king's daughters and all the people left in Mizpah, over whom Nebu-zaradan, chief of the guards, had appointed Gedaliah son of Ahikam; Ishmael son of Nethaniah took the captives and left to cross over to the Ammonites. (41:10)

It is astounding that a mere ten men manage to herd all these nameless, faceless refugees. For Ishmael, the king's daughters are most important. They are his entire purpose. He now aims to cross the Jordan and join King Baalis of Ammon in the Egyptian-led rebellion against Babylonia. The dream has not yet died.

Suddenly, Johanan son of Kareah and his officers reenter the picture. There is no record of where they have been during the fateful last few days, but now they pursue Ishmael and overtake him at the "great pool of Gibeon" (41:12), another site evoking an encounter that took place centuries earlier. It was precisely here, by the pool of Gibeon, that Joab son of Zeruiah – David's chief of staff – skirmished against Abner son of Ner, Saul's general (II Sam. 2). The people view Johanan as their savior: "all the people whom Ishmael had captured turned back and went over to Johanan." Now it is Ishmael's turn to flee for his life with his men, as Johanan remains to govern the remnant of the people.

If we consider the sequence of Judean leaders during Jeremiah's lifetime, we can see how the leadership collapses. First was Josiah, the "anointed one of God," who embodied all the hopes of restoring the glory of the Davidic line. After his death, his son Jehoahaz was exiled to Egypt, which installed Jehoiakim, under Egyptian influence, on the throne. He was an aloof king, estranged from his people, but a stable ruler and a strong and capable leader. His successor, Jeconiah, was quickly exiled to Babylonia, and Josiah's son Zedekiah ascended the throne with Babylonian backing. He was a weak-willed king, influenced by his inner circle. When he was deposed, the reins passed to Gedaliah, a member of a family of scribes, who was subsequently murdered by a member of the royal family. Now, as Ishmael flees to Ammon to plan the rebuilding of an independent Davidic state, the fate of the surviving remnant is in the hands of Johanan son of Kareah – an officer who tried in vain to stop the murder of the governor, knowing that Babylonia would not forgive such an offense.

Johanan faces a difficult dilemma. He knows Babylonia will wreak vengeance first and foremost upon him and his men, for they are officers. His only alternative is to continue the momentum of rebellion and lead the remnant into a voluntary and comfortable exile in Egypt. He first heads toward a neutral location: "Chimham, near Bethlehem" (41:17). While we do not know precisely where this place is, we can understand Johanan's route: He leaves the territory of Benjamin, heading south along the ancient route that leads toward Hebron and beyond. From there he can decide whether to continue to Egypt via Beersheba or return to Benjamin and face the wrath of the Babylonians.

CHAPTER 42: THE VERDICT – "YOU LIE, JEREMIAH"

> Then all the army officers, Johanan son of Kareah, Jaazaniah son of Hoshaiah, and all the people from youngest to oldest approached. They said to Jeremiah the prophet: Please accept our supplication and pray to the Lord, your God, on our behalf, on behalf of this entire remnant, for we, the few, remain of many, as you see. Let the Lord, your God, tell us which path we should take and what we should do. (42:1–3)

For the first time in this momentous affair, Jeremiah is mentioned. Where has he been until now? The last time we saw him, he was trying to chain himself to the convoy being led to Babylonia. Nebuzaradan did not allow him to do so, suggesting instead that he either travel to Babylonia in style or join the remaining Judeans under Gedaliah's patronage. Jeremiah chose the second option, but the text emphasizes that he "lived with [Gedaliah] among the people who were left in the land" (40:6). That is, Jeremiah never disconnected from the lower classes. He simply exited the stage. What else could he say? All his prophecies have come to fruition; the destruction has become part of history; Jerusalem is no more; the monarchy has been abolished.

Jeremiah is only fifty-five years old, but there is nothing left for him but to suffer his remaining days. Perhaps this is when he utters his most baleful lamentation:

> Cursed be the day I was born! May the day my mother bore me not be blessed! Cursed be the man who brought my father the news, who made him very glad, saying: A male child is born to you! May that man be like the towns the Lord overthrew without pity; may he hear wailing in the morning, a battle cry at noon. For he did not kill me in the womb, so that my mother would be my grave, her womb forever large! Why did I ever emerge from the womb to see trouble and sorrow and my days consumed with shame? (20:14–18)

Jeremiah dwells in Mizpah but does not sit at Gedaliah's table. His place is among the people. Together with them, he is shocked to hear of the royal Ishmael's usurpation. Together with them, he wanders toward Ammon as Ishmael's prisoner. Now, together with them, he is dragged along to a place near Bethlehem and waits for the new leader, Johanan, to make his next move. But then, out of the blue, the entire population turns to Jeremiah.

We should note several details of this plea to the prophet. Firstly, Johanan is not first on the list of those seeking guidance. Until now, he has been struggling against Ishmael. But now, having managed to seize control, he becomes indecisive. The internal debate is endless. So he and the other displaced persons in this "transit camp" gather around Jeremiah to hear God's word.

Second, this is the first time anyone has ever asked Jeremiah to prophesy. Even during the siege of Jerusalem, Zedekiah merely asked him to pray; the king did not want to hear any prophecy. He was rejected as a prophet. Now, when the people are trapped, they turn to him and his prophecy for a way out. An entire system had to collapse in order to glimpse the light of redemption. Perhaps now that everything has been shattered, the surviving remnant will heed God's word. But now the word of God does not come to him, and Jeremiah promises to pray to God to ask Him to show the people the right path to take.

> Jeremiah the prophet said to them: I have heard you; I will pray to the Lord, your God, as you have requested; whatever the Lord answers you, I will tell you; I will withhold nothing from you. Then they said to Jeremiah: May the Lord be a true and faithful witness between us if we do not act in accordance with whatever the Lord, your God, sends you to tell us. Whether it is favorable or unfavorable, we will listen to the Lord, our God, to whom we are sending you, that it may go well with us, for we will listen to the Lord, our God. (42:4–6)

Let us note the difference between Jeremiah's words and the people's. In the original Hebrew, he speaks twenty words; they reply with twice as many. He speaks cautiously and hesitantly; they answer excitedly, with complete commitment. The difference between Jeremiah and the people is clear but dismal: He has lost all desire to prophesy, while they have only just begun to crave the word of God. He, who has devoted his life to speaking God's word, now agrees to do them a favor by acquiescing to their demands. They, who have been estranged from God's word all their lives, now fervently vow to "listen to the Lord, our God."[5]

This request is followed by ten days of tense prayer, until Jeremiah is finally answered. He gathers the people and addresses them in an order

---

5. Hoffman, "Method of the Narrator," 106–7.

that differs from the one in which they presented their request. He first mentions Johanan, the hapless leader:

> After ten days the word of the Lord came to Jeremiah. So he called Johanan son of Kareah, all the army officers who were with him, and all the people from youngest to oldest. He said to them: Thus said the Lord, God of Israel, to whom you sent me to present your petition: If you stay in this land, I will build you up and not tear you down; I will plant you and not uproot you; for I have relented from the disaster I have inflicted on you. Do not be afraid of the King of Babylonia, whom you now fear; do not fear him – declares the Lord – for I am with you to save you and deliver you from his hand. I will show you compassion – he will have compassion on you and restore you to your land. (42:7–11)

Jeremiah speaks unambiguously and confidently, echoing his very first prophecy, when God charged him with his life's mission:

> I appoint you this day over nations and kingdoms: to uproot and tear down, to obliterate and destroy; to build and plant. (1:10)

Jeremiah has already witnessed the fulfillment of most of this prophecy. He has seen uprooting and tearing down, obliteration and destruction. But suddenly, he is filled with hope that the final part will now be fulfilled as well: "If you stay in this land, I will build you up and not tear you down; I will plant you and not uproot you; for I have relented from the disaster I have inflicted on you." Now, they must courageously overcome their fear of the Babylonians. The prophet promises that the ruler of Babylonia will "have compassion on you," just as Jacob, who sent his sons to the ruler of Egypt (before learning that he was none other than Joseph), prayed that "God Almighty will show you compassion before the man" (Gen. 43:14). This is an optimistic prophecy. Jeremiah is filled with new strength and hope that finally, after having drained the foul cup to its dregs, the days of peace and consolation have arrived.

Yet this prophecy is apparently not what the people want to hear. One imagines a murmur rising from the officers and the people. No one is willing to heed the prophet. They asked him to pray, but not so he would send them back to the lion's den in Benjamin, a place crawling with Babylonians. Already on their way to Egypt, they sought only a wayfarer's prayer and some moral support. They have waited ten days for God's blessing – can this really be it? This response can be inferred from Jeremiah's next words:

> If you say, "We will not stay in this land," and do not heed the voice of the Lord, your God. If you say, "No, for we will come to the land of Egypt, where we will see no war and hear no battle trumpets, nor will we hunger for bread, and there we will dwell." (42:13–14)

He hears them saying, "We cannot stay here." They have no real intention of heeding the word of God. Their oath of ten days earlier was meaningless. Egypt sits on the Nile in peace and prosperity and beckons them. Upon this they pin their hopes and dreams. They perceive themselves not as refugees fleeing for their lives, but as immigrants. Jeremiah's prayer on their behalf was thus based on a fundamental error. He flies into a rage against them:

> Now hear the word of the Lord, O remnant of Judah: Thus said the Lord of Hosts, God of Israel: If you are determined to go to Egypt and you go to sojourn there, then the sword you fear will overtake you there in Egypt, and the famine you dread will follow you into Egypt, and there you will die! (42:15–16)

Jeremiah holds nothing back. He vents his frustration, his disappointment, his sense of betrayal at their request for the word of God, and his willingness to believe that, finally, the people wanted to connect with the word of God. So begins one of Jeremiah's longest speeches, from verses 15 to 22. Everything finally bursts out – bitterness, humiliation, anger, and despair.

The leaders of the flock behave wisely. They do not interrupt the prophet as he pours out his heart.[6] Only afterward do they respond. Now, after the last hope, after they swore and turned to him, everything declined and worsened:

> When Jeremiah had finished speaking to the people all the words of the Lord, their God – what the Lord had sent him to tell them, Azariah son of Hoshaiah and Johanan son of Kareah and all the arrogant men said to Jeremiah: You lie; the Lord, our God, has not sent you to tell us not to go to Egypt to sojourn there. Rather, Baruch son of Neriah is inciting you against us to hand us over to the Chaldeans, that they may kill us or carry us into exile to Babylonia. (43:1–3)

The speakers respond to Jeremiah's boiling rage with chilling coolness: "You lie; the Lord, our God, has not sent you." The word "lie," *sheker*, hits Jeremiah like a knockout punch. No prophet uses this term more. Of the 109 times it appears in Scripture, thirty-five occur in the Book of Jeremiah. And this is the only time it is directed against him. The assembled point an accusing finger at Baruch son of Neriah, who presumably has silently accompanied Jeremiah ever since his imprisonment – a faithful disciple accompanying his tormented master. Baruch has not been mentioned since Jeremiah's purchase of his cousin's field. Perhaps the people are taken aback by the prophet's transformation from a broken and listless shell of a man to a newly inspired and energetic spirit. Perhaps they assume that this about-face has been engineered by his young accomplice, who, after all, hails from a family of scribes well-known for their opposition to activism and preference for passivity.

The decision to continue on to Egypt has been made. Jeremiah finds himself part of the convoy heading south. Could he have chosen to stay behind? It seems unlikely:

---

6. The sages found the wisdom of Johanan and Azariah instructive: "One should not interrupt his fellow's speech. As Scripture states: 'When Jeremiah had finished speaking... Azariah son of Hoshaiah and Johanan son of Kareah and all the arrogant men said...'" (*Kalla Rabbati* 4).

Johanan son of Kareah and all the army officers led away all the remnant of Judah – those who had come back to Judah from all the nations where they had been scattered: The men, women, and children, and the king's daughters; all those whom Nebuzaradan, chief of the guards, had left with Gedaliah son of Ahikam son of Shaphan; and Jeremiah the prophet and Baruch son of Neriah. And they went to Egypt, for they did not heed the word of the Lord; they arrived at Tahpanhes. (43:5–7)

Jeremiah's End

CHAPTER 44: THE SUPPRESSION OF JEREMIAH'S PROPHECY IN EGYPT

Tahpanhes, where Jeremiah arrives with his fellow exiles, is identified with Tell Defenneh (just west of El Qantara) in northern Egypt. One of the hills among the ruins is known locally as "the Castle of the Jews' Daughter." In Jeremiah's day, this area was most fertile, well-irrigated by the Pelusian arm of the Nile. An ancient caravan route from Egypt through the Land of Israel to Mesopotamia passed through here.[1] The convoy of displaced persons led by Johanan son of Kareah stops here, and the survivors of Jerusalem's destruction can finally rest. The immigrants are accepted readily by the locals, integrate smoothly, and settle in. Jeremiah wanders among them like a stranger. Then he is commanded to perform an act that will crush the hopes of the wanderers who think they have finally arrived at a safe harbor:

> Take some large stones and hide them in the mortar in the brickwork at the entrance to Pharaoh's palace in Tahpanhes, in the presence of Jewish men. Say to them: Thus said the Lord of

---

1. Based on Z. Beilin, "Egypt, Babylonia, and the Prophet Jeremiah," *A Volume in Honor of Yosef Braslavi* (Jerusalem, 5730), 89–93 [Hebrew].

Hosts, God of Israel: I will send for My servant King Nebuchadnezzar of Babylonia, and I will set his throne atop these stones I have buried; he will spread his royal pavilion over them. He will come and attack Egypt, bringing death to those destined for death, captivity to those destined for captivity, and the sword to those destined for the sword. I will set fire to the temples of the gods of Egypt; he will burn them and take [their gods] captive; he will fold up the land of Egypt as a shepherd folds his garment.... He will smash the monoliths at the temple of the sun in Egypt, and he will burn down the temples of the gods of Egypt. (43:9–13)

Even now, Jeremiah does not relent. He continues to call Nebuchadnezzar "My servant." Even those who sought refuge and peace in distant, mighty Egypt will feel the long arm of the Babylonian king. This prophecy will be realized some years later. Indeed, Josephus recounts that Nebuchadnezzar "invaded Egypt to suppress it, killing its king, recapturing the Jews there, and bringing them to Babylonia."[2]

The Jewish encounter with Egypt is fatal. Egypt is at the height of its power and glory. The broken Judean refugees are at their lowest point. Egypt embraces them, and they return its love, becoming infatuated with its luxurious lifestyle, unique culture, and pagan religion.

Jeremiah wanders around his people in shock. All the reformations of his beloved Josiah are instantly forgotten. The idolatry he had witnessed in his childhood, the legacy of Manasseh, has been resurrected in a different form. He finds himself back where he started forty years earlier, only now he is weary, broken, and drained of all hope. For the last time, he summons his strength to warn the people going astray in Egypt to learn from the sins of their forefathers. His history lesson soon turns to current events:

Now thus said the Lord, God of Hosts, God of Israel: Why are you doing such evil to yourselves, cutting off from Judah the men and women, the children and infants, and leaving yourselves without a remnant? Why arouse My anger with what your hands have

2. Josephus, *Antiquities* X, 9:7.

made, burning incense to other gods in Egypt, where you have come to sojourn, in order to destroy yourselves and make yourselves a curse and an object of reproach among all the nations on earth? Have you forgotten the wickedness of your ancestors, of the kings of Judah, of their wives, and your own wickedness and that of your wives, committed in the land of Judah and the streets of Jerusalem? To this day they have not humbled themselves or shown reverence, nor have they followed My Torah and the laws I set before you and your ancestors. (44:7–10)

Jeremiah concludes with words of rebuke, the likes of which his people are already weary of hearing: The sword shall find you here, as it found your ancestors there; only individuals shall survive the next onslaught.

Once Jeremiah would shout out his prophecies at the palace or the Temple, and none would pay him any heed. Here in Egypt, he receives an immediate, unanimous response:

Then all the men who knew that their wives were burning incense to other gods, along with all the women who were present – a large assembly – and all the people living in Pathros, in Egypt, answered Jeremiah: We will not listen to the message you have spoken to us in the name of the Lord! We will certainly do everything we said we would, burning incense to the queen of heaven and pouring libations to her, just as we and our ancestors, our kings and our officers did in the towns of Judah and in the streets of Jerusalem – when we had plenty of food and were well-off and suffered no harm. But ever since we stopped burning incense to the queen of heaven and pouring libations to her, we have had nothing and have perished by sword and famine. When we burn incense to the queen of heaven and pour libations to her, do not our husbands know that we make cakes in her likeness and pour libations to her? (44:15–19)

History has reached a new low. For the first time, the Jews feel no need to apologize for their actions. They are no longer on the fence. They are not blindly doing what they have seen others do, nor are they mistaken in their intentions. The women are prompting their families to burn incense to the gods of Egypt, while their husbands support their actions with theological justifications and accuse Jeremiah of speaking without substance. If, on their way to Egypt, they accused him of lying, now they simply inform him that they will not listen to him. Their decision is the result of the rational conclusion reached after years of trial and error. We have practiced what you preached, they tell Jeremiah, and it did us no good. We too were around in the days of Josiah, which you seem to perceive as a golden age. Until his reformation, all went well for us. We all served the gods of Assyria, King Manasseh cared for us, and no sword passed through the land for decades. As soon as we started with the reformation and the return to worshipping the God of Israel, everything changed for the worse. Babylonia rose up and exiled Jeconiah, we became subservient to Egypt, and then to Babylonia, and then came exile and destruction. It was a grave mistake to choose the God of Israel.

What can Jeremiah say? Once again, the truth of his prophecy is put to the test. When the people had to choose between his prophecy and that of Hananiah son of Azzur, they followed Hananiah, who sounded more convincing. Jeremiah had responded: We will see whose prophecy proves true. Now he faces a similar dilemma. His audience does not believe him and has no intention of listening to him. His answer is chilling:

> So hear the word of the Lord, all you Jews living in Egypt: I swear by My great name – said the Lord – that no Jew living anywhere in Egypt will ever again invoke My name or swear "as the Lord God lives." For I am vigilantly watching over them to their detriment, not to their benefit; the Jews in Egypt will perish by sword and famine until they are gone. Those who escape the sword and return to the land of Judah from Egypt will be very few; then the whole remnant of Judah who came to sojourn in Egypt will know whose word stands – Mine or theirs. (44:26–28)

Jeremiah repeats his previous prophecy, adding nothing. His words are similar to Moses' oath when he stood before Pharaoh after nine of the ten plagues. Pharaoh threatened that Moses would never again see his face. Moses repeated these words in agreement: "Indeed as you have spoken, I will never see your face again" (Ex. 10:29). Similarly, Jeremiah turns the people's own words back on them: You say you will never again invoke the name of God – indeed you will not, for you will all be slaughtered or exiled to Babylonia, and there will be no one left to invoke God's name.

Jeremiah continues with stinging words: "For I am vigilantly watching over them to their detriment, not to their benefit." Once again he returns to his prophetic initiation, but this time to its elements of rebuke, not hope. The almond blossom, the *shakeid*, had symbolized God's watchfulness, that He was *shokeid* (vigilant) over His people. Now it flashes before the eyes of a much older Jeremiah: God remains vigilant, but now it is for harm, not for good.

Jeremiah swears before his people that they will learn whose words are true – the women burning incense before their idols, or the word of God that he repeats to them. He concludes his prophecy with a sign:

> Let this be your sign – declares the Lord – that I will punish you in this place, that you may know that My words will be fulfilled against you for evil. (44:29)

These seem to be Jeremiah's last words. It is the only time he uses a sign, and this perhaps encapsulates his entire prophetic career. Never, not even in his final prophecy, does his audience believe him. The Torah describes the prophet who uses signs to try to convince the people to serve other gods:

> If a prophet, or one who foretells by dreams, appears among you and gives to you a sign or demonstration. And the sign or wonder that he told you of comes true, and he says: Let us follow other gods, which you have not known, and let us worship them – you must not listen to the words of that prophet or dreamer, for the Lord, your God, is testing you to find out whether you love Him with all your heart and soul. (Deut. 13:2–4)

Jeremiah knows his words will not be heeded. The only thing left to do is to anchor them in a sign that will prove that everything he has said is from God. With this dreadful statement, he exits the prophetic stage.

JEREMIAH'S END ACCORDING TO RABBINIC TRADITION

Where does Jeremiah go next? He certainly does not stay in Egypt – the people, so entrenched in idol worship, spit him out. A midrash has Jeremiah and his disciple Baruch son of Neriah going to Babylonia. This midrash applies a verse in Ecclesiastes, "the pitcher shall be shattered at the spring" (12:6), to these two figures. Rashi explains the metaphor:

> "The pitcher shall be shattered at the spring" – Baruch son of Neriah's pitcher at Jeremiah's spring, for they were both exiled to Babylonia and interrupted their studies due to weariness from the journey. They were first exiled to Egypt, as Johanan son of Kareah exiled them, and when Nebuchadnezzar conquered Egypt, he exiled them to Babylonia. (Rashi, ad loc.)

This tradition is reinforced by various sources that identify Baruch as Ezra the Scribe's teacher:

> Rav or R. Shmuel b. Marta said: Torah study is greater than building the Temple. As long as Baruch son of Neriah was alive, Ezra did not leave him to ascend [to the Land of Israel to rebuild the Temple]. (Megilla 16b)

These sources endeavor to connect the era of the prophets with that of the sages. Ezra was a founder of the Great Assembly, whose scholars received the Torah from the prophets: "and the prophets transmitted it to the men of the Great Assembly" (Mishna Avot 1:1). With Baruch son of Neriah linking Jeremiah and Ezra, the chain of the Torah's transmission is enhanced.[3]

---

3. The historicity of the posited link between Ezra and Baruch lies beyond the scope of the present work. After all, according to this tradition, Jeremiah and Baruch left Egypt after Nebuchadnezzar conquered it in 570 BCE. Ezra arrived in the Land of

A later and more enigmatic aggadic tradition concerns Jeremiah's descendants. Its source is *The Alphabet of Sirach* (*Alpha Beta DeBen Sirah*), a somewhat dubious work according to all scholars.[4] Early in his prophetic career, as noted, Jeremiah is commanded by God to remain childless. Despite this unambiguous statement in Scripture, the aforementioned source insists that the Egyptian sage Ben Sirah was a descendant of Jeremiah – not just a descendant, but a son *and* grandson. According to this tradition, Jeremiah's daughter took a bath right after her father and became pregnant from the semen remaining in the bath-water, eventually bearing Ben Sirah. This midrash seems determined to prolong Jeremiah's life, even if other sources say nothing about his end. Yet this tradition also has Jeremiah serving as a key figure in the transition from the era of prophecy to that of the sages.

JEREMIAH 52: THE CONCLUSION OF THE BOOKS OF JEREMIAH AND KINGS

The Book of Jeremiah ends by describing King Jeconiah of Judah much later in his Babylonian exile:

> In the thirty-seventh year of the exile of King Jeconiah of Judah, in the year Evil-Merodach became King of Babylonia, on the twenty-fifth day of the twelfth month, he lifted up King Jeconiah of Judah and freed him from prison. He spoke kindly to him and gave him a seat of honor above those of the other kings who were with him in Babylonia. So [Jeconiah] changed out of his prison clothes and for the rest of his life ate regularly at the king's table.

Israel in 450 BCE, more than a century later. It is thus extremely difficult to accept a close relationship between the two. Rather, this interpretation attempts to fuse the worlds of the Written Torah and the Oral Torah, and therefore links these two great figures, Jeremiah and Ezra, through Baruch. For a learned explanation of this tradition, see Gutel, "Prophetic Status."

4. Some years ago, A.M. Habermann published an introduction to a facsimile of the Constantinople 1519 edition (Italy, 1997), which was based on a unique manuscript. On pages 8–10 of this introduction, Habermann notes that medieval rabbis and modern scholars alike regard the book as nothing but a frivolous comedy. Nonetheless, generations of scholars have treated it as a halakhic source, especially regarding artificial insemination.

The King of Babylonia gave Jeconiah a regular daily allowance
until the day of his death, all the days of his life. (52:31–34)

The Book of Kings ends similarly. What message does such an ending
impart to us, after we have followed Jeremiah throughout his life, from
his childhood in Anathoth until he fades out of the picture in Egypt?[5]

Throughout his forty-year prophetic career, Jeremiah's lot is one
of bitter disappointment. Right at the start, he learns the secret of prophecy
and its disenchantment. As an idealistic, eager youth, he believes
that Josiah is God's anointed one, and that the Israelite clans will soon
reunite into a large kingdom. Josiah's fall at Megiddo and Jehoiakim's
ascent shatter his dreams and frustrate his hopes.

To Jeremiah, Jeconiah is a mere afterthought – a "despised, broken
vessel" (22:28). First and foremost, he is a child of Jehoiakim and his
haughty queen Nehushta daughter of Elnathan, symbols of evil. Jeremiah
does not regret the brevity of Jeconiah's reign or his exile to Babylonia.
However, the prophet has high hopes for Zedekiah, son of the admired
Josiah. He believes this weak king will remain faithfully submissive to
Nebuchadnezzar, thus allowing Judah to exist in tranquil submission. He
is gravely disappointed when Zedekiah begins listening to the chorus
of prophets demanding rebellion against Babylonia.

The book concludes by showing how salvation sprouts from the
unlikeliest places, from machinations that even prophets cannot predict.
In this case, it is the ephemeral Jeconiah – his reign so brief, hopeless,
and devoid of majesty – who flourishes in Babylonia. He is given a new
lease on life, and two generations later, his grandson, Zerubbabel son
of Shealtiel son of Jeconiah, leads the exiles back to build the Second
Temple. Jeremiah's prophecy about the obliteration of Jeconiah's dynasty
goes unfulfilled, but it is for the best.

---

5. See M. Avioz, "The Story of Jeconiah's Pardon," *Shnaton: An Annual for Bible and
Ancient Near Eastern Studies* 16 (5766): 29–41 [Hebrew].

Afterword

At the dawn I seek Thee,
  Rock and refuge tried,
In due service speak Thee
  Morn and eventide.

'Neath Thy greatness shrinking,
  Stand I sore afraid,
All my secret thinking
  Bare before Thee laid.

Little to Thy glory
  Heart or tongue can do;
Small remains the story,
  Add we spirit too.

Yet since man's praise ringing
  May seem good to Thee,
I will praise Thee singing
  While Thy breath's in me.

(Shlomo ibn Gabirol, "At the Dawn")

A new day dawns at the Ein Perat Academy for Leadership, in the community of Alon. Wadi Qelt, the biblical Naḥal Perat, flows just below this institution, whose students seek to take responsibility for the future of the Jewish state. Slightly upstream is Anathoth, Jeremiah's hometown. Here, during the month of Shevat 5770, I wrote the story of Jeremiah.

Some 2,600 years ago, Jeremiah was sitting in prison, mired in the depths of personal misery and national tragedy, when God commanded him to purchase a field in the town of his ancestors. This task seemed to him the culmination of forty years of humiliation suffered at the hand of God. In the earliest days of his career, during the promising reign of Josiah, the land shuddered at the fall of the great northern empire, Assyria. Everyone feared that the blessed tranquility of the Assyrian kingdom was over, but Jeremiah presented his brethren with glorious visions of the restoration of the Davidic dynasty and the reunification of the tribes of Israel. "It will be a time of strife for Jacob, but he will be saved from it," he promised. Yet nothing came of these visions – no glorious monarchy and no reunification; only a continuous descent into devastation and despair, culminating in the destruction of Jerusalem, and exile to Babylonia. Just before that nadir, God explained to Jeremiah why he was to purchase the field – God closes no door without opening a window.

This phase of the nation's history had come to an end. The fate of the Kingdoms of Judah and Ephraim was sealed – yet the nation was destined to resurrect itself, upon the land promised to its forefathers:

> I will surely gather them from all the lands where I banish them in My furious anger and great wrath; I will bring them back to this place and cause them to live in safety. They will be My people, and I will be their God. I will give them one heart and one path, that they may always revere Me, and that all may go well with them and their children after them. I will make an everlasting covenant with them: I will never stop doing them good, and I will inspire them to fear Me, never turning away from Me. I will rejoice in doing good for them and will assuredly plant them in this land with all My heart and soul. (Jer. 32:37–41)

The Babylonian exile eventually ended, followed by the limited independence of the Second Commonwealth. The Jews lived under the thumb of Persia, then Greece, and finally Rome. The destruction of the Second

Temple, at the hands of the latter, led to a new exile that lasted until the twentieth century.

We are now in the midst of a third attempt to establish a national home in our ancestral land, but often fear that history might be repeating itself: The leaders have sinned, and the prophets stray after worthless idols. The streets of Jerusalem still throng with false prophets who earnestly claim, "The tradition of our forefathers is in our hands; the Third Temple shall not be destroyed!" Once again, they seek to lull us into a sense of false security, to make us forget the grave responsibility we shoulder: to be worthy of this national home, this Jewish state.

The State of Israel has no insurance policy. It is our role to protect and maintain it. There are many good people who strive to rectify the ills of the Jewish state – to reduce socioeconomic disparity, to break down the walls that divide us, to bridge language gaps, to include rather than reject. I sincerely pray that this book inspires us to re-excavate the treasures of our past, drawing upon them to rebuild a Jewish identity, a Jewish culture that will shed light and goodness upon all it touches.

The fonts used in this book are from the Arno family

Other books by Binyamin Lau
available from Maggid Books:

The Sages: Character, Context & Creativity

Volume I: The Second Temple Period

Volume II: From Yavneh to the Bar Kokhba Revolt

Volume III: The Galilean Period

Maggid Books
The best of contemporary Jewish thought from
Koren Publishers Jerusalem Ltd.